THE LURE OF THE VAMPIRE

THE LURE OF THE VAMPIRE
GENDER, FICTION AND FANDOM FROM BRAM STOKER TO BUFFY

MILLY WILLIAMSON

 **WALLFLOWER PRESS** LONDON & NEW YORK

First published in Great Britain in 2005 by
Wallflower Press
6a Middleton Place, Langham Street, London W1W 7TE
www.wallflowerpress.co.uk

A catalogue for this book is available from the British Library

ISBN 1-904764-40-1 (pbk)
ISBN 1-904764-41-X (hbk)

Printed by Thomson Press (India) Ltd.

CONTENTS

ACKNOWLEDGMENTS

Many thanks to my close friends, Karen Blackney and Caroline Donald, for their friendship and support. Thank you also to Janet Golding, Kieran Kelly, Arthur Husk, and Danny and Jenny Coyle. I would like to thank the following colleagues for their advice and comments: Jo Entwistle, Don Slater, Martin Barker, Lyn Thomas, Elizabeth Wilson, Mike Chopra-Gant, Dee Amy-Chinn, Gholam Khiabany, Bill Osgerby, Matt Hills and the MeCCSA Women's Network. Thank you to the Media Research Capability Fund Committee at London Metropolitan University for funding my research trip to New Orleans and for funding eight weeks of research relief in the last stages of this book. A special debt of gratitude goes to Christine Geraghty, my PhD supervisor at Goldsmiths College. She was generous with her time and her ideas while I was her student and I would like to thank her for her intellectual guidance, support, patience and for all that she has taught me. My good friend Susie Coggles gave up one of her valuable holidays to travel with me to New Orleans to interview vampire fans. Throughout this project Susie has shared my enthusiasm for vampire fiction, has discussed ideas with me and sent me valuable insights via e-mail. She has also been a wonderful friend. I particularly want to thank her for looking after me in New Orleans when one of our key contact's German Shepherd dog bit me (I guess something with fangs had to get me). Finally, this book and the research it is based on would not have happened without the many daily sacrifices (large and small) made by John Budis over many years. His constant support and companionship, his belief in me, and his chicken risotto have kept me going. I would like to thank him with all of my love.

The author and publisher gratefully acknowledge the following permission to reproduce material: Pictorial Press for figures 1, 2, 4, 6, 7, 8, 9, 10; the Wellcome Institute Library, London, for figure 3, Anonymous print of a painting by J. H. Hasslehorst, *J. C. G. Lucae and his Assistants Dissecting a Female Cadaver*, 1864; the Mary Evans Picture Library for figure 5, 'The doomed Byron lays on a tombstone at Harrow'. Every effort has been made to trace copyright holders. The author apologises for any errors or omissions and would be grateful to be notified of any corrections that should be incorporated into the next edition or reprint of this volume.

This book is dedicated to my daughter Emmeline, with all my love.

We are told to be wary of vampires. Some critics remind us that vampires can infect us with their otherness, beguile us with their depraved intimacy and exhaust us with their embraces. Others warn us against accepting the images of fear that the vampire is held to represent. The vampire is a voraciously sexual woman, and a hyper-sexual African, a hypnotic Jewish invader, an effeminate or homosexual man. The vampires of the West exist to frighten us into acquiescence, to reassert patriarchy, racial superiority, family values and chaste heterosexuality. We have long been urged to exorcise the vampire from our imaginations, or, at least, not to get carried away with it. Bram Dijkstra warns:

> To fantasise about warlocks and witches, about vampires and werewolves
> ... is to perpetuate a world eager for war and to remain complicit in the
> fetishisation of others as 'evil', as 'alien', as 'inferior'. (1996: 443)

This is a book about why that warning has not been heeded and about why the vampire has more often fascinated us rather than terrified us. Since the vampire entered the English language over two hundred years ago, it has almost permanently existed either in print or visual culture and is an enduring figure in the Anglo-American cultural imagination. But far from the vampire frightening us into rejecting its difference (and thus all the differences that it symbolises), the vampire has become an image of emulation, a glamorous outsider, a figure whose otherness we find versions of (sometimes ambivalently) in ourselves. From Polidori's Byronesque Lord Ruthven, to peroxide-punk Spike, the vampire's otherness has lured us with its rebellious pose and its refusal (or inability) to live by the rules of the day. Nina Auerbach candidly explains this appeal for her:

> These shadowy monsters were a revelation to my best friend and me ...
> we did feel we had found a talisman against a nice girl's life. Vampires
> were supposed to menace women, but to me at least, they promised pro-
> tection against a destiny of girdles, spike heels, and approval. (1995: 4)

The vampire offers a way of inhabiting difference with pride, for embracing defiantly an identity that the world at large sees as 'other'.

But to embrace the vampire is also to embrace pain; a painful awareness of outsiderdom, a recognition of inhabiting an unwelcome self, a life at least partly lived at the edges. Richard Dyer elegantly captures this ambiguity in the vampire when he writes:

> If the vampire is an Other, he or she was always a figure in whom one could find one's self ... the despicable as well as the defiant, the shameful as well as the unashamed, the loathing of oddness as well as pride in it. (1993: 10–11)

Much of the vampire's pain is to be found in the pathos of its misrecognised identity; there is a long history of vampire fiction in which the vampire is sympathetically constructed; a reluctant symbol of evil whose innocence is hidden by the very fact that its body is seen to be the essence of evil. The vampire's troubling ontology resonates with many experiences of the self in Western modernity for those who do not occupy the normative identity – white, middle-class, male, able-bodied, heterosexual, and successful (and even most white men don't) and it combines arresting pathos and a glamorous pose. This book examines the way that the vampire's duality of repulsion and attraction resonates with the continuing dilemma of the 'self' found in Anglo-American culture, for this vampire (in a variety of incarnations) has generated enormous fan cultures in the twentieth and twenty-first centuries.

But the vampire's pain also symbolises another dilemma which faces us all – the desire to signify, to have meaning, to *matter* in the light of day and not just in the shadows. This desire stems from a 'success'-oriented culture which is also one that severely curtails the possibilities for the self. Vampire narratives today speak specifically to this contemporary dilemma of the 'self' and this is another reason for their appeal. However, the potential of the vampire to offer significance is rooted in the fame and renown that surrounded nineteenth-century vampire figures, whose ability to pique curiosity and obsess the public prefigures the contemporary fascination with fame. The vampire continues to address issues of fame and significance, but in a manner which resonates with today's experience of the self.

In this book I will chart the sympathetic vampire from its Byronic origins to its most recent incarnations on the small screen. In doing so I want to demonstrate the strong feminine appeal of the vampire which has received far less attention than the masculine concerns that the vampire is said to raise. This fiction has not traditionally been considered to be a 'female' form, but I will draw on literary theories of melodrama and the gothic, and on feminist accounts of melodrama, to offer interpretations of the vampire that are not male-centred, but which examine the structure of pathos and the use of excess to raise the 'unspeakable' existence of hidden injustice in vampiric guise. Chapter one will consider non-masculine and non-middle class readings of the so-called King vampire Dracula by drawing on ideas about the differing discourses that circulated in Victorian England and in chapter two I will examine the different gendered appeals of the vampire beyond (and in some cases, before) Dracula. This emphasis on 'readings' of the vampire also means that this book will offer an analysis of vampire fan culture and chapter three will draw on interviews with vampire fans to help to make sense of the vampire's appeal; many vampire fans have generously helped me to understand the significance of the vampire today and have helped me to clarify the way that it relates to our feelings about ourselves. I will also look at a variety of activities that this fandom inspires. I will consider the day-to-day dynamics of vampire fandom and will look at the experience of large vampire events in chapter's five and six. I will examine fans' accounts of vampire-inspired sartorial styles and the fan fiction that is produced in chapters seven and eight.

Because of the multifaceted nature of the activities involved in fandom (not to mention the complexity of the figure of the vampire itself), this book relies on interdisciplinarity and ranges from literary theory to film theory, and from television studies to theories of dress and fashion. Yet while the initial chapters of this book focuses on readings and re-readings of the vampire, Pierre Bourdieu will be a significant presence in the later chapters because there I will offer a theoretical model of fandom arising out of my observation and participation in vampire fan clubs that will be theorised through Bourdieu's analysis of the field of cultural production. Although many scholars have relied on Bourdieu to explain fandom, I will argue that the key dynamic that Bourdieu proposes marks the cultural field (and thus fandom as a subset of this field) is missing. Scholars have drawn on Bourdieu to suggest that fans are acquiring subversive sub-cultural capital, or else are invoking a cultural hierarchy to distinguish themselves from others. What is missing from these accounts is a recognition that the field of cultural production is structured by a destabilising struggle between two opposing, but dominant sets of cultural values which drive towards the aforementioned hierarchy. These opposing sets of values influence fandom which then reverberates with the struggles and the instability that mark the cultural field more widely. Thus Bourdieu's schema is able to account for the differences between 'official' and 'unofficial' fandoms with their differing cultural values and for the very real tensions and struggles that take place within vampire (and other media) fandoms. However, I do not rely on Bourdieu uncritically, for I will argue that there is something beyond the quest for distinction that motivates artistic and cultural engagement, which Bourdieu's schema cannot account for, despite his achievement in having identified the structure of relations into which cultural engagement necessarily enters. Part of this 'something beyond' for vampire fans is the wish for creative expression which is an affirmation of 'self' in the context of culturally imposed non-fulfilment.

Like any book, this one has two covers and there is much to be said about the vampire that you will not find between them. I have concentrated on the popular Western and Anglophone version of the vampire and its surrounding fan culture. This means that I have not addressed the numerous Eastern European, Indian, South American, French, Italian, Spanish and Mexican versions of this myth and its incarnation in many of these national cinemas. By concentrating on the 'other' at the heart of the Anglo-American West, I have made many exclusions, but I also hope to have demonstrated that what is alien to our Anglo-American rulers also exists within their own national boundaries and that in some way or another it is most of us – vampire fans or not. The vampire symbolises the pain of this condition and defiance in the face of it, even if in ambivalent and individualised ways, and like many of the vampire fans who offered their time and intelligence to me while I was researching this book, I would like to suggest that it is not *the vampire* that we should be wary of...

CHAPTER I

GENDER AND THE DRACULA: WHAT'S AT STAKE?

It has been said that we conjure the vampires that we want or need for the cultural and historical times that we find ourselves in.[1] Yet throughout the twentieth century, Dracula (both Bram Stoker's novel and the many screen adaptations) has dominated critical interpretations of the vampire, eclipsing earlier incarnations of the vampire and their many progeny. At least one commentator has suggested that Dracula's dominance has been an invention of the critics who are participating in 'a process of myth-making that has progressively foregrounded Stoker's novel as an arbitrary high point in the alleged evolution of vampirism in literature' (Hughes 2000: 144). The critical concentration on Dracula has been tremendously influential in staking out the symbolic and metaphoric territory that the vampire is considered to occupy. Even those critics who acknowledge that Stoker's Dracula was not the first vampire tale still suggest that 'it is largely due to Stoker that we owe the popular image of the suave, opera-cloaked bloodsucker now so familiar in films and television' (Parry 1977: 7).

This focus on Dracula reflects a tendency in literary and screen analysis to see psychic drives and historic periods as if they were '"summed up" in individual exemplary forms' (Moretti 1988: 26). The character of Dracula has come to stand for the vampire generally because this figure is seen as representative of a universal psychic condition or, alternatively, of the spirit of the age. Thus, despite the mutability of Dracula, from novel to stage to screen,[2] this figure has tended to be interpreted as a set of fixed metaphors and symbols which, particularly in the case in some psychoanalytic accounts, tend to universalise the nature of the psyche and foreground issues to do with masculinity. We shall see how such approaches have hidden the potential female engagements with the vampire figure, or readings of the novel. Socio-historical accounts of Dracula meanwhile, have tended to work with an analytical model that accepts the notion that the spirit of any age is shared by all members of society. This is what Franco Moretti terms the 'Zeitgeist fallacy' (1988: 25); the tendency to make sweeping generalisations about the era in which a work was produced, and thus about the work itself.[3] Dracula has, to some extent, fallen prey to the Zeitgeist fallacy. The Victorian age which produced Dracula (and its author) is considered to be one of sexual repression and the vampire represents the return of the (masculine) repressed. This chapter will begin by examining the foremost accounts of the original novel's meanings that have been produced on this basis. However, Bram Stoker's *Dracula* was written in a decade of 'sexual anarchy' (Showalter 1990: 3). As Elaine Showalter has argued, the 1890s were a time when male aesthetes and the 'New Woman' offered alternative definitions of what it meant to be male or female. Conflicting discourses circulated about proper conduct (sexual and otherwise) and gender roles. This chapter will re-examine *Dracula* in relation to these conflicting discourses and the contrasting Victorian interpretations of the novel that they point towards.

While there were undoubtedly dominant ways of understanding the world in Victorian Britain, various social groups were positioned quite differently in relation to those discourses. It is likely that this will have implications for the readings that different audiences might produce of the novel's articulation of, or engagement with, these discourses. Andrew Tudor warns against the assumption of homogeneity in horror, and criticises those approaches that '"explain" horror by reference to seemingly immutable characteristics of the genre or its consumers' (1997: 460). He suggests instead, that rather than offering universal accounts of meaning, critics should historicise and particularise the possible engagements of audiences. This chapter aims to provide such an account by considering potential female readings of *Dracula*, as well as other potential readings from Victorians who did not hold dominant social positions. For just as '*Zeitgeist* moment' analyses tend to generalise about the text, the 'reader' also tends to be over-generalised and forced into step with the spirit of his age. I use 'his' deliberately here because throughout the twentieth century, the ideal reader or viewer of horror has been assumed to be male, and this has been a crucial problem in such universalising approaches. The presumption that the reception of a work is shared results in a concealment of the possible interpretations of groups who do not correspond to the critic's assumed reading position. It is for this reason that *Dracula* has tended to be read through dominant discourses, from which readers are assumed to adopt the position of the middle-class male reader.

Taking an alternative approach, here I will consider the potential reading position of Victorian *women* (particularly the 'New Woman' who appears in the pages of the novel). I will also consider how working-class and lower-middle-class men and women might have interpreted the novel's key scenes. In this chapter I argue that that these groups did not necessarily inhabit middle-class, professional male discursive positions and did not adopt the reading position the novel is said to produce. Therefore, rather than accepting that dominant fears and anxieties are the only ones represented (and thus the only ones we must attend to), this chapter will suggest that the context in which *Dracula* was produced and received was typified by the collision of different values and discourses, each articulating (in often inconsistent ways) conflicting interests.

The re-examination of *Dracula* offered here will suggest the possibility of alternative contemporaneous readings of the tale by drawing on discourses circulating in Victorian England which clash with the governing ones that have been assumed to offer the only context for the novel. But because yesterday's audiences are not, as Andrew Tudor has pointed out, accessible to empirical research (1997: 5), it will not be suggested that these are the 'real' meanings of *Dracula* in contrast to the more familiar ones. Instead, this approach is interested in 'de-universalising' the *idea* of a singular Victorian audience for this widely popularised tale, and to consider the potential readings from those Victorians who have thus far been ignored; women, the working class and the poor. To begin with, however, this chapter turns to the key analyses of *Dracula*, and, because most critics agree that the novel's landscape is one of sexual repression and fear, it will discuss those sexual fears that are considered to be dramatised by the legend of the Count.

SEX AND THE VAMPIRE: MASCULINITY

Dracula, it seems, is a man's tale. And not just a man's tale, but a heterosexual man's tale. Numerous critical interpretations of the novel explain that it raises male (heterosexual) fears in order to ease them (see Richardson 1959, Jackson 1981, Astle 1980; Twitchell 1985; Bentley 1988). This view of the vampire stems from Freudian psychoanalysis with Ernest Jones providing the first critical Freudian landmark on the 'psychic shadow-land' (Skal 1990: 7) that the vampire is said to inhabit.[4] Jones' vampire is a classic Freudian symbol of sexual repression. By drawing on Freud's 'Oedipus Complex' (1925), Jones suggests that fear of the vampire stems from a combination of love, hate and guilt which results from the child's incestuous love for the mother and hatred of the father. For Jones, one of Freud's 'most important discoveries' is that love gives rise to fear when it is guilty and that 'morbid dread always signifies repressed sexual wishes' (1929: 315). Jones states: 'The psychological fact remains and must be faced, that the person who dreads the vampire is the person really afflicted by guilt' (1929: 320).

In the 1950s, Maurice Richardson drew on these insights to provide one of the first Freudian interpretations of *Dracula*. Richardson concurs that the vampire in *Dracula* represents male incestuous, infantile desire and he suggests that the novel presents two father figures in the characters of the Count and Dr Van Helsing. Van Helsing is the 'good father' who provides guidance for youthful masculinity in the shape of the four young members of the 'Crew of Light': Harker, Holmwood, Seward and Morris. Dracula, on the other hand, represents the 'evil father'; the father who keeps all of the women to himself. The good father steers youthful masculinity towards the destruction of the bad father thus ending his sexual monopoly. Richardson therefore sees *Dracula* as a 'blatant demonstration of the Oedipus complex' (1959: 427). Because the Oedipus complex is considered to emanate from masculine psychic drives, it is clear from this analysis that we are to understand the reader of the story to be male. It is also clear that 'he' is supposed to assume the point of view of the Crew of Light and thus experience the gratification of this position; guilt turns to triumph as the reader vicariously participates in the destruction of the vampire – the symbol of his anxiety.

Just over a decade later, Christopher Bentley's analysis of the sexual symbolism in *Dracula* draws directly on Jones. Bentley argues that Jones had identified in the tale of the vampire the 'perversions concealed by symbolism [which] are the dynamic of *Dracula*' and the reasons for its success (1972: 25). Bentley argues that Stoker was 'unaware of the sexual content of his book';[5] he was simply giving expression to his own unconscious desires and repressions. For Bentley, the sexual desires dramatised in the novel take the symbolic form of vampires because of the sexual repression of the Victorian age, of which Stoker's own repression is a part. Sexual repression means that the human characters are presented, and *must* be presented as chaste, so that it is only in the human character's interaction with vampires that they are able to engage in the desired, but repressed, 'perverted' encounters. This accounts for the way that such episodes are 'described in almost obsessional detail in *Dracula*, providing the means for a symbolic presentation of human sexual relationships' (1972: 26). To argue this point, Bentley turns to one of the most talked about scenes in the book; the seduction of Jonathan Harker by the three vampire women at Dracula's castle. Harker himself describes the encounter in highly erotic terms:

> All three had brilliant white teeth, that shone like pearls against the ruby of their voluptuous lips. There was something about them that made me uneasy, some longing and at the same time some deadly fear. I felt in my heart a wicked, burning desire that they would kiss me with those red lips ... I could feel the soft, shivering touch of the lips on the supersensitive skin on my throat, and the hard dents of two sharp teeth, just touching and pausing there. I closed my eyes in a languorous ecstasy and waited – waited with beating heart. (Stoker 1962: 41)

For Bentley, this scene dramatises the desire for 'immediate sexual gratification, though on illicit and dangerous terms' (1972: 26). The three vampire women are a 'tempting alternative to the socially imposed delays and frustrations of his relationship with the chaste but somewhat sexless Mina' (ibid.). Bentley notes that the vampires in the tale tend only to attack members of the opposite sex, thus 'suggesting that vampirism is a perversion of normal heterosexual activity' (1972: 27), presumably chaste, marital intercourse.

But Bentley seems to ignore the obvious masochism of this scene. Jonathan has just discovered that he is locked in Dracula's castle – he is a prisoner. He goes exploring and enters a forbidden room. Soon after, he falls into a state of dreamy languor and, against his will, is aroused by three voluptuous women whom he desires and fears, and whose erotic attack he can do nothing to prevent. However, to describe this scene as one of male masochism would upset the active-male/passive-female gender binary so prevalent in Freudian interpretation.

Like other commentators, James B. Twitchell suggests that the destruction of Dracula by the Crew of Light represents the destruction of the father by the sons. But for Twitchell, the tale is really a mythic lesson in proper sexual conduct for teenagers. Dracula's 'sexual violation' of young women apparently

Fig. 1 Jonathan Harker endures an erotic attack by Dracula's three vampire brides, in *Bram Stoker's Dracula* (1992)

offers double identificatory pleasures for the male adolescent; 'the primal young male audience witnesses the older man defile the virgin ... while at the same time imagining himself to be that powerful man' (1985: 136). However, he also identifies with the 'youthful throng that seeks his overthrow' (ibid.). Thus the vampire myth offers active, aggressive and sadistic identificatory pleasures for the male reader or viewer. Typical of Freudian insistence on the sadism of the male psyche, Twitchell sidesteps the question of male masochism so evident in the Harker seduction scene. The only masochism Twitchell acknowledges is female; the female audience, like the female victim, secretly wants to be violated and 'encourages her own defloration' (ibid.). Twitchell is quite clear that the 'vampire is a projection of the self for the male and the victim is a projection of the self for the female' (1985: 137). This linear view of audience identification insists, as Ken Gelder puts it, 'on a familiar gender distinction where boys are active and sadistic and girls are passive victims' (1994: 96). Constance Penley (1992) aims a similar criticism at psychoanalytic film theory, as does Carol Clover (1992). Nina Auerbach has rather succinctly argued that the 'best-known experts on American popular horror insist that it is and always has been a boy's game' (1995: 3) and in this comment she is directly referring to Twitchell.[6]

The assumption of the centrality of heterosexual masculinity in these accounts of *Dracula* and its readership is disrupted by Christopher Craft's analysis of gender inversion in the novel. Craft points to the novel's dramatisation of a fear of potential sexual mobility that disrupts the fixed gender roles of Victorian society. Craft reads Harker's seduction scene rather differently from the Freudian interpretation. He argues that there is an inversion of Victorian gender norms in *Dracula* which threatens the line between male and female, as in the seduction scene where 'Harker enjoys a "feminine" passivity and awaits the delicious penetration from a woman whose demonism is figured as the power to penetrate' (1990: 169).[7] Moreover, it is the vampire's mouth which is the site of this sexual mobility because it is both an 'inviting orifice' and a 'piercing bone' (ibid.). Yet, the male desire to be penetrated is enacted ambivalently in *Dracula*, and particularly, it is Dracula's potential penetration of Harker that provides one of the greatest anxieties in the novel; 'Dracula's desire to fuse with a male, most explicitly evoked when Harker cuts himself shaving, subtly and dangerously suffuses this text' (1990: 170). But, Craft suggests, the text also produces an 'anxious defence against the very desire it also seeks to liberate' (1990: 177).

Eve Kosofsky-Sedgwick's analysis of the expression of 'homosexual panic' (1985: 83) in the Gothic form might also disrupt the heterosexual assumptions of analyses of *Dracula*, as Gelder demonstrates. Drawing on Sedgwick's notion of an 'erotic triangle' in Gothic novels, Gelder argues that

> the bond which links the two rivals in such a triangle is as strong – or stronger – than the bond which links either of the rivals to their beloved (think, for example, of Dracula and the Crew of Light in their struggle over Lucy, and later Mina in *Dracula*). The former bond is always 'between men'; the latter between men and women. (1994: 59)

These challenges to the Freudian heterosexual tale return us to the idea of the 'Zeitgeist fallacy'. For a common theme running through each of the Freudian accounts of *Dracula* is the notion that the dominant spirit of the Victorian age was one of sexual repression; *Dracula* is seen to represent dominant attitudes towards 'the sexuality that Victorian England denied' (Hatlen 1988: 120). But Victorian age did not deny homosexuality (or sadism and masochism). On the contrary, as Robert Mighall points out, 'it invented these concepts' (1999: 285). Furthermore, while there may have been dominant values about sexual conduct, they were not totalising. Indeed it was the very existence of competing practices and discourses about gender and sexuality that provided the impetus for the Victorian medical establishment to label and categorise certain forms of sexual behaviour as 'deviant', in an effort to stamp its authority on a world of sexual turmoil. One might imagine that the 1890s, which saw Oscar Wilde sent to Reading Gaol as punishment for his sexual transgressions, was a decade of undeniable repression. But it was, as Elaine Showalter explains, a time when 'all the laws that governed sexual identity and behaviour seemed to be breaking down' (1990: 3). The 1890s not only saw the production of *Dracula*, it was also a time when 'New Women and male aesthetes redefined the meanings of femininity and masculinity' (ibid.). The Victorian establishment was undoubtedly as uneasy with these developments as it is likely that Bram Stoker was, but nonetheless, they provided alternative symbols of the male and female. A few years prior to this decade, at least one gay male writer used the image of the vampire to evoke homosexual love. For instance, Richard Dyer notes that in 1885 Carl Heinrich Ulrichs published a short vampire story, 'Manor', which tells of the love between a youth and a seaman, who gives his name to the story. The seaman is killed in a storm and returns as a 'spirit' to suck blood at the youth's breast. The villagers work out that he is a vampire and stake him, but the youth is so lonely without Manor that he wills himself to die; 'his last wish is that he be laid beside Manor in the grave and that the stake be removed from Manor's corpse – "and they did what he asked"' (1988: 47).[8] Dyer points out that from Manor in the 1880s to *The Vampire Lestat* in the 1980s, 'there is a line of vampire or Gothic writing that is predominantly gay-produced, or which at any rate forms part of a gay male reading tradition' (1988: 48). But the possibility of the vampire evoking male homosexuality, which, as Dyer points out, is redolent in the image of the vampire, is ignored in Freudian accounts of the vampire and the reading positions associated with it.

Like male homosexuality, femininity (including lesbianism) is ignored in Freudian accounts of the vampire, but the female was neither absent from the concerns of the Victorian world, nor indeed from the pages of *Dracula* and it is hardly surprising that feminists have returned to those pages with a view to examining the articulation of femininity to be found there.

SEX AND THE VAMPIRE: FEMININITY

Many feminist critics of *Dracula* grant that it is, as Gail Griffin puts it, 'essentially male' (1988: 137), but suggest that its maleness is usually misunderstood. Rather than considering femininity as a passive presence – a mere token of exchange between men and marginal to the 'real' masculine anxieties of the book – feminists argue that it is *femininity* itself that constitutes the novel's anxiety. From this perspective, what men really fear is active female sexuality and the vampires in *Dracula* symbolise that fear. For instance, Phyllis Roth argues that vampires represent the male fear and hatred of femininity. Roth suggests that the main focus of *Dracula* is the male fear of 'suddenly sexual women' (1988: 65) and the repressed desire to commit matricide. The reader is invited to identify with the male aggressors and their violent attacks on the women which dramatises the 'desire to destroy the threatening mother' (ibid.). Similarly, Bram Dijkstra argues that all vampires represent the female body in a distorted and monstrous form. He argues that the vampire demonstrates the way that Western culture simultaneously hates, fears and fetishises the female body, and he suggests that we should reject the 'mass media's lure of "evil sister" stereotyping' (1996: 443) and begin the 'daunting task of exorcising the vampires of misogyny from our imagination' (1996: 7).

However, some feminists read the link between monstrosity and femininity more ambiguously. For instance, Linda Williams argues that a 'strange sympathy and affinity' often develops between the monster and the girl which may

be 'less an expression of sexual desire and more a flash of sympathetic identification' (1984: 87).[9] In a similar vein, Barbara Creed suggests that the vampire *is* the 'monstrous feminine', and although it is shaped to help found the
patriarchal order, she is also interested in what the vampire might offer to a
female audience. She suggests that the vampire is always symbolically female
even if it is nominally depicted as male because it raises the 'abject' nature of
the female body. The vampire, like the female (particularly maternal) body, is
not clean and pure and closed. Instead, it transgresses boundaries and disrupts
ideas about where the body starts and ends. According to Creed, the vampire's
'blood-letting fangs' also invoke the 'mythic vagina dentata' (1993: 72). Thus,
while Creed's vampire may be abject, it certainly does not code the feminine
as 'passive'. Creed wonders, then, what the woman does on encountering the
vampire: 'Does she recognise herself in the figure of the monstrous feminine?
To what extent might the female spectator feel empowered when identify-
ing with the female castrator?' (1993: 155). Creed's questions disrupt the linear
Freudian model of identification (and the active/passive gender binary) by suggesting that the woman may identify with the vampire rather than the victim.
Yet, while it is clear that many twentieth- and twenty-first-century females
empathise with the vampire (and it is this audience to whom Creed is referring), it is difficult to provide evidence of this for nineteenth-century female
audiences and this position must remain speculative.

For many feminist interpretations of *Dracula,* however, it is the destruction
of the vampire Lucy that is considered to be the symbolic centre of the tale,
for it is in this scene that the fear and hatred of active female sexuality is most
fully revealed and then destroyed. For instance, Griffin contrasts the rather
elusive presence of Dracula in the novel with the highly erotic descriptions
of the vampire women, including Lucy. She argues that it is significant that
Dracula's 'reality explodes upon the other characters not in his own person,
but in Lucy's' (1988: 139). For it is only when Lucy becomes actively 'voluptuous'
and 'wanton' that she becomes a figure of horror in *Dracula*. Her vampirism is
sexual aggressiveness and her transformation symbolises 'the worst nightmare
and dearest fantasy of the Victorian male: the pure girl turned sexually raven-
ous beast' (1988: 143).

Lucy is clearly described in aggressively sexual terms in the scenes leading
up to and including her destruction. She is then is dispatched by her fiancé in
equally sexual terms, as described by Seward:

> Arthur placed the point over the heart, and as I looked I could see its
> dint in the white flesh. Then he struck with all his might. The Thing in
> the coffin writhed; and twisted in wild contortions; the sharp white teeth
> champed together till the lips were cut and the mouth was smeared with
> a crimson foam. But Arthur never faltered. He looked like a figure of
> Thor as his untrembling arm rose and fell, driving deeper and deeper
> the mercy-bearing stake, whilst blood from the pierced heart welled and
> spurted up around it. (Stoker 1962: 194)

The price Lucy pays for her 'wantonness' is a stake driven through her heart by the man she loved, followed by decapitation. While this scene is read by Freudian critics as symbolising sex with a virgin – Lucy's cries 'reminiscent of sexual intercourse and orgasm' (Bentley 1972: 30) – feminist critics read this scene as 'nothing so much as the combined group rape of an unconscious woman' (Senf 1987: 100).

Elaine Showalter links the scene of Lucy's staking with a number of earlier scenes in which the Crew of Light replenish the fast-fading Lucy with a series of blood transfusions. The sexual imagery is explicit, even from the point of view of the donors. Lucy shares bodily fluids with most of the men in the novel and even Van Helsing suggests that Lucy is a polyandrist following these transfusions. He asks the others to keep their blood donations secret from her fiancé, Arthur, who describes his own donation as a consummation of his marriage to Lucy. Meanwhile Dr Seward recalls his donation in terms of sexual conquest:

> It was with a feeling of personal pride that I could see a faint tinge of colour steal back into the pallid cheeks and lips. No man knows, till he experiences it, what it is to feel his own lifeblood drawn away into the veins of the woman he loves. (Stoker 1962: 119)

Showalter comments that Lucy represents the sexual daring of the New Woman, particularly in her desire to marry all three of her suitors; 'why can't they let a girl marry three men, or as many who want her?' Of the staking scene itself Showalter comments that

> the sexual implications of the scene are embarrassingly clear. First there is the gang-rape with the impressive phallic instrument ... Then there is the decapitation, a remarkably frequent occurrence in male *fin-de-siècle* writing ... the severed head also seems to be a way to control the New Woman by separating the mind from the body. (1990: 181–2)

Yet while the feminist reading of the staking of Lucy seems entirely convincing, it is sometimes accompanied by less sustainable assumptions about the reader. Griffin, for instance, collapses together the Crew of Light, Stoker and 'his audience' (1988: 141), as if horror at Lucy's *sexuality* is the only way to read this scene. But is it not possible that at least some readers were rather more horrified at what was happening to Lucy's body? Stoker tries to convince his reader that Lucy's violent destruction is necessary because of her 'monstrousness', and critics tell us (as we have seen) that this scene offers masculine pleasures, but would it not have produced terror in some readers? What, indeed, would Victorian New Women have made of this scene? Would they have been disturbed by the misogynistic sexual symbolism and the violence accompanying it? Would all male audiences have taken pleasure in the destruction of Lucy, even those, such as homosexual and poor men, whose own bodies were as much at risk by the patriarchal Victorian establishment? I would like to suggest that there is evidence of belief systems and values which are at odds with those of the Victorian patriarchal establishment and which provide the discursive ground for alternative readings of the staking of Lucy that is, as has been suggested, at the heart of *Dracula*. At the centre of this scene is a corpse – Lucy's corpse – and I would like to frame considerations about the different ways that Victorian audiences may have responded to this scene by examining differing Victorian attitudes towards the corpse.

DOCTORS, VAMPIRES AND DISSECTION

In the late eighteenth and nineteenth centuries the dissection of human corpses became more a widespread practice within the medical community, once legislation permitted this practice for medical purposes.[10] But the medical approach to the dissection of the human body was not gender neutral (nor was it class or race neutral) as we shall see. Ludmilla Jordanova, in a volume on medical images of the female body, has noted the connection between medical knowledge and sexual fantasy and has suggested that late eighteenth- and nineteenth-century medical imagery had an 'obsession with female corpses in particular' (1989: 98). Jordanova analyses the way that eighteenth-century wax models of female bodies reveal the medical view of the female form and of gender differences. These (female) models were always recumbent and excessively life-like, with such details as long hair, eyelashes and sometimes even a pearl necklace. They are also significantly termed 'Anatomical Venuses' and are positioned lying 'on silk or velvet cushions, in passive, yet sexually inviting poses' (1989: 44). Jordanova contrasts this to male anatomical models which are neither covered in flesh, nor recumbent; 'instead there are either upright muscle men, with no flesh at all, or severely truncated male torsos' (1989: 45). Jordanova also comments that the female wax models were constructed in layers which could be lifted up so that parts could be revealed and/or removed. She argues that 'the process of looking into the female ones by removing successive layers of organs' has distinct sexual resonances (ibid.). A viewer of the female anatomical model was intended to respond 'as to a female body that delighted the sight and invited sexual thoughts' and one form such thoughts can take is the 'erotic charge' of 'mentally unclothing a woman' (1989: 55).

The coupling of medical knowledge with the eroticised undressing of the female corpse and opening it up, persisted into the nineteenth-century in both medical texts and in painting. Showalter has commented that a popular theme in *'fin-de-siècle* painting, as in medical literature, was the doctor performing an autopsy on the body of a drowned prostitute' (1990: 134). Both Jordanova and Showalter suggest that a particularly vivid example of this is Hasselhort's German painting and lithograph of the anatomist J. G. C. Lucae directing the dissection on the corpse of a beautiful young woman who had drowned herself. Lucae is depicted in this dissection painting 'as if he were revealing the secrets of her sexuality' (Showalter 1990: 132). In the painting, the partially unclothed

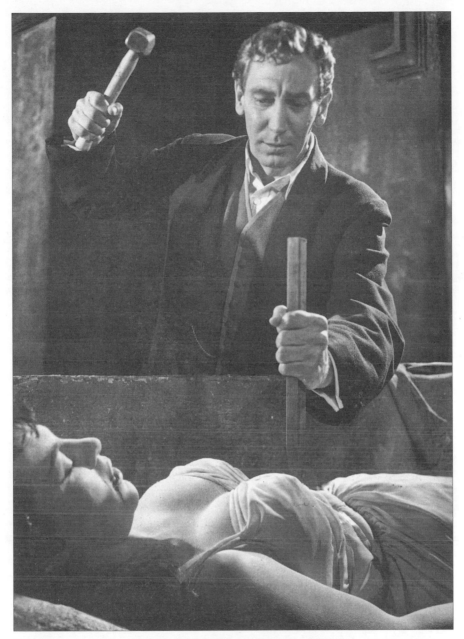

Fig. 2 John van Eyssen prepares to 'release' Valerie Grant in *Horror of Dracula* (1958)

body reveals the breasts and belly. A group of anatomists and artists stand watching as one anatomist performs the dissection. Jordanova comments that he is 'holding up a sheet of skin, close to her breast, as if it were a thin article of clothing so delicate and fine in its texture' (1989: 99). This painting is strikingly similar to Stoker's early scenes of Dr Van Helsing and Dr Seward examin-

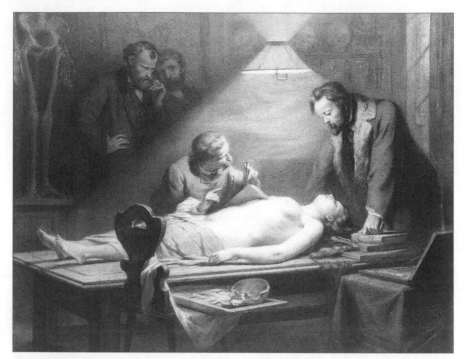

Fig. 3 Anonymous print of a painting by J. H. Hasslehorst, *J. C. G. Lucae and his Assistants Dissecting a Female Cadaver*, 1864

ing Lucy's prone body in her tomb. It has also been reproduced in countless *Dracula* adaptations on the stage and the screen.

This erotic fascination for unveiling and undressing female cadavers provides an alternative understanding of the medical and representational context for the staking of Lucy, for Stoker's novel is as fascinated with erotically charged revelations about female corpses as the Victorian medical establishment. Thus the scene of Lucy's staking simultaneously enacts a sexualised corpse mutilation as well as suggesting a rape. The whole episode of Lucy's despatch is one of the most drawn out in the novel, filling twenty pages of Dr Seward's diary between Van Helsing's first instruction to Seward that they must spend the night in the graveyard where Lucy is buried, to the final staking of Lucy by Arthur Holmwood in the company of Van Helsing, Seward and Quincy. Indeed, this part of the narrative is structured as a series of revelations – the literal unveiling of Lucy leads to the unveiling of knowledge about Lucy. This corresponds to what Jordanova considers to be one of the preoccupations of the medical world in the nineteenth-century – the notion that 'understanding' is brought about by the 'successful removal of layers' (1989: 55), knitting together medical knowledge production and sexual desire. Van Helsing must successively reveal what Lucy is to the other members of the Crew of Light in order to convince them to perform the act which at first they each abhor – the desecration and mutilation of Lucy's corpse. In fact, Van Helsing reveals the contents of Lucy's coffin no less than three times. The first is on the evening of 26 September, accompanied by Seward. Seward is initially horrified by Van Helsing's desecration of Lucy's tomb, and describes the act in terms of sexual violation:

'What are you going to do?' I asked. 'To open the coffin. You shall yet be convinced.' Straight away he began taking out the screws, and finally lifting off the lid, showing the casing of lead beneath. The sight was almost too much for me. It seemed to be such an affront to the dead as it would have been to have stripped off her clothing in her sleep whilst living;[11] I actually took hold of his hand to stop him. (Stoker 1962: 178)

Seward clearly considers this activity to be socially inappropriate and sexual; it is as if Van Helsing (like the anatomist Lucae) had 'stripped off her clothing in her sleep'. The erotic frisson is undeniable, and yet at this stage Seward's moral propriety and sensibility produce a hesitation. His response to the desecration of the tomb is – for the moment – framed by a non-medical and non-diagnostic mindset that emphasises conventional morality and his 'feelings' for Lucy. From this perspective any violation of a corpse was considered unspeakable. But Van Helsing begins to persuade Seward of his diagnosis of Lucy, and indeed of the *need* to subsume all of his feelings for Lucy into a diagnostic framework, for such detachment will prove necessary to perform her eventual destruction.

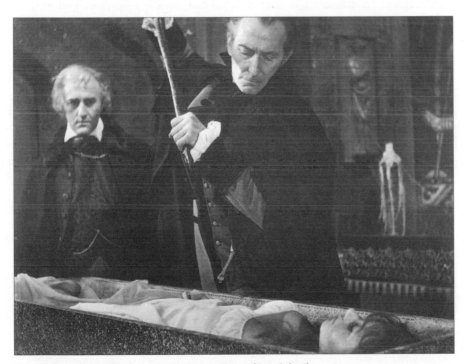

Fig. 4 Peter Cushing stakes the vampirised Lucy in *Horror of Dracula* (1958)

The following day before Lucy's funeral, the two men return to her coffin and Van Helsing opens it once again, this time Lucy's body looking 'if possible, more radiantly beautiful than ever ... The lips were red, nay redder than before; and on the cheeks was a delicate bloom' (1962: 181). When Seward asks Van Helsing what he means to do, Van Helsing answers 'I shall cut off her head and fill her mouth with garlic, and I shall drive a stake through her body' (ibid.). Seward's response to this is to admit that it makes him 'shudder to think of so mutilating the body of the woman whom I had loved' (1962: 182). However, his horror at the thought of mutilating the corpse has lessened overnight, and Seward admits 'the feeling was not so strong as I had expected' (ibid.). Seward's mindset at this stage begins to move from a moral one to a medical-diagnostic one, which is concurrent with his unfettered erotic projections onto Lucy's corpse. Significantly, it is at this stage that the corpse (which is even more beautiful than before) begins to turn from 'Lucy' into 'it' for Seward, a 'case' of vampirism to be solved. Lucy's body is thus both more sexually attractive in death and more objectified. The links between the New Woman and Lucy's sexual appetites have already been mentioned and it is pertinent to note Showalter's comments about the medical establishment's attitude toward the New Woman. She suggests that if the 'rebellious New Woman' could be turned into a 'silent body', her resistance to convention could be treated as a case to be solved. According to Showalter, this is best effected if the woman can be 'transformed from "she" into "it"' (1990: 128). By the third visit to Lucy's crypt, Van Helsing has completed Lucy's transformation into an 'it' in the minds of Seward, Quincy and the man who will perform the deed, fiancé Arthur Holmwood. Like Seward, Holmwood initially finds the desecration of the grave 'too much': '"Heavens and earth, no!", cried Arthur in a storm of passion. "Not for the wide world will I consent to any *mutilation* of her dead body"' (1962: 186; my emphasis). Once more, his horror stems from a moral and emotional mindset which considers the defilement of Lucy's corpse to be an act beyond the pale. However, at the third opening of Lucy's tomb, when all trace of Lucy's 'sweet purity' has been stripped away and she has finally been diagnosed as 'voluptuous', 'carnal' and 'unspiritual', all of the men 'shudder' again, but this time *not* with horror at the idea of defiling Lucy's corpse but with excitement and the *knowledge* of what Lucy has become – 'wanton' (1962: 192). The men have shifted from a moral and emotional attitude towards Lucy's corpse to a diagnostic one and in the process have collapsed together the issue of knowledge with covert and perverse sexual desire for female corpses.

For Jordanova, Victorian violence and idealisation of women 'constitute two sides of the same coin' (1989: 62); the female form is both venerable and profane. Lucy 'the pure' has turned into Lucy 'the thing', thus justifying the act to be committed. Furthermore, once the men have fully accepted the diagnostic approach to Lucy (and their 'feelings' for her have been replaced with 'knowledge' about her), the earlier images of undressing Lucy's corpse are replaced with images of a much more violent nature – her actual mutilation – and the men's expression of hesitation about unveiling Lucy in her tomb turns to grim satisfaction at the proposed violence on her body. Indeed Seward comments that were the task up to him he could now perform it with 'savage delight' (1962: 195). Thus, the staking of Lucy can be read as an erotically-charged corpse mutilation which mirrors the dissections being performed on female corpses throughout the Victorian era.

However, the availability of this reading does not suggest that all readers would have shared the grim satisfaction of the Crew of Light. While most branches of the medical and legal world accepted the practice of dissection, working-class Victorians regarded it as an unacceptable form of mutilation, and the practice was similarly troubling to sections of the middle classes. We shall see how dissection and the role of the anatomist was feared and loathed by the working-class population who generally deplored the possibility of their own bodies, or those of their loved ones, being cut up and disembowelled, and who associated the anatomist with the cruellest punishments meted out by the state.

As Jordanova suggests, there 'can be no doubt that violence [on the dissection table] has been focused particularly on women's genitals' (1989: 61).[13] Ruth Richardson's historical analysis of the Anatomy Act of 1832 confirms that 'sexual indecency' took place in the dissection room (1987: 95) and she comments upon one female anatomic model which was quoted as being 'chained down upon a table, as if opened alive' (ibid.). Richardson also suggests that the official language of 'detachment' and 'objectivity' found in dissection manuals concealed the evidence of the widespread 'disrespect and maltreatment of the dead in the process of dissection' (ibid.). Lucy's treatment at the hands of the Crew of Light mirrors the treatment of the corpse at the hands of the anatomist, both actually and in the perceptions of the working-class and lower-middle-class population.

The rhetoric of detachment, of seeing a corpse as an object (an 'it') accompanied the disrespectful and perverted treatment particularly inflicted on working-class and female corpses. But there was another population whose bodies and corpses were maltreated and made 'Other' by the Victorian medical establishment, the echoes of which can be read in the depiction of Lucy's corpse. It has been suggested that it is important that Lucy is turned into an 'it', an unconditional 'Other' in the minds of the men. But her Otherness, and the violence it permits, is importantly linked to racial otherness, and indeed links sexual and racial Otherness. The idea of aggressive and excessive female sexuality was predominantly projected, not onto white middle-class women, but onto black African women, Native American women (as well as poor women).[12] Black African and Native American women were considered to have larger sexual organs than white middle-class women and throughout the eighteenth century and into the nineteenth century African women in particular were exhibited in the parlours of the rich and at parties to demonstrate that the source of their 'excessive' and 'deviant' sexuality was to be found in their physiology. In 1819, J. J. Virey wrote that the vaginas of black women evinced a 'voluptuousness' that was 'developed to a degree of lascivity unknown in our climate, for their sexual organs are much more developed than those of the whites' (quoted in Doerksen 1997: 139).[14] In 1892 an American gynaecologist, Robert. T. Morris, published an article entitled 'Is Evolution Trying to Do Away With the Clitoris?', where he claimed that Nature intended to 'do away with the clitoris in highly civilised varieties of *homo sapiens*' (1892: 848), and he offered this as an explanation for his view that the clitoris in white women was being covered over by the prepuce. The following quote demonstrates the way that Morris expresses the Victorian mix of ideas about racial hierarchy, racial purity, animalism and female sexuality:

> In negresses the glans clitoridis is free ... excepting a few individuals who probably possess a large admixture of white blood ... In highly domes-ticated animals the glans clitoridis is free ... I presume that the glans clitoridis is free in wild tribes generally, but my attempts at getting data from the Indians are as yet a failure, because agency physicians to whom I referred state that Indian women would not allow them to collect sta-tistics such as we wanted. (1892: 849–50)

The link between sexual lasciviousness, savagery, animalism and race expressed by Morris was widespread in the nineteenth century. Furthermore, his Othering of Native American women is connected to his dehumanising view of them, articulated through his clinical detachment; seeing them as an 'it', simply the (unwilling) object of his research.[15]

This linkage of the rhetoric of detachment and the sexualisation of a racial Other is also found overtly in the world of medical dissections as can be seen in the case of Sarah Bartmann (Saartje Baartman). Bartmann was an African woman who was exhibited in England in the early nineteenth century in order to display her 'prominent buttocks, which were imagined to be a sign of her overdeveloped sexuality' (Doerksen 1997: 139). Significantly, she was labelled the 'Hottentot Venus' which alludes to both the name for female wax anatomical models of the time (implying the dissectability of her body) and to Bartmann's racial difference. When Bartmann died at the age of 25, her body was indeed dissected and her buttocks and external genitalia were removed and donated to the Musee di l'homme in Paris where they continue to be displayed today. Victorian anatomical science and the medical world generally were clearly grue-somely fascinated with what they considered to be 'savage' and 'excessive' sexu-ality, but deployed pseudo-scientific and racist discourses to rationalise this projection of illicit desires onto an Other, and crucial to this project was seeing a variety of women as 'cases', as 'its', and thus dehumanising them.

The surrounding context for Stoker's novel then, is not one that can be ade-quately understood from a 'gender-neutral' or 'race-neutral' perspective (which inevitably implies a white, middle-class and male view at any rate). The medical field, which had an enormous impact on the culture of the era, was troubled by the 'unknown continent' of female sexuality, black and native female bodies, and by their own unacknowledged desires. Indeed Teri Ann Doerksen argues that Victorian writings about Africa and Victorian vampire tales served similar functions; they create a mythos of race, Otherness and sexuality based on assumptions of superiority and inferiority. Doerksen argues that Lucy 'like Sarah Bartmann, is transformed from a woman to a half-woman/half-animal' (1997: 142). This transformation is based on the way that Lucy's body has been metaphorically turned into that of a sexual wanton, even before her death. Her wantonness is, according to Doerksen, akin to the 'Hottentot Venus', but instead of 'evidence of a less evolved culture, Lucy represents a devolution ... away from the Victorian concept of civilisation – and towards the savage, the primitive, the sexual, the uncontrolled' (1997: 142). Lucy's vampiric corpse, it seems, is a repository of all that the patriarchal medical and legal establishment loathed and desired. But what of the loathings and desires other sections of society?

One of the concerns of this book is to investigate the gap that often exists between critical interpretations of texts and popular ones. That the vampire tale was a very popular tale amongst the British working class by the mid-nineteenth century is well established. By the late 1830s, three quarters of the working-class population had learned to read and the level of literacy grew steadily throughout the nineteenth century. Working-class readers consumed large quantities of 'penny dreadfuls' which were serialised eight-page Gothic horror tales that sold for a penny a piece. One of the most popular of the 'penny dreadfuls' was *Varney the Vampire* by James Malcolm Ryder. *Varney* was a best-seller which ran to 108 instalments between the years 1845–47 when it was finally published as a novel. It is this tale that popularised the vampire for the English-speaking reading public and its depiction of the *suffering* vampire was the one that working-class Victorians would have been most familiar with, not the monolithic force of evil that Dracula will come to signify at the end of the century. Nina Auerbach suggests that Varney is faithful to a 'key attribute' of his predecessor, Polidori's Lord Ruthven, in that he offers mortals 'the lure of his friendship' (1995: 28). Auerbach also reminds us of the huge readership for *Varney the Vampyre* and comments that 'Varney's friendship, like his audience, is broader than Byronic intimacy; it embraces not a sole chosen spirit, but an entire society' (ibid.). Also, unlike Dracula, Varney's female victims are not transformed into vampires; 'instead, the vampire and the socialised characters become increasingly difficult to distinguish', with 'infection' giving way to 'friendship' (1995: 29–30). It is the depiction of this rather different fear, the fear of intimacy, that would have been recognisable to Varney's large popular audience, contrasting considerably with the vampirism readers were to encounter in *Dracula* at the turn of the century.

Large numbers of working-class Victorians probably would not have read *Dracula* as soon as it was published, because the first-edition hardback copy would have been too expensive at six shillings (although some might have read it through lending libraries). However, the publisher, Constable, brought out a paperback edition three-and-a-half years later in 1901 that was aimed at a less affluent readership at six pence a copy – not significantly dearer than a penny dreadful – indicating that there was a sizable readership for the novel beyond the well-to-do middle classes (see Miller 2002). I would like to suggest that *Dracula* may have been read by a poor, working-class and female audience rather differently to the dominant discourses as represented by the Crew of Light, not only because of the tale's divergence from *Varney*, but because of these groups' attitudes towards, and experiences of, the medical establishment that the Crew of Light represent. Indeed, both Carol A. Senf (1988) and Robert Mighall (1999) suggest that the narrative structure of Dracula is unstable, and the accounts of the diarists regularly coded as unreliable. There may be enough instability in the narrative to suggest that other readings were possible, even to a Victorian audience, particularly on the question of what happens to the body of Lucy. So to what extent would the activities of the Crew of Light in Lucy's tomb have deeply troubled the reading public, who themselves feared and hated the possibility of their own dissection?

There is considerable evidence to show that throughout the nineteenth and into the twentieth century, dissection was associated in the popular mind with gross defilement. According to Richardson, early nineteenth-century popular belief considered that 'dissection represented not only the exposure of naked-ness, the possibility of assault upon and disrespect towards the dead – but also, the deliberate mutilation or destruction of identity, perhaps for eternity' (1987: 29). It is worth noting that until the 1832 Anatomy Act, dissection was part of the punishment meted out to a convicted murderer, following hanging, and thus the fear of dissection was not only to be found on superstitious or religious grounds. It was a violently unpopular punishment and at times contributed to riots at the gallows or the razing of institutions where dissections were performed. Similarly, because of the anatomist's role in performing dissections at the gallows, popular belief associated anatomists with the state machinery of death and punishment after death. Richardson comments that the role of surgeons at the gallows 'was a material aggravation of popular hostility towards anatomy and dissection and promoted distrust of the medical professions' (1987: 53).

Furthermore it was not only the poor who feared dissection; the middle classes also abhorred it and took great pains to ensure that their own bodies remained intact after death. Just like the poor, the well-off feared grave-rob-bing and associated this activity, justifiably, with anatomy – for it was in the process of supplying newly-dead human corpses to anatomists that grave-rob-bing flourished. Even medical doctors 'assured the integrity of their own (and their relatives') bodies after death' (1987: 98). To the bereaved of every class,

> the conception of their spouse or child dragged out of the coffin, shoved into a sack, manhandled in transit, stretched out on a slab, decapitated or dismembered, and cut by (possibly irreverent) training anatomists, may in many cases have resulted in profound psychological disturbance. (1987: 78)

The 1832 Anatomy Act, however, lessened the fear of grave-robbing for the wealthy by legalising the use of the bodies of the poor for 'anatomical exam-ination' – a euphemism for dissection (1987: 125). The Act declared that the unclaimed paupers' bodies, of those who died in the poor house, the work house, in prison, or in hospitals for the poor – 'those who during their life have been maintained at the public charge' – would qualify for dissection.[16] In an atmosphere of brutality towards the poor (culminating in the New Poor Act two years later), poverty was criminalised and the poor could expect the same treatment as the worst of criminals after their death. In fact, dissection as punishment for the criminal was only repealed by the 1832 Act as an attempt to mollify parliamentary opposition to the Bill by attempting to disentangle *overt* associations of dissection with punishment; its covert role as a punishment for the poor was retained. But as Richardson puts it, 'there cannot have been much comfort to a pauper in the knowledge that he or she would be dissected on the slab *instead* of a murderer, rather than *alongside* one' (1987: 207). The Act only incidentally 'endorse[d] the respectability of scientific medicine'. Its main purpose was as an 'instrumental and symbolic degradation of poverty' and it 'served as a class reprisal against the poor' (1987: 266). And the poor knew it. Dissection retained its association with punishment, so that 'in the public mind, the word "dissection" could not fail to have been associated not only with the death sentence, but with the punitive destruction of the body' (1987: 204).

The Anatomy Act terrorised the poor, and, at the same time, provided the basis for a long-lasting public hatred of both the practice of dissection and those who engaged in it. Throughout Victorian times there remained a discrepancy between the attitudes of parliamentarian and medical 'reformers' towards the working-class corpse, and the attitudes of the working classes themselves. While the working-class corpse was an 'object' and a 'nuisance' (1987: 262) to health reformers, the working class themselves considered insuring themselves for proper burial services to be more important than health insurance, and spent 'disproportionately large' amounts of their 'meagre budgets' on such insurance and on funerals in an effort to avoid the anatomist's knife (ibid.).[17] Numerous cases, such as Rosanna Rox, who called upon the Mayor of Newcastle to aid her in 1841 when her mother's corpse was forcibly taken by men working for the local anatomist, fuelled popular outrage at the Act and its contraventions. The mother's body had been quickly immersed in near-boiling water before flaying in order to remove all traces of identity. This story and others like it would be told over and over again in public houses, thus intensifying the fear of dissection and of anatomists. Richardson comments that the 'poor endured the experience of powerlessness and swallowed feelings of hurt and injustice, though they did not forget' (1987: 264). Yet in 1896 (the year before *Dracula* was published) James Bailey claimed, with a familiar lack of sensitivity, that 'the best tribute to the success of the Act, is the very small alterations which have been made between 1832 and the present day' (from *The Diary of a Resurrectionist*, 1896: 118, quoted in Richardson 1987: 265). In fact, hardly any alterations were made to the Act in the 1890s; the poor continuing to be the sole fodder for the dissector's slab. Meanwhile, by the 1890s, the working class had developed a tradition of holding funeral raffles and other such events in public houses for acquiring donations in order to ensure a respectful funeral for the local dead, demonstrating a continuing hatred at the idea of, and fear at the possibility of, dissection. According to Richardson, the fear of dissection occasioned by a pauper's death and burial, 'infected and afflicted the entire working class in the Victorian era' (ibid.).

I would like to suggest that these popular attitudes towards dissection and the fear of the anatomist's knife constitute an alternative reception context for *Dracula* the novel amongst the working class and the lower-middle classes, who began reading what Stoker himself called 'a shilling shocker' (perhaps overly modestly) in large numbers by 1901 with the abridged publication of the Constable paperback edition aimed specifically at the less well educated. It is also worth remembering that these attitudes were not restricted to the lower end of the economic stratum but also had currency amongst the wealthy, particularly those outside of the scientific and medical world, the safety of whose own graves directly benefited from the Anatomy Act and the degradation of the poor. For some, at least, this was a source of guilt.

Victorian society had conflicting discourses about death and the proper conduct towards human remains, which suggests that it is possible that the mutilation of Lucy's corpse in the novel may have been one of the most troubling episodes for many of its Victorian readers, playing directly on their own fears of going under the anatomists knife in death. It is not only twentieth-century critics who consider the staking of Lucy to be the most significant event in the book. Indeed, one American review from 1899 claims that 'Nothing in fiction is more powerful than the scene at the killing of the vampire in Lucy's tomb' (quoted in Auerbach and Skal 1997: 367).[18] Furthermore, contemporary reviewers certainly did draw distinctions between different types of readers. For instance the *Daily Mail* reviewer of June 1897 recommended that the novel should be avoided by 'persons of small courage and weak nerves' (quoted in Auerbach and Skal 1997: 363-4). Similarly, the *Bookman* of August 1897 warned its readers to keep *Dracula* 'out of the way of nervous children', but commented that a 'grown reader, unless he be of unserviceably delicate stuff, will both shudder and enjoy' (quoted in Auerbach and Skal 1997: 366). Presumably, these 'manly' readers would have been Stoker's ideal reader (shuddering along with the Crew of Light), but clearly not his only reader. While neither contemporary reviews nor an indication of the context of popular beliefs about death and dissection that surrounded the reception of the novel can give us immediate access to a reading public now long gone, it is possible to suppose, given the distrust of surgeons and anatomists generally, that readers *may* have been more suspicious of the Crew of Light than Stoker intended, and not at all reassured by their triumph. The actions of the Crew of Light were not dissimilar to those of a rash of nineteenth-century corpse mutilators who were themselves dubbed 'modern vampires' by the popular press.

CORPSE MUTILATION AND 'MODERN VAMPIRES'

Throughout the nineteenth century there were famous cases of so-called 'modern vampires'; men who dug up corpses in graveyards and mutilated them with erotic intent. These cases captured public attention and were well publicised in the press because of the way they gruesomely played upon the widespread fear and loathing of body-snatching and dissection. These cases were also thoroughly examined by the emerging psychiatric medicine. Sexology and psychiatry were branches of medical science that were gaining respectability and prominence by the 1890s. Freud had yet to publish his first significant work in psychoanalysis (*Three Essays on the Theory of Sexuality*, 1905) and so it was sexology (rather than psychoanalysis) that supplied Victorian society with its definitions and categorisations of 'deviant' behaviour. However, according to Robert Mighall, sexology did not simply 'discover' that certain behaviours were sexual, instead it actively '*produced* [the sexual] meaning' of conduct (1999: 212). He argues that activities that would have been ascribed to monsters in folklore came to be labelled as sexual perversions in sexological discourse. The monstrous was eroticised in the writings of Victorian psychiatrists and sexologists in order, argues Mighall, to replace the concept of 'evil with sickness and mystery with perversion' (1999: 227).

Many high-profile cases of corpse mutilation not only found their way into the press, but also into sexological manuals such as Richard von Krafft-Ebing's *Psychopathia Sexualis* (1893) and one particularly famous case being that of Sergeant Françoise Bertrand. Bertrand became renown in the late 1840s for digging up bodies from graveyards in Paris and mutilating them, and he was dubbed 'the vampire' in the popular press because of the authorities' inability to catch him. Yet he was eventually arrested and court-martialled in July 1849, and he received a jail sentence. A number of medical experts examined this case and, aware of Bertrand's 'vampire' label, intervened to 'provide this "vampire" with a more appropriate scientific label' (Mighall 1999: 213). In other words, modern science took the opportunity of this sensational case to assert its own authority to explain, classify and sexualise monstrous behaviour, whilst simultaneously distancing itself from the 'ignorant' belief in vampirism. This case enters English sexological discourse via the *Journal of Psychological Medicine and Mental Pathology*, through an article entitled 'Impulsive Insanity – The French Vampire'.[19] There was, however, some disagreement among experts as to whether Bertrand's insanity was predominantly destructive monomania or erotic monomania. But Bertrand's condition would eventually be catalogued as 'Case 23' (1893: 69) under 'Sadism' in 1886 in Krafft-Ebing's *Psychopathia Sexualis*, under the heading 'Mutilation of Corpses' (1893: 67), and its designation as a sexual perversion was secured. Perhaps revealingly, Krafft-Ebing retains the link between sexual perversion and vampirism by referring to Bertrand as a 'modern vampire', who 'dug up bodies with his hands', and 'when he obtained a body, he cut it up with a sword or a pocket-knife, tore out the entrails and then masturbated' (1983: 70).

For Mighall, it is cases like these which first provide us with the sexual explanations for vampirism that have come to dominate critical accounts of *Dracula*. Through the discourses of sexology and psychiatry the vampire of folklore is 'transformed into a sexual deviant' (1999: 217). There is a problem with this very interesting analysis, which is that there does not seem to be a folkloric tradition of vampirism in the English language to be transformed in this way. It is widely acknowledged that the word (and the concept) 'vampire' did not enter the English language until the late eighteenth century, and thus simultaneously with the medical discourses that were deemed to have transformed it. In other words, in the English language, the vampire is a modern idea, not a folkloric one, and if it is a metaphorical creature, it is one that in the English language at any rate, relates to a modern sensibility (see Twitchell 1981). Also, if Victorian sexological discourses linked corpse mutilation with vampirism, does this not shed rather a different light on to the activities of the men in Lucy's tomb? A reading of the staking of Lucy scene which reflects this historical situation, that is, which reflects the contemporary sexological discourses that were responsible for interpreting such actions, would suggest that the men in the Crew of Light are *mutilating* Lucy's corpse, an act that renders them as vampiric as Lucy herself and destabilises the narrative justifications for their actions. This is not a reading that Mighall is prepared to entertain, however, because he insists that the sexual symbolism in the novel exists only in order to mask the 'real' fear of Victorian society – the fear of the supernatural itself. For Mighall, it is essential that 'vampirism really *is* vampirism, and that "sexuality" does not enter the picture' (1999: 247). If not, Mighall argues, the men must be seen as necro-sadists, and 'therefore subversive of Victorian morality' (1999: 246). Yet, as we have seen, the actions of the Crew of Light are not out of step with the anatomical branches of the medical world, nor the legal one which enshrined their hated practices in law as part of an overt punishment of the poor and of women. This is precisely the point that Doerksen makes when she suggests that *Dracula* is, 'framed by a scientific narrative structure ... that would not have been out of place in ... Krafft-Ebing's *Psychopathia Sexualis*' (1997: 140). In contrast, it may be the case that Bram Stoker himself deployed the language of the *supernatural* in order to justify and legitimate that which was unacceptable to the non medico-legal world, who were, after all, his readers. Either way, it is unavoidably the case that the actions of the Crew of Light are perilously close to the necro-sadism of the 'modern vampire' – indeed as we have seen, the men themselves describe their actions as 'mutilation' and they take pains to avoid detection. The Crew of Light perform an attack on Lucy's body not unlike those of the 'modern vampire', Sergeant Bertrand. But their mutilation of her corpse shares important features with the practices of the Victorian medical establishment itself, members of which were also conducting acts on dead female bodies that would not have been out of place in the very medical manuals that diagnosed these pathological behaviours in others.

The dividing line between the erotically-motivated corpse mutilations carried out by Bertrand and scientific dissection (including the genital mutilation of corpses such as Bartmann's) was established primarily in the discourses that surrounded each. Indeed medical science actively produced these discourses partly because of the popular association between dissection and gruesome activities, such as grave robbing and body-snatching. As Jordanova points out:

we know that popular associations between butchers, barbers, surgeons, vivisectionists and even murderers have led medical practitioners to present themselves as distinctive: as rational, scientific, in alliance with polite culture, and clean, for instance, and to strive for enhancement of their social status. (1989: 138)

Anatomists and surgeons avoided Bertrand's sexological label of 'perversion' through the deployment of scientific discourse, and this (at least in part) was constructed around dehumanising and thus Othering the dissection 'cases' (while at the same time keeping the female ones highly erotic). Similarly, the Crew of Light attempt to avoid those connotations through their own Othering of Lucy. What is common to both discourses is that the Othering takes place on the grounds of supposed excessive 'voluptuousness' (associated with the Otherness of black and native women) and a motivation to reveal 'the truth' about female 'wantonness'.

Stoker may have stirred – and then assuaged – the deepest fears of bour-geois patriarchal England (the 'manly' reader described above), by destroying a voraciously sexual female body, which is justified on the grounds that they were saving her from a fate worse than death. But he may have stirred quite different fears amongst other classes of readers by subjecting Lucy to the mutilation of her corpse, which was in itself considered to be a fate worse than death. It was a fate, no less, potentially inflicted not only on Lucy but on an entire class of people, though no fault of their own, by the very medico-legal establishment that the Crew of Light represents. Just as Lucy's 'only crime' was her beauty, 'a blatant' sign of her sexuality (Cranny-Francis 1988: 68), the black woman's crime her colour, another blatant sign of her sexuality, the pauper's only crime was blatant poverty, itself a form of Otherness to Victorian England. Thus, the destruction of Lucy's body may have produced terror of the action itself amongst many readers.

In this chapter I have attempted to disassemble the idea of a unified Victorian reading public and its seemingly singular interpretation of *Dracula*. I have suggested that this work could not produce a uniform response from Victorian readers, because this epoch, like any other, is marked, not by uncon-tested values and belief systems, but by dominant values subject to their own contradictions and the opposing pulls of other ideas; the world which *Dracula* belongs to is a world that is 'inevitably of permanent conflict between immiti-gable interests or values' (Moretti 1988: 28). Conflicts in belief systems and discursive formations provide the ground for suggesting a variety of interpreta-tions of the vampire in the Victorian world.

Twentieth-century readings of *Dracula*, however, do demonstrate the unavoidably troubling nature of the staking of Lucy. This part of the novel has received more critical attention than any other scene in the novel with most feminists considering it 'one of the most brutal and repulsive in the book' (Cranny-Francis 1988: 217). The linking of race, poverty and femininity in the figure of Dracula may or may not have produced overt sympathy in nineteenth-century readers, but does offer insights about why the vampire should return in the twentieth-century as a figure that overtly inhabits these identities *and* is written to elicit sympathy, by a new generation of writers.

Throughout the twentieth century, the depiction of the vampire becomes increasingly sympathetic and the fan culture surrounding vampire fiction becomes increasingly large. This vampire, however, speaks less to us about fear and tends to elicit other emotional responses. The vampire genre shifts significantly in the mid- to late twentieth century, with the vampire character, more often than not, acting as the narrator, or at least the narrative point of view, offering us Otherness from the inside. The next chapter will discuss these twentieth-century vampire transformations and consider how they continue to impact on our vampires today.

CHAPTER 2

Vampire Transformations: Gothic Melodrama, Sympathy and the Self

Dracula no longer holds centre stage in the world of vampires. The twentieth century produced a new generation of morally ambiguous, sympathetic vampires who lure audiences with the pathos of their predicament and their painful awareness of outsiderdom. While the previous chapter questioned the extent to which it was Dracula's 'otherness' that provoked fear in nineteenth-century audiences, 'otherness' returns in the vampires of the twentieth century as a source of empathy and identification. This signals one of the most important transformations in our perception of the vampire – it is no longer predominantly a figure of fear in Western popular culture, but a figure of sympathy. Thus, rather than a manifestation of our 'grisly nightmares' (Dickstein 1980: 67), this chapter will suggest that the vampire today speaks instead to our undead desires.

The mutability of the vampire and its various transformations has been identified by a number of literary and film critics (Silver and Ursini 1975; Pirie 1977; Senf 1987; Carter 1988; Gelder 1994; Auerbach 1995; Botting 1996; Punter 1996; Skal 1996; Gordon and Hollinger 1997; Holte 1997). In contrast to critics who have considered the vampire to manifest fixed psychic fears, these predominantly socio-historical accounts of the changing face of the vampire remind us that vampires are 'personifications of their age ... always changing so that their appeal is dramatically generational' (Auerbach 1995: 3).

A number of critics have identified a late twentieth-century tendency to depict the vampire sympathetically (Senf 1987; Carter 1988; Tomc 1997; Zanger 1997), yet fewer have examined the longevity of the pathos-ridden sympathetic vampire, and consider Anne Rice's *Vampire Chronicles* to represent a key moment in the sympathetic transformation of the vampire (Gelder 1994; Gordon and Hollinger 1997). Yet a year before the publication of Anne Rice's first chronicle, *Interview With the Vampire* (1976), Alain Silver and James Ursini offered a landmark account of a group of sympathetic male vampires whose roots go back to Lord Ruthven in 'The Vampyre' and Varney in 'Varney the Vampyre' – figures who are 'driven by a disease of the mind and body; and no matter how sedulously they try to rid themselves of the curse of the undead, they are always unsuccessful' (1975: 89).

This chapter will examine the historical roots of the sympathetic vampire and will suggest that, rather than a late twentieth-century phenomena, it is an incarnation of this figure that goes back two hundred years to Lord Byron. This chapter will also suggest that it is *this* vampire legacy, rather than that of Dracula, which has inspired the twentieth- and twenty-first-century versions of the vampire that have produced enormous vampire fan cultures.

Finally, this chapter will suggest that one important aspect of contemporary vampire fiction has been neglected or underplayed; the deployment of melodramatic themes and conventions across a range of the most popular vampire texts has been overlooked in critical accounts of vampire transformations, yet points importantly not only to the cultural form, but to the nature of the desires that our vampires dramatise today. This chapter will therefore examine melodrama in the modern vampire tale to suggest that it is now a crucial feature of the vampire's construction.

RE-READING THE VAMPIRE'S OTHERNESS

Carol A. Senf has observed that 'vampires in the twentieth century have been perceived as more or less attractive rebel figures, ones who *choose* to live outside society' (1987: 150). She suggests that the vampire-as-attractive rebel is a twentieth-century figure, but comments that 'a kind of latent rebellion exists in all vampires ... [because of their] refusal to live by the rules of their society' (1987: 152). For Senf, this latent rebellion transforms vampires into heroes and heroines in the twentieth century because of a 'changed attitude towards authority' (1987: 150). Margaret Carter similarly suggests that while the nineteenth-century vampire might have inspired sympathy *despite* its curse, in the late twentieth century it 'appears as an attractive figure precisely *because* he or she is a vampire' (1997: 27). For Carter, the vampire's otherness in the nineteenth century renders vampirism a terrifying threat, but late twentieth-century America finds itself in a mood to perceive otherness as attractive:

> As rebellious outsider, as persecuted minority, as endangered species, and as member of a different 'race' that legend portrays as sexually omnicompetent, the vampire makes a fitting hero for late twentieth-century popular fiction. (1997: 29)

Senf and Carter have identified important shifts in the depiction of the vampire and have related it to enormous changes in attitudes brought about by the tumultuous decades of the post-war era, in particular, the counter-culture of the 1960s. And significantly, both Senf and Carter link the sympathy for the vampire with notions of rebelliousness and outsiderdom. However, the *overt* treatment of the vampire as a glamorous and rebellious outcast is not solely a twentieth-century phenomenon, nor is the idea of a public that adores a famous figure of notorious repute; previous centuries were also of a disposition to be fascinated by glamorous notoriety and it was in the turbulent late eighteenth century that notorious fame and public adoration became fused to the image of the vampire through the figure of Lord Byron.

However, while Senf and Carter link the sympathy for the vampire with notions of rebellious outsiderdom, other critics consider the 'new' sympathy with the vampire to be a sign of its 'domestication' (Gordon and Hollinger 1997; Tomc 1997; Zanger 1997). Joan Gordon and Veronica Hollinger suggest that 'whether we mourn or celebrate' the domestication of the vampire, 'the contemporary vampire is no longer only that figure of relatively uncomplicated evil so famously represented by Count Dracula' (1997: 2). Yet there is a sense in the accounts of 'domestication' that it is equivalent to degeneration. Sandra Tomc is one who takes a negative stance towards the sympathetic or domesticated vampire. Tomc remarks upon the 'bland domestication' (1997: 96) of the contemporary vampire, particularly in relation to the vampires of Anne Rice. For Tomc the process of domestication revolves around the eradication of femininity and markers of female sexuality from Rice's texts, through the deployment of the 'twin paradigms of androgyny and weight loss' (ibid.). She suggests that Rice's vampires' refusal to feed is a form of self-abnegation which is central to the narrative of dieting and the female quest for thinness. For Tomc, then, 'ridding the vampire of his desire and self-deprivation is at the heart of his eventual domestication' (1997: 105).

From a different perspective, Jules Zanger mourns the demotion of the vampire from its status as a figure of metaphysical and cosmic evil to that of a 'demystified ... next-door neighbour (1997: 19). Zanger bemoans the arrival of a 'new' vampire whose cravings and motivations have become individualised and personalised rather than the 'cosmic conflict between God and Satan' (1997: 18) that Dracula characterised. Instead of the appropriately narrow range of emotions displayed by Dracula – 'hunger, hate, bitterness, contempt' (1997: 22) – the new vampires' 'communal condition permits them to love, to regret, to doubt, to question themselves, to experience interior conflicts and cross-impulses - to lose, in other words, that monolithic force possessed by Dracula, his unalterable volition' (1997: 22). For Zanger then, the 'new' vampire narratives provide an experience that readers and viewers engage in, 'not voyeuristically, as in the case of *Dracula*, but as conjoiners and communicants' (1997: 25). The 'new' vampire has ties of family and friendship, which locate it problematically in the realm of the emotions. This is a humanised terrain, which is more ambiguous in its depiction of good and evil.

It is significant that Zanger regrets those changes in the genre which shift it into areas that are conventionally associated with women's fiction, melodrama and with feminine (and therefore devalued) reading pleasures; the depiction of emotional states and the experience of interior conflicts. Yet this is not a new aspect to vampire fiction.[1] The vampire has long had ties of intimacy that has complicated the emotional investments surrounding the figure; as Nina Auerbach argues, 'intimacy and friendship are the lures of Romantic vampirism' (1995: 14). The vampire's hold over its early nineteenth-century victim was not to do with the mesmeric powers later found in Dracula. Instead, it was to be found in 'a bond between companions that is shared and chosen' (ibid.). Polidori's 'vampyre' Lord Ruthven conceals his true vampiric nature by extracting an oath from his young travelling companion. Although this oath is binding, it avoids the compulsion found in Dracula, and is 'frightening because it involves not raw power, but honour and reciprocity' (ibid.). It is therefore not the case that the vampire has degenerated *since* Dracula.

The differing perspectives on the 'new' sympathetic vampire as either 'rebellious' or 'domesticated' points to a deep ambiguity in the lure of the vampire that stretches back to its Byronic roots in the English language over two hundred years ago. Although Rice's vampires (and later *Buffy the Vampire Slayer*'s ensouled vampires) may epitomise the appeal of the sympathetic vampire, this figure has a much longer history in both the nineteenth and twentieth centuries. Indeed in the twentieth century Rice's first-person vampire narratives were pipped at the post by Dracula himself. The year before Rice published *Interview With the Vampire* (1976), Fred Saberhaagen published *The Dracula Tape*, a first-person retelling of the events of 1897 from Dracula's perspective, complete with accounts of the bumbling incompetence and cruelty of the Crew of Light and their terrible destruction of Lucy.[2] Dracula reminds readers, 'Lucy I did not kill. It was not *I* who hammered the great stake through her heart ... only reluctantly had I made her a vampire, nor would she ever have become one were it not for the imbecile Van Helsing and his work' (1975: 7).

In the previous decade, it was the small screen that introduced a sympathetic vampire into the homes of the American viewing public. In 1966 ABC aired its new series *Dark Shadows* (1966–71; 1991). This began as a daytime Gothic soap opera, but was close to cancellation because of falling ratings. Its fortunes were turned around by the introduction of the vampire Barnabas Collins (played by Jonathan Frid), who was cursed to roam the earth forever, loveless and suffering. Collins' predicament was sympathetically constructed as a vampire looking for a 'cure'. He had been turned into a vampire in 1795 by a spurned lover who used her powers of witchcraft to have a bat attack him and effect his transformation. The show had a large following and produced a loyal fan culture which persists to this day.[3] This pre-Rice vampire fiction interestingly garners the same pejorative association with the domestic and feminine as future reluctant vampires, its spin-off books are characterised as 'vapid Gothic romances aimed primarily at women readers' (Frost 1989: 107).

Even earlier in the twentieth century, motion pictures offered us sympathetic vampires. Universal's *House of Dracula* (1945) brings together the wolfman Lawrence Talbot, Frankenstein's monster and Dracula, in what Silver and Ursini call 'one of the last gasps of the Universal monster factory' (1975: 89). In this film 'the vampire is characterised as seeking a remedy for his affliction' and is 'portrayed as genuinely longing for release from his vampiric "malady"' (1975: 90). Dracula is undergoing treatment for his vampirism, but unlike the wolfman who is eventually cured and redeemed, the pull of vampirism ('the call of Thanatos') is too powerful for Dracula to resist, and he reverts to his vampiric ways.

1945 also saw the release of *The Vampire's Ghost*, which entirely ignored the renowned Dracula figure, and drew its inspiration instead from Varney and

Lord Ruthven. The 300-year-old vampire, Webb Fallon, has been cursed with vampirism because he has committed a terrible crime. Webb is introduced as the attractive, suffering and soft-spoken owner of a seedy bar in an African outpost, where his sympathetic status is ensured when he saves the life of the protagonist, Roy, in a bar room brawl. Like Varney and Ruthven, Webb has the power to hypnotise and it is his use of this power that saves Roy's life. Also, like Varney and Ruthven, he can be revived by moonlight. He is also without doubt the most appealing figure in the tale and enthrals not only Roy, but his fiancée, Julie. It is Fallon's passion for Julie which leads to his eventual demise as he is hunted and slain by Roy and a priest.

The sympathetic vampire in twentieth-century film also comes to inhabit the body of Anglo-America's others. *Ganja and Hess* (1973), *Blacula* (1972), *Scream Blacula Scream* (1973), *Vampire in Brooklyn* (1995), *Blade* (1998), *Blade II* (2002) and *Blade III* (2004) each depict a sympathetic black vampire who takes the form of a wronged African or African American. The black vampire is sympathetically presented as an unwilling victim of circumstances and a complex mix of rage, retaliation and redemption infuses the sympathetic construction of character. For example, *Blacula* is a 'blaxploitation' movie, starring William Marshall as an African prince, Prince Mamuwalde, who is doubly wronged. Mamuwalde's human life ends in 1780 as he tries to find a way of halting the slave trade in Africa, when he encounters Dracula who attacks him and his wife, Luva. Dracula infects Mamuwalde with vampirism, seals him in a tomb and leaves his wife to die. Mamuwalde is released as Blacula into 1960s America by two Americans who unwittingly have purchased the coffin that entombs Blacula. Silver and Ursini argue that Blacula is, 'caught in a double bind between desire for release and a compulsion to spread the vampiric plague', which is 'complicated in both films by the presence of love objects whom he does not want to turn into his victims' (1975: 95). Blacula's new love, Tina, is identical to his lost wife, and it is only when she becomes the victim of a shooting incident that he turns her into a vampire to save her. Tina is eventually destroyed by those hunting Blacula, whose grief is such 'that he walks out into the sunlight, and becomes a suicide in the manner of Varney' (Silver and Ursini 1975: 95). By the sequel, in which Blacula is revived by voodoo magic, the familiar symbols of the vampire's innocence and sympathy are conveyed in Blacula's attempt to cure himself of his vampiric condition, just as in Universal's 1945 depiction of Dracula and Barnabas Collins in the 1960s. Despite the sympathy accorded to this 'doubly other' vampire, Leslie Tannenbaum argues that the films can 'be read as an assimilationist narrative' (1997: 74). Tannenbaum argues that the heroes of the film are the 'young African American professionals who ... triumph over the seductive African vampire-prince' (ibid.) rendering him other in a manner which disavows racism. She comments that there is 'little overt reference to racial tension' (ibid.). Yet Blacula's history as one heroically fighting against the slave trade combine with his ability to love deeply to produce empathy with his otherness. Tannenbaum, however, compares Blacula with Eddie Murphy's portrayal of the vampire in *Vampire in Brooklyn*, which, she argues, 'foregrounds problems of race relations and racial identity in its very generic transgressions' (ibid.). For instance, each of the vampire's victims is racist towards him just before he attacks. His first victim calls him 'eggplant', his second calls him 'Sambo', and a liberal white lady had been remarking about the 'black servant problem' to her friend moments before the attack. She even tries to save herself with liberal political correctness by telling the vampire that she 'understands the plight of the negro'. For Tannenbaum

> it is clear ... that Murphy's vampire is really being provoked, and that – unlike Blacula – the vampire in this movie is being invoked as a hero figure, as one who lashes out at modern racism, whether blatant or more subtly liberal. (Ibid.)

The sympathetic vampire's otherness has long been imbued with ambivalence, and this is evidently marked even more so in depictions which overtly inhabit one of the bodies of Anglo-America's others.

With a longer history in vampire fiction of articulating the marginal self is the lesbian vampire. This figure has produced male-centred titillation movies *and* genuine pathos, it has provided an alternative image of romantic female eroticism and it has been used to censure friendships between women. Andrea Weiss notes that a 'spate' of lesbian vampire novels appeared in the first half of the twentieth century in order to pathologise women's friendships and to 'enforce the transition from nineteenth-century socially accepted close female friendships to the redefinition of such relationships as deviant in the first half of the twentieth century' (1992: 87). However, the source of many lesbian vampires has been Sheridan le Fanu's *Carmilla* (1872). A number of theorists have pointed to the sympathetic treatment of the vampire in *Carmilla* (Zimmerman 1984; Weiss, 1992; Auerbach, 1997). Carmilla is a lesbian vampire who comes to haunt the 19-year-old Laura. Laura lives alone with her father after her mother's death, isolated from other society on a remote mountain. Laura's father invites Carmilla to stay with them after a coach accident and Laura and Carmilla become intimate friends. Ken Gelder points out that Carmilla produces an uncanny effect in Laura who recognises her from a dream she had in childhood, and there is a blending between the two such that 'ultimately, it is difficult to tell who had been haunting who' (1994: 45). Weiss points out that Carmilla 'falls in love with her so-called victims' (1992: 87) as Laura does with her. Thus Carmilla is 'characterised sympathetically in that she acts out of compulsion rather than malice. Auerbach reads this blending between Carmilla and Laura as offering the image of 'self-accepting homosexual' (1995: 41) desire. For Auerbach, Carmilla is much less wary than her male vampire predecessors:

> Everything male vampires seemed to promise, Carmilla performs: she arouses, she pervades, she offers a sharing of the self. This female vampire is licensed to realise the erotic, interpenetrative friendship male vampires aroused and denied. (1995: 39)

Unlike her male predecessors whose intimacy with other men evades questions of desire, Carmilla 'feeds on women with a hunger inseparable from erotic sympathy' (1995: 41). Carmilla is an earlier vampire to Dracula, and she is also his antithesis. She is not remote and solitary, but intimate and connected, and she suggests a sharing and a blending that can occur only outside of patriarchal sexual mores.

Despite Carmilla's sympathetic portrayal of lesbian desire, Bonnie Zimmerman argues that this figure's translation into film has reinforced the view that lesbians 'are narcissists capable of making love only to images of themselves' (1984: 155). The Hammer films *The Vampire Lovers* (1970), *Lust for a Vampire* (1971) and *Twins of Evil* (1971) are all based on Carmilla and each depicts vampires who 'seduce young women strikingly similar to themselves' (ibid.). Weiss concurs that the story of Carmilla in twentieth-century cinema is a 'muted expression of lesbianism, no longer sympathetically portrayed but now reworked into male pornographic fantasy' (1992: 87). Yet Zimmerman argues that despite the hostility to lesbianism found in these films, the power of lesbian love to provide an alternative model of love to patriarchal norms cannot be overlooked. She suggests that the plethora of lesbian vampire films produced in the 1970s relates to the beginnings of the women's movement where women were bonding together and challenging male domination. Male directors were simultaneously flirting with the thrill of lesbianism as a male fantasy *and* as a threat to (still secure) male power.

The sympathetic treatment of the vampire has spanned the twentieth century. This figure may have reached new heights of popularity in the late twentieth century, but the inspiration for this figure is to be found in the pre-Dracula sympathetic vampires; not a figure of monolithic evil, but one where the relationship between the vampire and its human 'victim' is pivotal. Vampires before Dracula were not isolated from humanity, but were, 'singular friends' (Auerbach 1995: 13). Auerbach suggests that 'in the nineteenth century, vampires were vampires because they loved. They offered intimacy, a homoerotic sharing, that threatened the hierarchical distance of sanctioned relationships' (1995: 60). But while Auerbach suggest that these offerings are repudiated by the vampires of 'our own century' (ibid.), it can be argued that there is a strong strand of continuity between the pre-Dracula vampire companion, and our own vampire's today. The most popular of twentieth-century and early twenty-first-century vampires have been those whose ancestors are the sympathetic vampires of the nineteenth century. However, it was not just sympathy but also a sense of personal rebellion that made the vampire an object of fascination to the audiences of the past, as well as its entry into the twentieth century as an object of emulation. That the vampire figure has transformed from a figure of fascination to a figure of emulation signals not so much changes in attitudes towards authority, as it implies how those broader social changes are related to changes in attitudes towards the 'self' in the twentieth century. The vampire suggests an attractive outsiderdom – even a bohemianism – in a culture where a dominant experience for the self is predominantly marginalisation and outsiderdom. This chapter will now turn to examine the roots of the vampire's bohemianism which emerged from the explosive culture of the late eighteenth century.

THE VAMPIRE AND THE BOHEMIAN

Four figures emerge out of the volatile eighteenth century to be rolled into one: the Romantic poet, the bohemian, the Gothic vampire and Lord George Byron. In the early nineteenth century, it was Byron who, surrounded by an air of doom, contributed deeply to the Romantic idea of vampirism; the outsider, the fatal man, the sexual deviant (Wilson 2000). It is widely acknowledged that John Polidori, who was Byron's physician and travelling companion to the Villa Diodati in 1816, modelled his vampire, Lord Ruthven, on Byron. In a highly engaging account of the tensions between Byron and Polidori, the confusion over the authorship of *The Vampyre*, and the vicissitudes of Byron's celebrity, James B. Twitchell comments that 'the vampire was not just born in the novel but given an instant popular audience' (1981: 103). *The Vampyre* was snapped up by the reading public of the day because of its association with Byron. But the tale was Polidori's revenge on Byron who began to find Polidori tiresome and who sacked him that summer after subjecting him to weeks of humiliating ridicule. As Twitchell notes, '*The Vampyre* is more a slander of Byron than a plagiarism' (1981: 108), and Bryon becomes the widely recognised anti-hero of the tale. Simultaneously, Bryon had become a figure of shocking repute. Rumours of infidelity, incest, homosexuality and debt dogged Byron so that the London society that had 'lionised Byron, now cast him out'. Twitchell further comments: 'As he earlier "awoke to find [himself] famous", now he awoke to find himself infamous. He was exiled from drawing rooms, spat upon in the streets, and cast in the role of the social pariah, almost a vampire among men' (1981: 104).

Byronism thus becomes fixed to the vampire an image of notoriety, of flouting social conventions, of radicalism, infamy *and* the sinister aristocrat. It is a figure which is deeply ambivalent, pointing simultaneously in opposing directions, from political radicalism to aristocratic elitism, from fascination to contempt.

Byron's image is also infused with an aura of fatality and doom and this too is merged with vampirism. Despite his social ostracism, the bourgeois public remained fascinated by Byron, for he seemed to live the role of glamorous outcast 'better than he wrote it' (ibid). Twitchell comments that Byron was no longer writing about the melancholy outcast: the lusty libertine in the open shirt whose peculiarities made him live forever on the fringe of lawlessness; he had overnight become that character, and he played it in wondrous style (ibid.).

In a landmark account of bohemia, Elizabeth Wilson suggests that Byronmania had become an industry and provided an icon for future bohemia, whose members began to dress and behave in a manner 'calculated to shock and

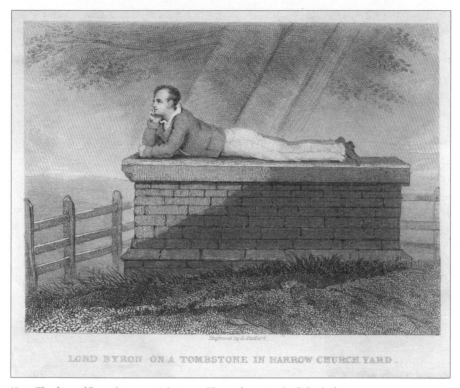

Fig. 5 The doomed Byron lays on a tombstone at Harrow (engraving by G. Stodart)

outrage his or her audience' (2000: 9). Byronism helped to shape a new kind of rebel who comes to enter the twentieth century – the bohemian – a figure who was very much about cutting *the figure* of the rebel, and the vampire also comes to adopt the pose of this emerging bohemianism. For Wilson, Byron was 'perhaps the first of a pantheon of individuals who become bohemian icons', precisely because he was 'becoming the mysteriously flawed hero about whom he wrote' (2000: 53). After he became famous overnight with the publication of his poem *Childe Harold's Pilgrimage*, Wilson suggests, 'every woman wanted to meet, and if possible get to bed with, the poet who, it seemed, was the living embodiment of his own doomed hero' (ibid.). Four years later Byron had left England for good in a storm of scandal and debt. But, according to Wilson, Byron's life was the most intense distillation of bohemian themes:

> His reputation anticipated twentieth-century forms of fame, glamour and notoriety, his personality generating a legend that became more important than his work, although crucially bound up with it. (2000: 54)

From its earliest incarnation in the English language, near the beginning of the nineteenth century, the figure of the vampire has become fused to Byronic images of glamorous outsiderdom, morose fatalism, social and artistic rebellion, and, crucially for twentieth-century developments of the myth, a subversive posture and notorious fame that prefigures much modern-day stardom. Also, through Byronic bohemianism, the vampire's rebel-status comes to belong to the arena of the self, or rather, of making a spectacle of oneself – of making the 'self' a spectacle of the unconventional and rebellious. Predictably, Byron's own vampire creation, Augustus Darvell, is imbued with roguish charisma. As Nina Auerbach suggests, Darvell is endowed with a 'glamour at once familiar and unattainable' so that the narrator of the tale, Darvell's travelling companion, 'hopes implicitly to become equally uncommon' (1995: 13). It is Byronism then, rather than the ubiquitous Dracula, that is the ancestor of those vampires who question the centre of society by standing on the margins.

The sympathetic vampire today produces enormous fan cultures. As has been indicated, some of the most popular are the ever-growing cast of Anne Rice's *Vampire Chronicles*. The humans they encounter are as besotted by them as any human companion of old. Indeed, like Darvell's travelling companion, many are converted to the idea of a vampiric existence. In *Interview With the Vampire*, Daniel, the boy reporter who has been interviewing the vampire Louis exclaims at the end of Louis' narrative,

> 'Don't you see how you made it sound? It was an adventure like I'll never know in my whole life! You talk about passion, you talk about longing! You talk about things that millions of us won't ever taste or come to understand ... If you were to give me that power! The power to see and feel and live forever.' (Rice 1976: 343)

The boy refuses the conclusion of despair in Louis' tale and demands from the disappointed vampire, 'Make me a vampire now!' (ibid.). Like those drawn to the melancholy of Byron or the bohemian outcast, Rice's vampires offer the allure of glamorous pathos.

Rice's vampires are also very much the image of the dandy and carry over the bohemian themes of adopting a cultured and rebellious pose. As Ken Gelder points out, in Rice's world 'to be a vampire is to *be* "cultured"' (1994: 119). Lestat and Louis express this in the two modes common to modernity; Lestat with his conspicuous consumption and addiction to luxury and Louis' bookish asceticism. Both vampires and their kith and kin spend much of their time in philosophical contemplation (of the meaning of their existence), in appreciation of the arts, and in travel and adventure. David Punter writes of the *Vampire Chronicles*, 'here Paris is certainly "the capital of the nineteenth century", and the vampires who stroll its night-time, gaslit streets are nothing but the very image of the *flâneur*' (1996: 162).

Lestat and Louis, also, in different ways, convey the bohemian idea of personal rebellion. Their posture is that of one who is at odds with all society; their rebellion is against any constraints which inhibit individualism. As vampires they are tangential to human society and they are at odds even with their own vampire world. Louis' refusal to embrace his vampire nature and his despair

Fig. 6 Tom Cruise plays the wickedly roguish Lestat de Lioncourt, in *Interview With the Vampire* (1994)

at his ontological predicament are a form of rebellion, as he refuses to live by rules set by other vampires. Sympathy and personal rebellion are the twin attractions in the construction of the vampire for the surrounding fan culture. However, while the vampire's rebellion draws on bohemian themes, its sympathy is structured as pathos, which is as much derived from the heroine of the Gothic novel and melodrama, as from the bohemian outcast. Rice's vampires, like the heroine of the gothic novel (and like each of the vampires mentioned in this chapter), suffer from circumstances they did not choose even if, at times, they revel in their outsiderdom. While the *Vampire Chronicles* have received a

great deal of critical attention, the melodramatic structuring of the protagonists has been underplayed. Most critics ignore the melodrama of these tales
entirely or consider the 'women's themes' such as the 'search for fulfilment, for
a "complete" love relationship' to be 'dispersed'; an insistence that 'these novels
are·not *just* romances' (Gelder 1994: 109). However, melodrama is central to an
understanding of the appeal of today's popular vampire tales.

MELODRAMA AND THE VAMPIRE

The sympathetic vampire has been considered to be rebellious, domesticated,
intimate – and indeed it is all of these things at one time or another – but most
of all the sympathetic vampire is *melodramatic*. I would suggest that melodrama
is the inevitable home for the vampire, for melodrama is not just a set of conventions; it is, as Peter Brooks has established, a mode of the modern imagination concerned with the dilemmas arising out of the struggle for meaning
and significance in a post-sacred society devoid of a unifying transcendence. I
want to demonstrate the way the vampire both embodies and articulates the
melodramatic imagination by turning once again to Anne Rice's sympathetic
vampires, for melodrama emerged as a literary form in order to dramatise for
the modern sensibility the kinds of dilemmas faced by these vampires.

It is now well known that Rice's novels narrate the tale of the vampire from
the vampire's point of view.[4] We hear, as Gelder puts it, 'the "other" speaking
first hand'. The result is that the vampires, rather than signifying a fear of the
dangerous and taboo, are presented as sympathetic and knowable 'outsiders'.
We learn from Louis' tale that he is a reluctant vampire, he did not choose
his ontological status, but had it thrust upon him unwillingly. He was made a
vampire against his will. Thus, like many other sympathetic vampires, Louis
has more in common with the heroine of melodrama and the Gothic tale than
he does with their villains, for like the heroine of melodrama and the gothic
novel, what Louis suffers is as a result of one caught in circumstances beyond
his control and understanding; he is a pathos-ridden creature and as such represents one of the key emotional and ethical categories of melodrama – the
depiction of misrecognised and persecuted innocence, voicing incomprehen-
sible wrongs, and ultimately, the recognition of that innocence. Brooks argues
that melodrama actually shares many characteristics with the Gothic novel;
both are 'equally preoccupied with nightmare states, with claustration and
thwarted escape, with innocence buried alive and unable to voice its claim to
recognition' (1995: 19–20). And indeed, it is not Louis who is able to recognise
his innocence, but the reader.

Louis' vampiric body itself is filled with melodramatic meaning. Brooks
suggests, in the preface to the new edition of *The Melodramatic Imagination*,
that melodrama, in order to articulate the full stakes involved in the drama,
utilises 'somatic meaning – meaning enacted on the body itself' (1995: xi). In
commenting upon why melodrama has a tendency to deploy non-verbal signs,
Brooks suggests

words ... however transparent as vehicles for the expression of basic relations and verities, appear to be not wholly adequate to the representation of meanings, and the melodramatic message must be formulated through other registers of the sign. (1995: 56)

Melodrama therefore has a tendency to use extreme physical conditions ('muteness', 'blindness', 'paralysis') to 'represent extreme moral and emotional conditions' (ibid.). The body becomes a central site of signification in melodrama, where the possession of a physical flaw can evoke innocence and victimhood.

Indeed, Louis' entire unwanted ontological status is his flaw, and thus his flaw is excessive and taken to the extremes that are appropriate to melodrama. His unwelcome vampirism is not a sign of evil, but a sign of victimhood; he is the (mostly unwilling) prey of an evil doer, the vampire Lestat (although Lestat's own status as 'evil' shifts and crumbles in the course of the tale), and only comes to inhabit the formal category of 'evil' vampire as a result of Lestat's actions and not his own. Misrecognised innocence is often coded as passive in the heroine of melodrama, so it is crucial to the establishment of Louis' status that he remains passive in the act of transformation. Lestat's first attack on Louis was unexpected although Louis lived like someone who wanted to die. He tells the boy reporter that he 'truly wished to be murdered':

'And then I was attacked. It might have been anyone – and my invitation was open to sailors, thieves, maniacs, anyone. But it was a vampire. He caught me just a few steps from my door one night and left me for dead, or so I thought.' (Rice 1976: 10)

Later, Lestat returns to Louis to complete his transformation, to give Louis the 'Dark Gift'. He forces Louis to watch him feed on the plantation overseer, and insists that Louis depose of the body. Louis responds:

'I want to die: kill me. Kill me ... Now that I am guilty of murder, I can't live.' He sneered with the impatience of people listening to the obvious lies of others. And then in a flash he fastened on me just as he had on my man. I thrashed against him wildly. (1976: 17)

There are clearly homoerotic connotations to the scene in which Lestat 'turns' Louis, giving the *Chronicles* a sizable gay following and complicating further the moral categories at play. Gelder describes this as one of the tale's many '"queer" scenes' in which Lestat is 'like a "lover", and Louis is "taken" ... in a drawn-out ecstatic moment which has them mingling their fluids together' (1994: 112).

However, while Louis is entwined in his new 'queerness' by his enchantment at how his physical transformation has opened out his senses, his status as an innocent and a victim is pressed further by his refusal to drink human blood. Rather than his rejection of blood-drinking representing an eradication of markers of femininity and symbolic of female self-abnegation, as Sandra

Fig. 7 Lestat toying with a young prostitute, in *Interview With the Vampire* (1994)

Tomc suggests, this is a sign of sacrifice (generally coded through a female body in melodrama) which is crucial to melodrama's establishment of virtue. Melodrama is concerned with articulation, with exteriorising ethical conflict and making it legible, so that the signs of innocence and virtue are made visible. The signs of virtue and innocence are often, as with Louis, written in sacrifice. Louis' refusal of blood-drinking marks him as suffering and as deserving of our sympathy. This is in contrast to Lestat, who in this novel at least, is the sign of that to which virtue is opposed – villainy. His delight in blood-drinking and his wanton destruction of human life are emblematic of his villainy, made overtly legible. Louis wakes one evening to find that Lestat has not one, but two prostitutes in their rooms. He feeds on one quickly, but toys with the other in a manner that horrifies Louis:

> He took the girls wrist again, and she cried out as the knife cut. She opened her eyes slowly as he held her wrist over the glass. She blinked and strained to keep them open. It was if a veil covered her eyes. 'You're tired, aren't you?' he asked her ... and he picked her up softly and took he into the bedroom ...˙ Lestat did not put her on the bed; he lowered her slowly into the coffin. 'What are you doing?' I asked him coming to the door sill. The girl looked around like a terrified child. 'No...' she was moaning. And then, as he closed the lid, she screamed. She continued to scream within the coffin. (Rice 1976: 84)

Louis is dismayed at this cruelty and wilful destruction of human life. The girl has lost too much blood to live and as Lestat continues to toy with her and terrify her, Louis decides he must intervene and he finishes her life quickly and quietly. Louis' body, however, at this point cries out for more of the blood now coursing in his veins, an appetite he struggles to refuse: 'My agony was unbearable, never since I was a human being had I felt such mental pain' (1976: 87). It is this mortal anguish that marks Louis off from other vampires and provides the reader's point of sympathy. However, Lestat is not the sign of evil in subsequent novels (and significantly shifts his blood-drinking only to 'evil doers'), and the inability of serialised melodrama to sustain categories of good and evil in these serialised novels is akin to the serialisation of the televised gothic soap opera *Dark Shadows* and more recently *Buffy the Vampire Slayer*. Punter suggests that although Louis is a good vampire he is 'not very good to be sure, since he kills nightly, but he does make an attempt to kill only animals, like a kind of vegetarian bloodsucker' (1996: 161). Yet Louis is more 'good' than he considers himself to be, and his virtue is misrecognised. But Punter has importantly gestured towards the idea that there is a sense of ambivalence in the sympathetic vampire's innocence and we shall return to this point later. Punter does note that the 'human' has not been 'entirely burned out' of Louis as it has from 'the conventionally violent Lestat and the terrifying child-vampire' (ibid.).

Reluctance and the refusal to 'feed' has become an important development in the conventions of the sympathetic sub-genre of vampire fiction and are symbolic of the vampire's misrecognised innocence. Although Rice is the first novelist to make full use of this sign of innocence, vampires throughout the twentieth century have sacrificed the imbibing of blood – the source of their sustenance and of their evil – and this refusal has become an overt sign of their innocence. Even the Dracula of *House of Dracula* is attempting to cure himself of the desire to feed on the blood of humans and although he is ultimately unsuccessful, his struggle is a harbinger of the coming sign of the vampire's innocence. Both Barnabas Collins, the vampire of *Dark Shadows*, and Nick Knight of *Forever Knight*, sacrifice their thirst and Knight makes good use of blood banks. More recently, the most popular vampires of the twenty-first century – Angel and Spike from *Buffy the Vampire Slayer* – are both signed as 'good' and 'virtuous' at those moments when they possess a 'soul' and thus forsake the gratification of blood. According to Brooks, virtue and innocence in melodrama is often construed as 'apparently fallen' (1995: 31) so that it cannot fully articulate itself, and, paradoxically, the vampire cannot fully articulate its innocence because it is a sign of evil to the world. For Brooks,

> the violation and spoliation of the space of innocence stands as a recurrent representation of the dilemma confronting innocence. Expulsed from its natural terrain, its identity put into question through deceiving signs, it must wander afflicted until it can find and establish the true signs in proof of its nature. (1995: 30)

The reluctant vampire embodies this melodramatic impulse as fully as any fictional figure. Its unwanted vampirism is the violation it has suffered, it is expelled from humanity, is misrecognised as evil by a world to which it does not belong and its innocence and virtue are obfuscated by its very ontology, until we the readers or viewers come to understand the vampire's predicament (and therefore innocence), even if the world at large does not. Vampirism, paradoxically, has become an extreme physical sign of one of melodrama's core impulses – the struggle for innocence to be acknowledged and virtue to be recognised. As we shall see later, the vampire Spike, of *Buffy the Vampire Slayer*, is a twenty-first-century version of misrecognised innocence, but his anguish, like Blacula's, is the anguish of love. For Brooks, the importance of 'virtue recognised' in melodrama stems from its impulse to act out ethical choices, so that melodramas 'tend to move toward a clear nomination of the moral universe' (1995: 17). Melodrama personalises these ethical positions by depicting them through individual characters so that 'good and evil can be named as persons are named' (ibid.). Louis, like the melodramatic heroine, is virtuous, even as society misrecognises that virtue for guilt or villainy.

There is a further sense in which the sympathetic vampire's ontology pushes towards what is considered to be the fundamental concern of melodrama – the problem of significance; of how to be meaningful in a post-sacred world. The vampire embodies non-signification because it is neither dead nor alive. Being undead, the vampire signifies a lack of signification – it does not have meaning in the cold light of day. But the vampire presents us with a dilemma because it continues to exist despite a lack of meaning. It is this dilemma that is at the heart of Louis' quest and it structures the narrative of *Interview With the Vampire*. Louis and his companion, the girl vampire Claudia, travel to Europe to find out about the significance and origins of vampirism, and of what it means to *be* a vampire. Instead what they find is a troupe of Parisian vampire actors – real vampires who act as vampires in the Théâtre des Vampires. What Louis learns is that vampirism indeed has no overarching significance in the scheme of things, it is not part of a cosmic conflict between the forces of good and the forces of evil, it simply exists. Louis tells Armand, 'I tell you, after seeing what I have become; I could damn well believe anything! Couldn't you? And believing thus, being thus confounded, I can now accept the most fantastical truth of all: that there is no meaning to any of this!' Ken Gelder reads this scene as part of Louis' disillusionment and his lapsed Catholic faith: 'he both believes in nothing and is (therefore) able to believe in *anything*, including the unbelievable – vampires' (1994: 111). It is the manner in which the novel collapses the distance between belief and disbelief, between being (a vampire) and acting (the part of a vampire) that Gelder proposes produces a 'new kind of faith' which results in 'a closing conversion (in)to the fiction itself' (1994: 112). Gelder suggests that it is 'hard to imagine a more effective way of accounting for fandom, in this closing image of the converted reader/listener' (ibid.). I would like to suggest, however, an alternative reading of this scene and an alternative way of accounting for the huge fandom that surrounds these tales. The first point is that Louis does not believe in *anything* at the end of the novel, he precisely believes in *nothing*. Louis is an embodiment of, and acts out in the structure of the novel, what Peter Brooks has termed the 'moral occult'. Brooks suggest that the 'melodramatic mode in large measure exists to locate and articulate the moral occult' (1995: 5). In order to illustrate how it is that sympathetic vampires dramatise the moral occult, a full discussion of this concept is needed and its relation to melodrama.

VAMPIRES, THE PROBLEM OF SIGNIFICANCE AND THE 'MORAL OCCULT'

Although Brooks centres his discussion of melodrama in relation to its opera-tion in the texts of Balzac and Henry James, his wider points about melodrama continue to be pertinent today:

> As Walter Benjamin argued, it is from the 'flame' of fictional representa-tions that we warm our 'shivering lives', and this is nowhere more true than in the most enduring popular fictions, which suggest over and over again that we do not live in a world completely drained of transcendence and significance. (1995: 205)

The vampire is one of the most enduring of popular fictions in modern Anglo-American culture, and its sympathetic plight points to the melodramatic con-cern with significance. Indeed, for Brooks, melodrama 'appears to be a peculiarly modern form' (1995: 15) and its roots can be traced historically to the French Revolution. The repercussions of this event have indelibly marked artistic and cultural modes of expression because it inaugurated a secular age, where tradi-tional beliefs in hierarchy and unity have broken down. Brooks argues that the French Revolution is the epistemological moment that melodrama illustrates and contributes to:

> the moment that symbolically, and really, marks the final liquidation of the traditional Sacred and its representative institutions (Church and Monarch), the shattering of the myth of Christendom, the dissolution of an organic and hierarchically cohesive society, and the invalidation of the literary forms – tragedy, comedy of manners – that depended on such a society. (Ibid.)

Society no longer has a sense of the sacred, nor a system of beliefs that relate to a notion of transcendental truths. In our post-sacred society, humans have had to find new ways to make life matter and produce new ways of understand-ing how we are meaningful in the world. Melodrama expresses this condition by both conveying a desire to restore a sense of the sacred, the transcendental, and by recognising that this is not possible. For Brooks, melodrama

> comes into being in a world where the traditional imperatives of truth and ethics have been violently thrown into question, yet where the promulgation of truth and ethics, their instauration as a way of life, is of immediate, daily, political concern. (Ibid.)

Fig. 8 Brad Pitt as the sympathetic vampire Louis in *Interview With the Vampire* (1994)

Melodrama develops out of modernity and expresses the anxiety brought about by a frightening new world in which the traditional patterns of moral order no longer provide the necessary social glue: 'It demonstrates over and over that the signs of ethical forces can be discovered and made legible' (1995: 20). It is for this reason that melodrama is 'not only a moralistic drama but the drama of morality: it strives to find, to articulate, to demonstrate, to "prove" the existence of a moral universe' (ibid.). Brooks suggests that the impulse to restore the existence of a larger ethical dimension is dramatised in melodramatic conflicts between good and evil; the conflict between heroine and villain articulating the desire for the presence of significance and meaning greater than ourselves, for 'at its most ambitious, the melodramatic mode of conception and representation may appear to be the very process of reaching a fundamental drama of the moral life and finding the terms to express it' (1995: 12).

Hence Brooks suggests that melodrama refuses to allow 'that the world has been completely drained of transcendence' and locates that transcendence 'in the struggle of the children of light with the children of darkness, in the play of the ethical mind' (1995: 22).

When Brooks describes the melodramatic mode as a 'central fact of the modern sensibility' he considers it to be the 'sensibility within which we are still living', a central mode of modern art that has 'typically felt itself to be constructed on, and over, the void, postulating meanings and symbolic systems which have no certain justification because they are backed by no theology and no universally accepted social code' (1995: 21). There exists no transcendent meaning, only the void left by de-sacralisation. Melodrama addresses the 'decentring' (1995: 200) of modern consciousness, its lack of a central plenitude by searching for 'a new plenitude and a new ethical centring'. Brooks suggests however, that

> the melodramatic imagination at its most lucid recognises the provi-
> sionality of its created centres, the constant threat that its plenitude
> may be a void, the need with each new text and performance to relocate
> the centre. (Ibid.)

Modern cultural expression is a reaction to the 'vertiginous feeling of standing over the abyss created when the necessary centre of things has been evacuated and dispersed' (1995: 21). This is what Brooks terms the 'moral occult', and it indicates a sense of humans feeling cut off from intense and transcendental ethical forces and meanings. For Brooks, the moral occult is not a metaphysical system, 'it is rather the repository of the fragmentary and desacralised rem-nants of sacred myth' (1995: 5). By the end of the Enlightenment, there was, according to Brooks, a 'renewed thirst for the Sacred' which took the form of Romanticism and reasserted a need for 'some version of the Sacred [but] offered further proof of the irremediable loss of the Sacred in its traditional, categorical, unifying form' (1995: 16). Furthermore, there was a

> desperate effort to renew contact with the scattered ethical and psy-
> chic fragments of the Sacred through the representation of fallen reality,
> insisting that behind reality, hidden by it yet indicated within it, there
> is a realm where large moral forces are operative, where large choices of
> ways of being must be made. (1995: 21)

I want to suggest that the modern sympathetic vampire is a personification of the dilemmas implied in Brooks's notion of the 'moral occult'. While the reluctant vampire expresses the urge for meaning greater than ourselves, it demonstrates the impossibility of such a worldview. The vampire (a supernatu-ral creature) expresses and embodies this urge, but cannot come to signify the transcendental (even of evil), because what the reluctant vampire learns, and we learn through it, is that they do not signify the cosmic category of evil, in fact they do not signify at all. To return to *Interview With the Vampire*, it is evi-dent that the 'moral occult' is central to the narrative drive of the tale – Louis' quest for meaning. Louis' quest both dramatises the desire for wider meaning and demonstrates its impossibility. He returns to New Orleans at the end of the tale forsaken. For Louis this emptiness produces an inexpressible sorrow. When he finds the ruined creature that is now Lestat, he becomes 'conscious of an overwhelming sadness' (Rice 1976: 334). Louis tells the boy reporter:

> Only, it didn't seem to be a sadness for Lestat, for that smart, gay vam-
> pire who used to live there then. It seemed a sadness for something else,

something beyond Lestat that only included him and was part of the great awful sadness of all the things I'd ever lost or loved or known. It seemed then I was in a different place, a different time ... And I was on the verge of knowing that place and knowing with it a terrible pain, a pain so terrible that my mind veered away from it, said, No, don't take me back to that place – and suddenly it was receding. (Ibid.)

Louis has faced the void of meaningless; he has approached that 'place' of 'terrible pain' and has confronted the missing transcendental. Yet Louis manages to persist, to go on, even if it is only living in the senses. On his final night in Paris, he goes with Armand to the Louvre, to 'lay down' his soul, 'to find some transcendent pleasure that would obliterate pain and make me utterly forget even myself' (1976: 324). Of course, he does not find that solace in art and even loses the meaning of the human heart which he had held so dear. Instead he says: 'I drank of the beauty of the world as a vampire drinks. I was satisfied. I was filled to the brim. But I was dead. And I was changeless' (ibid.).

It is important to note that the *Vampire Chronicles*, as in much serialised melodrama, are not a straightforward melodramatic tale with a clear Manichean impulse to name good and evil. Serialisation as a narrative form is unable to sustain the clear categorisation of the moral universe through the unambiguous depiction of good and evil. Serialised narrative produces shifting perspectives and extended middles that, as many feminists have noted in relation to soap opera, contribute to the moral complications that surround characters. Although these stories come to an end, the *Vampire Chronicles* share the moral complication of the serialised genre. The point of view shifts from Louis to Lestat in the second *Chronicle*, when we discover that he too is a victim of circumstances who cloaks his pain in fiendishness. As the series continues we are offered the perspective of another vampire, Armand. Rice also began a new series of vampire tales told from the perspective of minor characters from the *Chronicles* as well as introducing new characters. Each of these contributions extends the imaginative universe and destabilises the point of view of any character. Crucially though, like many other late twentieth-century vampires, rather than embodying 'otherness' as evil, Rice's vampires are ambiguous but sympathetic, they are reluctant and roguish. They blend the characteristics of the Gothic heroine, locked in circumstances outside of her control with those characteristics of what Maggie Kilgour terms the 'Gothic hero-villain', 'a rebel and rogue; a fatal man operating outside the limits of social norms' (1995: 53). They are pathos-filled creatures, but they also have the preternatural strength and longevity to aid their predicament (like the gothic hero-villain); they are strong individuals even in their communal arrangements.

For Brooks the moral occult arises from a desire to give meaning to meaninglessness through the cosmic depiction of good and evil. But, if, as suggested here, modern Gothic melodrama does not pit good against evil but complicates such moral categories, then what is the transcendent category which fills the void of meaning? I would like to suggest that in the contemporary vampire tale, the void is filled by the category of the 'self'.

Louis, like all reluctant vampires, sounds the depths of the void, he confronts the abyss, and seems, as Gelder puts it, 'to come back empty-handed' (1994: 110). But actually, he does not return completely empty-handed. When Louis sounds the depths, he is confronted, not with emptiness, but with *himself*. Brooks argues that as modernity attempted to find a new morality, it replaced the 'sacred' with the 'self' as a central category of meaning. The discourses of individualism, which continue to mark the modern condition, arose as part of the larger bourgeois challenge to the old order; science over superstition, merit over rank, man over nature, so that the individual comes to be the repository of moral life and significance. Brooks argues:

> Mythmaking could now only be individual, personal; and the promulgation of ethical imperatives had to depend upon an individual act of self-understanding that would then – by an imaginative or even terroristic leap – be offered as the foundation of a general ethics. In fact, the entity making the strongest claim to sacred status tends more and more to be personality itself. From amid the collapse of other principles and criteria, the individual ego declares its central and overriding value, its demand to be the measure of all things. (1995: 16)

Louis' moment of disillusionment, his experience of believing in nothing, produces in the novel, not a pacified reader, as Devon Hodges and Janice L. Doane (1991) suggest, nor a conversion into the fiction itself as Gelder suggests (1994: 112). Gelder is correct in suggesting that the novel produces a 'conversion', but the conversion that is invited is a belief in the self, or rather, a belief that the self can and does matter. This is the very stuff of melodrama, for as Brooks has suggested, melodrama 'tells us that in the right mirror, with the right degree of convexity, our lives matter' (1995: xi). The curve of this mirror is such that it reflects back to the self an image of the vampire, for it is in this undead image of selfhood that meaning resides. This is the lesson of *Interview With the Vampire*, although it is not a lesson that Louis can learn; he cannot believe in himself, for he still wrongly considers himself to be evil, and he cannot even believe in a universalism that a grand concept of evil might bring, for he considers his own evil to be quotidian rather than cosmic, part of the grubby business of taking human life. Louis' sorrow has blinded him to the meaning of his own goodness. When he leaves Lestat, he takes with him the baby that Lestat's vampire 'nurse' has snatched from its crib to nourish Lestat. Louis returns the baby to its crib unharmed, all the while proclaiming his inability to 'feel'. This is a significant final reminder at the end of the novel of Louis' innocence – a reminder to the reader rather than to himself. Infancy and childhood are both important motifs in vampire fiction. Recall in *Dracula* that a major part of Van Helsing's armoury in persuading Seward of Lucy's evil is the notion that she is about to feast on a baby. If this is a sign of the epitome of evil, then conversely,

Louis 'saving' a baby from the same fate is a sign of his virtue. Virtue here, as in melodrama more broadly, comes to stand for the meaningfulness of the self. Again, it is not a lesson that Louis' sorrow allows him to learn. Rather it is the lesson learned by the boy reporter, who, like the reader, attains a sort of omniscient point of view, able to 'see' what the protagonist himself cannot. The boy declares to Louis 'You don't know what human life is like' [i.e. meaningless] ... 'You've forgotten. You don't even understand the meaning of your own story, what it means to be human like me' (Rice 1976: 343). For the boy reporter, as for the reader, Louis has shown a life that has meaning, that the self can have significance, paradoxically, because for Louis, his life has no meaning. His meaningfulness is open to us to see for it resides, melodramatically, in his unrecognised virtue – only we have the sense to recognise it.

The personalising and individualising of the spiritual and moral imagination stamps an imprint on the gothic form which persists in today's vampire fiction. Contemporary vampire tales share the themes of personalising and individualising moral dilemmas; only now the vampire is both innocent (because it has vampirism unwillingly thrust upon it), simultaneously glamorous and an outsider, and a victim of circumstances outside of its control. This vampire can thus be seen to personify dilemmas of the self: how to have meaning in the world which demands it, how to act in circumstances we did not choose, how to be a good human. Misrecognised innocence and virtue return with great force in the small-screen sympathetic vampires, Spike and Angel. Their appeal, just as Louis and Lestat's appeal, is the offer of the pain of outsiderdom as a route to the possibilities of the self and of individual significance. Audiences place possibilities for the self in these attractive, but undead, characters whose unwanted ontology is the clearest sign of their meaning.

CHAPTER 3

FANS RE-READING THE VAMPIRE: ISSUES OF GENDER AND THE PLEASURES OF PATHOS

A BRIEF HISTORY OF READING THE VAMPIRE

Reading the vampire has long been a popular activity. The vampire became an instant Gothic success with the publication of Polidori's *The Vampyre* in 1819 in Henry Colburn's *The New Monthly Magazine*. Colburn (who had published Lady Caroline Lamb's novel, *Glenarvon*, with its thinly-disguised portrait of Byron) was astute in exploiting the enormous public interest surrounding the figure of Byron and he published *The Vampyre* under Byron's name. Colburn also passed the tale onto five other London publishers who published it in book form in the months that followed, all of whom made a good deal of money from the sales. *The Vampyre* soon took off in Europe and America. Three editions were published in America. A French publisher, Galignani, issued three editions from Paris in English, quickly followed by French translations from Henri Faber later that year. A German edition was also published in 1819, followed by an Italian version in 1824, a Swedish version in 1827, and a Spanish one in 1829. The tale also prompted a number of theatrical adaptations. Charles Nodier adapted it with great success for the Paris Theatre de la Porte-Saint-Martin, and there were at least six other adaptations for Parisian theatres. *Der Vampyre* was also produced as an opera by Wilhelm August Wohlbruck and Heinrich August Marschner in 1828 and went on to be performed in German, Russian, French, Dutch and English.

Whether Polidori willingly participated in the exploitation of Byron's name or was a victim of Colburn's fraudulence is still debated, but it is clear that Polidori was unsuccessful in establishing his authorship of the tale and only ever received £30 in total from the various publishers who profited so well from it. It is also the case that *The Vampyre* was an unprecedented success and became a model for subsequent English vampires, as has been suggested in the previous chapter. Its popularity even prompted Polidori to give up his medical career in order to pursue a literary one. Polidori never did establish his literary reputation and *The Vampyre*, despite its popularity, came to be regarded as inferior melodrama, comparing badly to Byron's Romanticism, even though the figure of Byron is crucially bound up with it.

The critic Michael Gamer suggests that the Gothic in general became critically dissociated with the Romantic Movement and comments on the Gothic's 'widespread but uneasy presence in romantic writing' which contrasts sharply with its 'almost unanimous critical vilification after 1795' (2000: 23). In the early nineteenth century the public taste for all manner of Gothic tales was at its height. But, as Gamer has suggested, the critical reception of the Gothic was highly disparaging, and he suggests that this offers us 'some indication of the extent of the gulf between critical and popular audiences' of the late eighteenth and early nineteenth centuries (2000: 4).

The Gothic from its inception was regarded as of low cultural status, despite – or perhaps partly due to – its immense popularity; for it emerges concurrently with an expansion in the literate population. The extension of literacy and the proliferation of the press produced 'a wariness of the potentially pernicious influence of literature on a broad but naive market' (Kilgour 1995: 6). Indeed, the early nineteenth century witnessed an outpouring of 'bluebooks' – short, cheap derivatives of the Gothic novel which could be purchased for sixpence, taking their name from the flimsy blue paper that covered them. These publications have become more commonly known as 'shilling shockers', and they were considered to cater to 'the perverted taste for excitement among degenerate readers' (Haining 1978: 12). As a schoolboy Percy Bysshe Shelley was just one of the 'hundreds of thousands of men, women and young people of all classes [who] were eager customers of the multitude of titles which flowed from a host of publishers' (Haining 1978: 8).

One vampiric example was *The Bride of the Isles: A Tale Founded on the Popular Legend of the Vampire* (Anon.), which is an interesting case of the various modifications of Polidori's tale. This sixpenny bluebook was published by J. Charles around 1820. It was an adaptation of the highly successful stageplay of the same title. The play itself was actually an adaptation of Nodier's *Le Vampyre* (itself one of the adaptations of Polidori's *The Vampyre*), but which shifted the background to the Scottish Hebrides. The bluebook adaptation was also set in the Scottish islands, but regardless of its departure from Polidori's tale, also credits the story to Lord Byron, and its vampire possesses the body of a man named Ruthven (the name of Polidori's vampire). The front cover of the tale was 'complete with a dramatic hand-coloured frontispiece' (Haining 1978: 113), for the front covers of all bluebooks were important in attracting a semi-literate readership and often were 'daubed with red, yellow, blue and green colours' showing 'some sensational incident ... a bare-bosomed girl threatened by a grinning monk ... a dark and gloomy hero in the clutches of a group of bandits' (Haining 1978: 11).

According to Maggie Kilgour, early critics thought shilling shockers encouraged an 'amoral imagination that was a socially subversive force' (1995: 7). In particular there were concerns that the imaginative fairytale world created by the gothic offered a 'tempting alternative to the mundaneness of everyday life' (ibid.). Bluebooks were said to have corrupting effects among their lower-class and youthful readership, but for their readers they offered both the *frisson* of the forbidden and a convenient four-by-seven-inch size for slipping into a pocket, unseen.

Singled out as particularly vulnerable to the pernicious influence of blue-books were young women, particularly of the lower classes. Indeed there was a close association between the Gothic's devalued status, notions of 'pulp popularity' and femininity (Gamer 2000: 8). Indeed, Anne Williams (1994) has hesitated about defining the Gothic because of the way that critics have used this label to scorn texts as feminine. Fred Botting suggests that the Gothic actually depended on women readers and writers who were excluded from 'the male-dominated "high arts" of poetry and politics' (1996: 6). For Botting, there was a 'feminisation of reading practices and markets' (1996: 4) which in a patriarchal age helped to keep the gothic at a low status in the eyes of the critical establishment. The Gothic's cheap spin-off bluebooks were replaced in the 1820s by monthly magazines which continued the tradition of terror, but they provided the initial bridge between the Gothic novel and the mass circulation of horror tales in the twentieth century, including a pejorative association with femininity and related concerns about the effects of such fiction, which persist into our own time. Kilgour points out that while early conservative moralists found the 'gothic's offer of an imaginative retreat from reality' a potentially dangerous amoral threat, 'to many modern critics this, contradictorily, has proved it to be a reactionary, socially conservative form' (1995: 8). According to Kilgour, 'the gothic was seen as encouraging a particularly intimate and insidious relationship between text and reader, by making the reader identify with what he or she read' (1995: 6). Martin Barker's well-known research into campaigns against 'horror comics' in the first half of the twentieth century and 'video nasties' in the second demonstrates the way that horror continued to be an arena for misguided 'concerns' about 'effects'; his work has systematically challenged the concept of identification upon which many such claims are made (1984a, 1984b, 1989, 1997). Recently, as Lisa Parks has noted, *Buffy the Vampire Slayer* was 'one of the many sites of popular culture to be scapegoated after the Columbine shootings' (2003: 118), demonstrating that even a television text that has garnered a reputation as 'quality' can become part of the fuel for a moral panic. The CEO of Warner Bros. (the network that aired *Buffy*) cancelled two episodes of *Buffy*, 'Graduation Day' and 'Earshot', in May 1999 because they both were seen to contain scenes that were thought to 'resemble the traumatic events that unfolded in American schools during the spring of 1999' (Parks 2003: 120). Parks demonstrates the media effects research that still dominates the debates about violence in American high schools and comments that 'the 1990s has generated a culture of moral panic that is unable to recognise that youth-oriented television might actually confront the issue of violence rather than encourage it' (2003: 129). The idea of compulsive identification has not disappeared today and continues, as we shall see, in the case of vampire fiction, to be associated in particular with the feminine.

However, vampire fandom has a history that spans the twentieth century, at least. Bela Lugosi as Dracula received enormous amounts of fan mail – mostly from women – revealing a great deal of sympathy with Lugosi's portrayal of the vampire. In the late 1960s a new sympathetic vampire, Barnabas Collins, appeared the Gothic television soap opera, *Dark Shadows* (1967–71; 1991), which spawned a huge fandom that persists today. According to one scholar of this fandom, the appeal of its Gothic characters and its evolution 'has kept *Dark Shadows* alive in the minds of its fans for over twenty years' (Benshoff 1998: 200). Harry Benshoff notes that fan clubs for the show began with the initial series but grew in the following decades: 'for the last 25 years, fans have been successful in bringing *Dark Shadows* back to television via syndicated re-runs ... and home video releases' (ibid.). The fans hold an annual Dark Shadows Festival and there are fan clubs in at least ten US cities (see Melton 1994). Benshoff also suggests that fans were 'instrumental' in producer Dan Curtis's decision to remake *Dark Shadows* as a primetime television series in 1991. Similarly, the television series *Forever Knight* (1989; 1992–93) has generated a large and longstanding fan culture. Nick Knight was a sympathetic vampire detective who wanted to return to his mortal condition and who only drank bottled blood. The show has produced numerous fan clubs and also has an annual convention.

In the late twentieth century, it was Anne Rice's *Vampire Chronicles* that produced a large fan culture and numerous fan clubs. The fans of Anne Rice's *Vampire Chronicles* were singled out by scholars as susceptible to these texts' conservative messages, as well as being caricatured by media commentators. Just prior to the release of *Interview With the Vampire* in Britain in January 1995, there was a flurry of interest in 'real' vampires in the British press which accompanied the mixed reviews of the film. An article entitled 'Simply Batty' in the *Scottish Sunday Mail* on 15 January 1995 describes members of the Scottish Vampire Society (accompanied by large photographs of the vampire gang) as 'dressed to kill' with the sideline reading in large bold letters, 'Ghouls keep a coffin in the living room!' The article makes use of the tabloid pun to finish with, 'As I left, I was invited to join – "No fangs", I replied. And fled like a bat out of hell.' On the same day an article in the *Independent on Sunday* entitled, 'Interview with a few vampires', describes members of the Vampyre Society as 'a huddle of white-faced figures', one woman having 'astonishing hair', and a young man having 'black hair, black lipstick, a face paler than the moon'.

The press treatment of the vampire fan-as-curiosity is actually rather mild in comparison to some academic comments. For instance, David Skal's otherwise excellent writing on horror is marred by his contempt for its surrounding fan culture. Revealingly, it is female fans who take the brunt of his ridicule. Skal comments on the 'the striking preponderance of obese women drawn to horror literature, gothic music and Anne Rice in particular' (1996: 175). He continues:

> Don't take my word for it: check out the marathon-length lines for Rice's next autograph signing (or any other 'gothic' event) and come to your own conclusions about the displaced oral aggression, the relationship between vampirism and eating disorders, and the curious gratification presumably straight women (commonly, if uncharitably known as 'fag hags') derive from fantastically neutered depictions of male/male sex.

Fig. 9 'Simply Batty', interviews with members of the Scottish Vampire Society, in the *Scottish Sunday Mail*, January 15, 1995

> The plunging necklines and corpse-white makeup these women typically affect for their moment of communion with Anne Rice says it all; 'I want to be sexual, but my sexuality is dead.' (Ibid.)

Skal's language of ridicule may belong to the twentieth century, but his sexist diagnosis of femininity and his pejorative association of the feminine with Gothic excess have a much longer history. One might suggest that he is invoking a cultural hierarchy (cf. Jensen 1992) in order to distinguish between his own interests in the vampire and those of the female (or 'feminised' male) fan.

Other scholars are less unpleasant about vampire fans, but retain a sense that fans are vulnerable to the insidious influence of these texts. For example, Devon Hodges and Janice L. Doane argue that Rice constructs vampire narratives which prematurely pose the end of stable gender categories and that readers 'greedily ingest' (1991: 158) these conservative fantasies, taking pleasure in the early disavowal of 'disturbing differences' (1991: 168) which none the less continue to assert the values associated with that difference. Also, Ken Gelder's impressive analysis of the vampire nevertheless implies a similar sense of compulsive identification amongst readers. He suggests that the reader of *Interview With the Vampire* wants to become a vampire at the end of the novel, because, like the boy journalist, s/he 'gets carried away' by the tale and 'is recuperated through a closing conversion (in)to the fiction itself' (1994: 112).

However, there is something of compulsion in the formulation of the fan/text relationship as one which 'converts' the reader, (which also leaves aside why some readers do *not* become fans).

The response to this characterisation of 'the fan' in early fan scholarship (Bacon-Smith 1992; Fiske 1992; Jenkins 1992) was to conceive of the fan as a hero of popular culture, a rebellious figure who was likened to a guerrilla fighter, invading the territory of mainstream culture and poaching meaning from texts. But this book also challenges this designation of fandom and considers not only how attitudes towards fandom are changing (not least since it has become an established sub-field of cultural studies), but also how fandom has never been 'outside' of culture, but has always fitted into the dynamics and politics of the cultural field, and the struggles therein to designate cultural worth.

However, before analysing the place of vampire fandom in the field of cultural production in subsequent chapters, I would like to consider how female vampire fans engage with the vampire. This is in order to demonstrate, in contrast to much of the theoretical material on femininity and the vampire (discussed here and in chapter one), that the female viewer/reader of the vampire *does* exist and does not adopt a masochistic spectator position, nor is she as sexually dead as Skal implies. She is also not a dupe of mass culture ingesting conservative messages or being converted to texts. Indeed female vampire fans are occupied in active and thoughtful engagements with vampire texts and have well thought-out likes and dislikes. This chapter will discuss how female fans read the vampire, how they talk about their readings and how they relate to them. This analysis will demonstrate that female fans are neither some revolutionary vanguard of audiencehood (because there is no such thing), nor are they passive victims. I want to consider fan interpretations of the vampire both in terms of activity and in terms of the constraints on the act of fan reading.

Paradoxically, while femininity has been made absent from Freudian interpretations of the vampire, there has long been a devalued association of femininity with the Gothic vampire and this is linked to the feminisation of 'popular' or 'mass' culture more generally which can be found in critical and even fannish discourses. In his excellent discussion of the process of taste distinctions in operation among horror fans, Mark Jancovich comments on the way that that male horror fans who consider themselves to be 'authentic' fans in contrast with those audiences duped by 'mainstream' Hollywood horror, often associate such films 'with inauthenticity through the familiar trope of "mass culture as woman"' (2000: 29). The following discussion of female fan engagements with the gothic and melodramatic vampire challenges such tropes while demonstrating a persistent connection between Gothic melodrama's ability to speak the unspeakable in contemporary vampire tales, and the gendered experiences of the self that female fans live through, for just as eighteenth- and nineteenth-century gothic writers raised un-askable questions about 'individualism and sexual separatism' (Punter 1996: 200), contemporary Gothic is, as Punter puts it, 'still an arena for related questions' (ibid.).

FEMALE FAN EMPATHY AND THE RELUCTANT VAMPIRE

At odds with much theorising about popular vampire fiction, female fans do not identify with the vampire's female victims, but rather, empathise with the vampire figure itself. But the vampire with whom the fans empathise has its ancestry in the early Byronic tradition of Lord Ruthven and the popular 'penny dreadful' *Varney the Vampyre*, rather than *Dracula*. This chapter draws on interview material with women vampire fans in New Orleans and various parts of Britain between 1997 and 2001. As in much of the surrounding fan culture, all of the fans shared an interest in those vampire narratives where the central vampire characters are constructed sympathetically. Most of the fans I talked to in New Orleans had been members of the Anne Rice Vampire Lestat Fan Club, although not all had remained members. In Britain the fans interviewed are, or had been, members of The London Vampire Group, The Vampyre Society, or regularly post on one of the many news groups dedicated to *Buffy the Vampire Slayer* and its spin-off, *Angel*, as well as various other smaller fan groupings. All of the female fans quoted in this chapter have a long-standing interest in the vampire going back to their teenage years, and occasionally before. The difference between the women fans in the US and those in Britain has to do primarily with the vampire texts available when their interest in vampires was first aroused. For the American fans, this interest in the sympathetic vampire found early expression in television series such as *Dark Shadows* (ABC Television, 1966–71) and *Forever Knight* (CBS Television, 1992–93) and only the few *Dracula* films from Universal Studios in which the vampire is considered to be treated as persecuted and soulful. The central vampire characters in *Dark Shadows* and *Forever Knight* are at odds with their ontological status as vampires. Either trying to return to human form or (as precursors to *Angel*) using their vampiric powers to solve crime and help the innocent, these vampires are depicted sympathetically. The American fans when discussing their early favourites comment enthusiastically about such portrayals. For example, Diane says of Barnabas Collins, the central vampire character in *Dark Shadows*:

> I just absolutely loved him – what attracted me – the vampire type that I like is the romantic type … you know he was a soulful creature, and he wasn't even very good looking, it was the romance of it.

Shirin makes a similar comment about her liking for *Forever Knight*:

> They're human but they have this problem. They happen to be a vampire. Like in *Forever Knight* you know. He's trying to become human again.

The American fans' preference for sympathetically portrayed vampires is accompanied by an interest in a concept of 'romance' that has little to do with romantic love. Melinda sums it up thus:

Romance not in the sense of a love interest, romance as in something that stirs the passions of the soul ... now I'll get on to the more base version of it later [laughs].

American fans also find sympathy in Frank Langella's version of *Dracula* (Universal 1979), and they also draw on the vocabulary of melodramatic pathos and the Gothic when discussing it. For example Dana comments about the film:

Oh, I liked that 1977 *Dracula* with Langella ... I could watch it again and again, it's just so filled with pathos, it's really dark Gothic – 'oh, the night' [laughs].

Melinda concurs:

Frank Langella ... again, very similar. Now the *Dracula* version – it bothers me a bit, and even as a child I was rooting for the vampire, so the fact that he dies in the end just breaks my heart. It always does.

This version of *Dracula* resides in the American vampire fan cultural canon and it is referred to repeatedly. For these women fans though, its merits stem specifically from a melodramatic and gothic reading of the vampire rather than the film's production values or style. The American female fans, then, refer explicitly to an alternative vampire myth, one with the gothic roots of pathos and sympathy. These fans, rather than somehow being converted to vampire texts, demonstrate considerable cultural competence in their discussion of their favourites, and the ability to deploy complex concepts in their judgements of texts.

The appeal of a pathos-filled vampire who elicits sympathy is shared by the majority of the women fans in Britain. However, while the American fans were watching television series and vampire films from Universal Studios, British fans were watching late-night re-runs of the horror films from the Hammer Studio stable. Many of the British fans interviewed and spoken to in the course of this research had watched Hammer horror films on television either in their early teens or twenties and the majority comment with approval on those Hammer films where the vampire offers more than an image of menace. Interestingly, for British female fans Hammer is primarily remembered for its sympathetic female vampires who were often depicted with lesbian overtones. Cheryl for example, comments that she favoured the Hammer films which drew on the Carmilla strand of the vampire idea (such as *Vampire Lovers* (1970) and *Lust For a Vampire* (1971)). She explains why:

I like the mystery about it, and the sort of innocence about it. It's got sensuality about it, which again for the time would have been quite shocking, and she doesn't understand the feelings that she is having ... you can empathise with her.

The empathy that Cheryl and the fans on both sides of the Atlantic feel for the sympathetic vampire is matched by their articulation of derision for Dracula. British and American women fans hate Dracula for the very reasons that some critics offer for the success of this figure.

ON DISLIKING DRACULA: GENDER AND FAN INVOLVEMENT

The pleasure of reading *Dracula*, critics claim, is afforded the reader through the hunt and destruction of Dracula (Pirie 1977; Astle 1980; Twitchell 1985; Bentley 1988; Richardson 1991; Skal 1993, 1996; Zanger 1997). Yet there is a widespread disapproval among female fans of the depiction of vampirism in 'Dracularised' modes. This finds expression in distaste for Bram Stoker's novel *Dracula* (1897). Melinda says of the book:

> I never could actually sit through the book, because the book was always ... he is a monster, he is walking like a lizard, he turns himself into a bat, he is a grotesque creature ... I was only eleven when I saw that version of the movie, or twelve. Back in this very impressionable age, and I just decided that is the version that I wanted to cling to. And when I tried to go back and read that *Dracula* again – before I realised how much of a difference there generally is between the book and the movie – I was horrified, and so I never actually made it through, I just couldn't.

Andrea also could not 'sit' through the book because

> Dracula is just mean and nasty, so I don't like the ones with all the gore and I really don't think that that's a true portrait. That's not really what a vampire is like.

These two fans deploy different vocabularies of involvement. Melinda clearly distinguishes between the different versions of the vampire and articulates her desire to 'cling' to one. Andrea's vocabulary draws on the widespread notion of verisimilitude in popular culture. One might imagine from this quote that Andrea thinks that vampires are real, but I asked her directly and she does not. Instead she is using the vocabulary at her disposal to articulate her dislike – i.e. 'its not realistic'. These differences in vocabulary of involvement may be directly related to the women's different levels of education and cultural capital.

Hannah also describes reading *Dracula* only as a result of her already engaged interest in the vampire via Rice. Her account of this experience demonstrates clearly the way her interpretation of the text is shaped by what she has already learned from her melodramatic favourites, her expectations are patterned by her existing involvement and pleasure in the vampire tale:

> I hated it, it was not everything I liked in Anne Rice ... I just didn't like the way the character was portrayed, they were too interested in making

him a villain, I didn't like it ... [Rice's vampires] were anti-villains, or the
sympathetic sort of villain at least that you could get into even if they
were killers and whatnot. You could at least have sympathy for them;
they were not there just to be despised.

This comment demonstrates not only the importance of sympathy in her
vocabulary, but also an awareness that this feature of the vampire is a textual
creation; she articulates the sense that the character of Dracula was constructed
to be despised. This is reiterated in the following exchange from two British
fans who explain their dislike of most of the Hammer films:

Pam: Those ones just show that they're hunters and killers and they
       kill, kill, kill indiscriminately and they just always seem to por-
       tray [Vampiricism] is as evil and bad and the church and the
       crosses and the garlic...
Janet: That's 'cause the church were always hunting them down, weren't
       they? Hunters with their stakes going after them 'cause they
       don't understand them...
Pam: Yeah, the vicars are always up there with them [both laugh].

Despite the difference between fans' vocabularies of involvement, the central
criteria that they all deploy is that the vampire be sympathetically constructed.
   These women vampire fans demonstrate an understanding of the way that
Dracula has, as Gelder puts it, undergone a process of the 'cultural remodelling' (1994: 92). Shirin, like most women fans involved in this study, is 'not a big
Christopher Lee fan' but she demonstrates a knowledge of the transformations
of *Dracula* from page to screen which echo Gelder's comments about *Dracula*
and she identifies the 'vein of sympathy' (Punter 1980: 348) for the screen vampire found in some academic accounts:

Frankenstein is a better book than *Dracula*, but the Dracula movies are
better. I don't think the Frankenstein movies are so good. He's *just* a
monster and he's not like that in the book. But Dracula you see, he *is*
like that in the book, but it seems like they got it all turned around in
the movies.

Without using academic language, Shirin both cogently explains the cultural
remodelling of *Dracula* (and *Frankenstein*) and engages in textual discrimination;
she judges texts as 'good' or not, on the basis of her existing sympathetic reading of the vampire, and whether or not a text conforms to a depiction as something more than 'just a monster'. Diane's comment about *Dracula* 'the book'
and Dracula in the movies repeat those of Shirin. She states:

I loved the later *Dracula* movies, especially the most recent one with
Gary Oldman ... *Dracula* the book, you hated Dracula, *he was a monster*

and you wanted him to die. But the movies are so ... the 1977 one I can watch again and again, it's so romantic – I just love it.

Once again, this fan recognises the shifts and movement in the depiction of the vampire which is articulated alongside existing aesthetic criteria. Like Diane, Pam and Janet in Britain praise Gary Oldman as Dracula because of the pathos of his circumstances:

Janet: It was another sad story wasn't it...
Pam: That was also very good because that again went away from the normal sort of angle didn't it...
Janet: Yeah, well, look at how emotional he was.
Pam: Yeah, no. He wasn't just evil, he was so emotional he loved her with such a passion...
Janet: And that carried him through the centuries...
Pam: All the centuries just waiting for her to come back ... Well I hope Winona Ryder is *not* at the end of it [laughter].

Also, fans have other vocabularies at their disposal which are not derived from the strategies of orientation towards particular texts, or even context of fandom, but stem from their understanding of, and experiences in, wider cultural and social processes. For instance, many of the women fans deploy vocabulary from the feminist movement. Even though many of these fans would not label themselves as feminists, nonetheless, the language produced by the feminist movement enables certain vocabularies to be brought to bear on their understanding of texts. The following comment from Karen demonstrates the combination of feminist and fan vocabulary, which revealingly directly applies the interpreted meaning of the text to the self:

Lee – the ways things progressed – how can I put it? He was good for his time, but he was very male chauvinistic, there was no equality and that was what I don't like about him, there's this vampire and it's all very male-dominated. The females he made into vampires were cowering little things kept down in the cellar ... whereas with him it was control, um, and I will *not* be controlled.

Karen concludes that the Lee vampire was 'very much a predator, there was nothing kind or gentle or sensuous about him. He really was just a killer, you know.' It is interesting how Karen relates judgments about Dracula as 'predator', lacking in gentility and sensuality to her feminist vocabulary – 'male chauvinism' and 'male domination'. This folding together of different interpretive vocabularies begins to indicate that the women fans' choices are to do with the way they relate to one's experience of self. For many female fans on both sides of the Atlantic, it is the *Vampire Chronicles* that, until very recently with *Buffy*, provide this link most fully.

61

Fig. 10 Gary Oldman plays a sympathetic Dracula, in *Bram Stoker's Dracula* (1992)

FAN FAVOURITES: GENDER AND THE PLEASURES OF PATHOS

The vampires' unwanted plight and persecuted innocence are aspects of the *Vampire Chronicles'* melodramatic structuring that ensures it a place as a firm favourite with the majority of women fans. Many of the women comment that their sympathy with Louis and Lestat derives from the knowledge that these characters did not choose to become a vampire but had it thrust upon them. For example, Diane says:

> With Lestat and Louis, it's against their will and so long as those condi-
> tions are met, it's okay, you know? I don't like it when they start liking
> what they're doing or if they become a vampire because they like killing
> or they like blood, you know? ... I like the 'can't help it', you know, 'got
> into this by accident but soldiers on', you know? That's what attracts me
> and it seems as long as those conditions are met I can be sympathetic.

Shirin also 'likes the more thoughtful ones' and Andrea comments that she is a fan because 'there are characters that you can care about, in comparison to some of the other vampires that are just sadistic and like hurting people'. In Britain, Cheryl favours Louis because of the pathos of his circumstances: 'I like the way that he is really unhappy with his existence. I like that he's not happy with himself and that he's got to kill people.'

Janet and Pam concur:

> Janet: I think Anne Rice's books have woken a lot of people up to the
> concept of vampires. It makes them seem as if they're not so dif-
> ferent from us, they're not monsters, they're not ghouls...
> Pam: They're just different...
> Janet: That's why I like the way that someone eventually portrayed
> them finally as very loving people, not monsters. They are very
> loving, they have got deep feelings, they've made them seem, you
> know, not the old Nostradamus [sic] and all the old monsters
> – vampires that were terrifying and, and with the fingernails
> and...
> Pam: Yeah, it's all Hollywood.
> Janet: I mean these were beautiful people and they got such intense
> passion and feelings for life.

The fans' comments about their favourites demonstrate the importance of the construction of the vampire characters through melodramatic modes of pathos and sympathy. It is also interesting here that Pam is deploying the same process of distinction ('its all Hollywood') as other fans who would ridicule her interest in both Francis Ford Coppola's film and Neil Jordan's film of *Interview With the Vampire* (1995). One might consider Pam as deploying elitist taste distinctions even though her preferred cultural objects are not those conferred status, even in horror fandom. However, fannish taste distinctions between their own tastes and 'mainstream' tastes are not simply devices to accrue subcultural capital. Fannish responses are (like all responses) complex and contradictory in this respect because the texts that we all engage with stem from the commercial domain, but the different responses towards a text come not just from differing levels of cultural capital, but also from engagement with our experiences. It seems as important in the discussion from fans above that a figure that is supposed to embody monstrousness and Otherness is not considered to be a monster and is seen as not so 'different from us'.

The previous chapter examined the way that Gothic melodrama has the ability to force to the surface what are often submerged injustices, through the portrayal of a misunderstood and wrongly damned protagonist. Many feminist scholars have suggested that this portrayal often resonates particularly with women's experiences. Christine Gledhill, for example, argues that melodrama is a 'public enactment of socially unacknowledged states' (1987: 31) articulated through the persecution of the protagonist and the eventual recognition of innocence. It is this narrative trajectory which structures the *Vampire Chronicles*, and many other tales which feature sympathetic vampires. The women fans' articulation of their involvement with these texts follows the melodrama of the narrative. This is evidenced in the many comments about the 'pathos' of the vampires and their 'soulful' existence; the designation of the vampires as victims of forces outside of their control and – crucially – the desire for their innocence to be recognised: 'finally someone has portrayed them ... not [as] monsters'. It is the notion that the vampire is 'not happy with his existence' that is a key aspect of the sympathetic vampire's attraction as a character. For female fans of the vampire, the notion of 'innocence buried alive and unable to voice it claim to recognition' (Brooks 1995: 20) is the central melodramatic pull of the Gothic vampire and the fans relate it directly to experiences of the self.

Rice's *Chronicles* did not teach all of these fans to read the vampire sympathetically, for many were already fans before they encountered her work (again, indicating that Rice also 'learned' about the vampire's potentially sympathy prior to sitting down at her typewriter), and subsequently a new generation have learned about sympathetic vampires from Joss Whedon's *Buffy the Vampire Slayer* (the topic of the next chapter), who acknowledges his own influences in the sympathetic depiction of the vampire Blade. However, there are important developments in the depiction of the vampire in Rice's texts which provide new lessons in the pleasure of involvement with the sympathetic vampire and which re-emerge in *Buffy*. The final exchange quoted above (between Pam and Janet) demonstrates not only that it is important that the vampires are recognised as innocent, but also that they express 'intense' emotional states such as 'passion' and 'feelings for life'. It is vital that Louis and Lestat are not simply victims of circumstances, but that, unlike the gothic heroine of old, they also have preternatural powers with which to intervene in those circumstances and to 'live' fully. For Rice's characters, vampirism may be agony, but it is also, as

Punter puts it, 'rich, glowing and lustrous' and the world is newly 'open to the vampire's vastly expanded senses' (1996: 161). A contemporary sensibility is found in the transformations of the vampire which now combine the long-held attributes of the innocence attributed to the melodramatic heroine, with a modern ability to intervene in circumstances outside of one's control and to do so with glamour. In the past, the vampire may have provided a reactionary mirror of self-loathing (see Dyer 1988). Rice's first-person narratives, however, celebrate polymorphous sexuality (perhaps prematurely, as Hodges and Doane (1991) suggest) and turn self-loathing into pride – 'what fools these mortals be' (Dyer 1988: 59). The vampires in Rice's serial blend the characteristics of the melodramatic heroine with a contemporary glamour and strength, but each embodies one aspect more fully than others. So while Louis' appeal is primarily his embodiment of an anguished morality, Lestat is a rebel and a rule-breaker. It is clear that fans associate rule-breaking with glamour; as Melinda says: 'Louis is sorrow and Lestat is glamour.' Thus, for many fans, favouritism shifts from Louis to Lestat by the second *Chronicle*. Louis is a sensitive one on whom everything leaves a mark, but Lestat is one who leaves his mark on everything. Like Louis, he desires personal significance and meaning in the world, but this propels him into ever more shocking (and glamorous) escapades. Lestat moves from being a vampire rock star to stealing a human body to inhabit, to re-animating the terrible original Egyptian goddess-vampire and is finally wooed by a quasi-Miltonian version of the Devil that he follows into Hell. His power and zest for adventure combine with the sympathy produced by the pathos of his circumstances. Many fans find this mixture most appealing. Dee, for example, explains why she favours Lestat:

> Oh I loved *The Vampire Lestat*. I actually loved it better than the first one. I don't know, he's had a rough time, but he just gets on with it.

Melinda offers a full and lucid account of why this is her favourite *Chronicle*:

> It goes into the creation of Lestat and how and what he went through. Again, we've got the emotions, we've got the pathos. He's a normal kid, he was abused, he ran away. He's doing well for himself, he's not doing bad, I mean he's doing what I'm doing here, right? Just eking out a living, but he's happy. Suddenly he gets snatched off the streets and vamped! Whoa! You know, how did he deal with it? How did he rise above it? And this happened to so many others. Louis got snatched off the streets and vamped. But what did he do? He spiralled down. Lestat spiralled up, he overcame, he conquered. Yes! Go baby! Um, so I admire the book because it delves deep into the heart of what every human is capable of and watches them rise above everything – no matter how fantastic.

Both Peter Brooks and Ien Ang have commented on the pleasures of self-pity that is afforded by melodrama, and Louis does seem to embody this aspect of melodrama, indeed Rice herself has proposed that Louis emerged as a response to her pain at losing her young daughter to leukaemia (Ramsland 1991). Lestat however, emerges as the central character of the *Chronicles* at the height of the 'self-help' culture of the 1980s which banished self-pity and promoted individualistic and apolitical solutions to problems faced by the self. The 'get on with it' vocabulary produced by this culture is evidenced in the language of some of the fans. For example Diane comments:

> Well, when I first read the books Louis was my favourite and I thought Lestat was a terrible, terrible, guy. But then in the next book – you just wanted to say 'Louis – get a life', you know what I mean?

The 'get a life' vocabulary emerged in the increasingly individualistic 1980s which told us that society no longer existed, only individuals, and this is reflected both in *The Vampire Lestat* and in fan engagements with it. However, the fan involvement with Lestat is also bound up with his status as a rule-breaker and the glamour this affords. The vampire's ability to intervene in its unasked-for circumstances is a transformation that *simultaneously* relates to the increasingly individualistic culture of the 1980s *and* to the hopes for meaning for the self that reach beyond. The duality of anguish and hope for the self symbolised in the vampire has long been figured as personal rebellion (as argued in the previous chapter), but in Lestat, personal rebellion is figured as the quest for renown, exhibitionism and the achievement of a kind of celebrity status. This too speaks to the cultural moment, but it also speaks to a much wider experience of the marginalised self – the desire to make a mark, to have an effect, in short, to have meaning.

The idea of the ability to intervene also has particular resonances with femininity because of the cultural imposition of passivity on the feminine. Intervention, as we shall see in the following chapter, becomes a crucial feature of today's vampire tales, and it is one of the central organising themes of the female-centred narrative of *Buffy the Vampire Slayer*. Yet we also see sympathetically (and glamorously) depicted vampires in this television series, and this continues to be a central aspect of the vampire's construction and its appeal.

READING THE LOST BOYS: SYMPATHETIC VAMPIRE AS META-TEXT

So strong is the sympathetic aspect of the vampire's appeal that fans will often read it into texts lacking overtly sympathetic vampires. Fans have a meta-exegetic reading of the sympathetic vampire; that is, a meta-interpretation that overarches any single text and informs their selection of texts (as we saw in the case of *Dracula*). At times however, fans reproduce the (meta-exegetic) reading of the vampire for text where it does not quite 'fit'.

The 1980s saw a number of vampire films that were aimed specifically at a youth audience and seemed to be directed primarily at male youth rebellion. One of the most popular was an American vampire biker-gang film, *The*

Lost Boys (1987). It is one of the first of a series of vampire films that directly addresses rebelliousness and youth culture and at its centre is a vampire punk-biker gang, a glamorous subculture who tear through America's west coast town, Santa Carla (Santa Cruz), wreaking havoc. The leader of the vampire gang, David, played by Kiefer Sutherland (the epitome of 1980s unconventional youthful cool), develops an interest in a town newcomer, Michael, who has recently arrived from Arizona with his divorced mother and younger brother. At the same time, Michael develops an interest in an enigmatic girl named Star, a half-vampire who turns out to 'belong' to David. David tries to persuade Michael to become one of the gang, as Michael struggles against his vampiric transformation. Some critics read the tale as one of homosexual panic (Showalter 1991; Gelder 1994), where vampirism stands for homosexuality and Michael's eventual defeat of the gang is symbolic of his re-entry into 'normal' heterosexuality. Others read it through the lens of the reactionary politics of the Reagan/Thatcher era in which it was produced. Nina Auerbach argues that 'the Lost Boys', like other vampires of the 1980s, were 'depressed creatures ... constricted in their potential, their aspirations, and their effects on mortals' (1995: 165). *The Lost Boys*, according to Auerbach, presents 'transformation as self-imprisonment rather than exaltation' (1995: 166):

> The lost boys of 1987, dull-eyed, stunted, and pale, have become casual-
> ties of the Republicans' war against drugs; they are so burned out that
> the anti-drug message of official culture seems to have stifled all trans-
> formations or transforming perceptions. (1995: 167)

Auerbach concludes that the film features 'young men and their women with neither the energy nor the dreams of change; even vampirism, their sole rebellion, is an impermanent condition governed by the respectable patriarch Max' (1995: 169). However, Auerbach underestimates the pull of the vampire biker gang, and the appeal of its rebellious and glamorous punk-rock image. For fans of the vampire, the biker gang in *The Lost Boys* provides alluring images of west coast rebellion as the following exchange from fans demonstrates:

Pam: *The Lost Boys* were good in a different sort of way, 'cause there
         were rebels...
Janet: They were total rebels, they knew what they had and they
         just got on with it. They did flaunt it a bit, they were just
         rebellious. Michael was my favourite...
Pam: He pulls back from it, which was a pity. I liked all the others,
         yeah the bad boys, yeah, they were good.

For these fans, as for others, the snarl and swagger of the vampire gang is not a sign of burned-out depression, but is entirely in tune with the youthful disenchantment of the day, in which rebellion was expressed as petty lawlessness and an insolent personal manner with a sartorial image to match. This demonstrates (as Auerbach has persuasively argued) that because of vampiric mutability, its appeal is in tune with each generation, as are the images of personal rebellion that often accompany its depiction. But Auerbach's comments are also apt, for the rebellion of the vampire has always been highly ambiguous, tending to fold together the possibilities for the self outside of conventional life with the ever-present potential for elitism in the act of standing out.

Comparing fan readings of the vampire gang in *The Lost Boys* with Auerbach's account, then, is not to suggest a 'wrong' academic reading of the film and a 'correct' fannish one. Instead I want to suggest something about the character of *fannish* interpretations of vampire narratives: the meta-interpretive framework for vampire fiction within vampire fan cultures that provides fans with an important lens through which to read the vampire, despite the specificities of, or differences between, vampire texts. This meta-interpretation is linked to texts – many texts conform to the meta-interpretation of the vampire – or, to the way that fans read the vampire, and this can overlay the explicit characteristics of a text. Much fan scholarship would call this a fannish subtext, linked to an interpretive community which reads 'against the grain' of a text in order to produce their own meaning (Bacon-Smith 1992; 2000; Fiske 1992; Jenkins 1992; Cartmell *et al.* 1997; Merrick 1997; Watson 1997; Baym 1998; Classen 1998; Dell 1998; Harris 1998; Tankel and Murphy 1998; Jenkins *et al.* 2002). Fan scholarship has produced numerous claims of fannish rebellion on the basis of the idea that fans subvert authorial meaning. For instance, one early and very influential study of fandom characterises fans as 'poachers' (Jenkins 1992). Henry Jenkins suggests that fans overturn 'sanctioned' interpretation and resist dominant culture by reworking texts to suit their own needs (1992: 25). However, as Sara Gwenllian Jones (2000; 2003) has argued, the subtext of a television show is now something that is actively encouraged on the part of the producers, rather than simply on the part of fans. Fans do not have to 'read against the grain' to produce subtextual readings – they are encouraged to do so by the nature of television texts which

> employ a range of textual and narrative devices that make an explicit address to the immersive, interpretive and interactive viewing practices that characterise fan cultures. Intertextuality, metatextuality, self-referentiality, story-arc ... are knowingly employed. (2003: 166)

I would also add that serialised novels like the *Vampire Chronicles* also produce an intensification of the audience's 'imaginative engagement with the text' (Gwenllian Jones 2000: 11) and can impact on fannish interpretations of single films such as *The Lost Boys*. Indeed, fans take considerable pleasure in the serialised format of the *Chronicles*. Hannah in New Orleans explains the appeal:

> You asked me if I like Poppy Brite and I said not as much as Anne Rice and part of the reason why – it's a single book – I pick it up, I read it, I

Fig. 11 'Sleep all day. Party all night. Never grow old. Never die. Its fun to be a vampire.' Kiefer Sutherland leads the vampire gang in *The Lost Boys* (1987)

put it down and I'm never gonna read anything with these same characters in it again, because she doesn't write a series, she writes a book.

The sense that fans are engaging with a 'vast, multilayered cultural territory which is only ever partially mapped ... and yet which constantly presents the promise of fulfilment' (ibid.) not only challenges the notion that fannish interpretation is an act of rebellion by pointing to the subtextual invitation of many texts, it also suggests a plausible explanation for the huge fandom surrounding these novels which does not rest on ideas about 'conversion' or 'compulsive identification'.[1] The vampire fans quoted above are reading 'with the grain', not of a particular text (although often they are), but of an interpretive strategy, a meta-interpretation of the figure of the vampire that is in excess of any single textual construction, although it can be found in many. This reading is produced within fandom, but is a product of the way that fans learned what they like about the vampire from the imaginative universes that most fully expressed them, and this feeds back into textual constructions. The popularity of certain conventions, both historically and currently, have produced a way of reading the vampire amongst many vampire fans which is connected to important genre conventions, but partially disconnected from specific texts (and of course, authors, producers and directors learn them too which is why they persist as explicit characteristics).

In a sense, we might say that the sympathetic vampire is a character who has become a 'virtual star' (Gwenllian Jones 2000: 20) in vampire fan culture; and one that has more meaning than any flesh and blood star or celebrity who plays the part of the vampire in any specific film or television programme. Gwenllian Jones develops the idea of the textual character as 'star' in her analysis of *Xena: Warrior Princess*. She argues that while the actor Lucy Lawless, who plays Xena, is 'undoubtedly a star, her stardom is secondary to that of the character she plays. The pre-eminent star *of Xena: Warrior Princess* is Xena, Warrior Princess' (2000: 10). She comments that Xena is one of many characters who seem to 'assume 'lives' and 'identities' of their own, about which the audience knows far more than it does about the actors who play them' (2000: 11). This is an inversion of the way that stardom is usually understood. Unlike Hollywood, where a film is understood as part of the actors repertoire, 'cult film and television audiences are more likely to understand actors as part of the cult text's repertoire, wherein the character rather than the performer is all-important' (ibid.). The sympathetic vampire is, like Xena, a 'virtual star' in its own right, but unlike Xena is disconnected from any individual actor. Instead it is connected to particular conventions, which depict the vampire as a sympathetic and pathos-filled character because of its unwillingness to *be* a vampire and its lack of control over this aspect of its destiny. Added to this is the vampire's bohemian rebellion and unconventional cool. The examination of female fans' accounts of *The Vampire Chronicles* above demonstrates that these tales are favourites because of their deployment of these conventions.

However, this is not the depiction of the vampires in *The Lost Boys*, who, unlike Louis, are *not* at odds with their ontological status. The vampires in *The Lost Boys* revel in their fiendish lawlessness, yet the fans read the film's vampires sympathetically because they are reading them through the sympathetic vampire lens that overarches any particular text; the sympathetic vampire is a 'virtual star' that exceeds the stardom of any performer's star image. In this sense, as Gwenllian Jones puts it, 'the performer's star image is not so much "entangled" with the fictional character as exceeded by it' (2000: 12). Fans know that the fiendishness of sympathetic vampires is (as in the overtly depicted case of Lestat) part of its cover for its deep-rooted pathos. Also, *The Lost Boys* does show Michael as vampiric, but unwilling and traumatised by the vampiric transformation coming over him. The fans quoted earlier pursue their point:

Pam: It is a shame he pulls back from it though, innit? I just wanted him to become one of them and for it to go on and on.

Janet: Yeah, the vampire gang are good, but it's good that he didn't want to be a killer, I don't like it when they just enjoy killing...

Pam: Well, I just wish David would have jumped on him and done it, just get it over with, so that he can be one of them. [laughter]

The lure of the vampire for these fans is bound up with its melodramatic structuring as a victim of forces outside of its control, and thus its vampiric transformation must be enacted unwillingly. However, the 'virtual' vampire star *always* becomes a vampire in the end and the fact that Michael does not is a source of disappointment to the fans. One fan, who comments that she has watched the film repeatedly on video, explains that she stops the video before the ending, because it interrupts her understanding of the film:

Dee: I was disappointed at the ending actually, but it didn't entirely ruin it for me. Anyway, I usually stop the film at a certain point, because I've seen what I want and I know how it is going to end.

Milly: *So at what point do you usually stop it?*

Dee: Before all of the silly stuff at the end, you know? When he is still one of the gang.

Throughout the film, the vampire gang leader David repeatedly enjoins Michael to 'be one of us', and in a crucial scene revving his motorcycle engine at the edge of a cliff asks, 'How far are you willing to go, Michael?' Ken Gelder suggests that this question carries the film's 'homosexual subtext' (1994: 106). For Gelder, *The Lost Boys* offers Michael the 'pull' of the gang, and the film's dwelling on the traumatic experience of his vampiric transformation can be read as the lure of homosexuality which gives rise to 'homosexual panic' (ibid.) in Michael. Gelder suggests, as part of an analysis of this film's depiction of youth anxiety, that there is an erotic triangle between Michael, Star and David, where Star 'is there to tip the balance: she literally guides him "back" to heterosexuality ... and back to the family home' (ibid.). However, for the women fans, Michael's trauma at his vampiric transformation is not a narrative avenue back to the family and heterosexuality, but is a prerequisite to becoming a sympathetic vampire. It is the depiction of this process of transformation which conforms to many fans' expectations. The ending of the film is a disappointment to fans because they read Michael as a sympathetic vampire, even though he is not 'fully fledged', and they cannot fathom his eventual rejection of the gang, even though they know that his unwillingness is a key component of the sympathetic vampire. The point at which David asks Michael how far he is willing to go is, for these fans, an impossible question to answer – they want him to 'go all the way' but they do not want him to want to 'go all the way'. The fannish meta-interpretation of vampire narratives circumvents this unanswerable question; Michael is still seen as a sympathetic vampire. The 'silly stuff' at the end does not resolve the film for the fans; they choose to ignore it, avoid it, or simply dislike it. The fan meta-interpretation of *The Lost Boys* pulls on its overt depiction of the vampire-as-glamorous-rebel as part of the equation of the sympathetic and reluctant vampire, for we have long understood that the two go together; that the 'vampire star' is a virtual figure that involves glamour, a lack of respect for rules, as well as a certain amount of doom, and that the trappings of vampirism's dangerous allure is attained *against one's will*. This (particularly female) fan meta-interpretation of the vampire stems from a complex blend of the historical Romantic and gothic vampire, a knowledge of the development of the genre, and the appeal of a vampire constructed as a classic melodramatic heroine – as subject to forces outsider of her control – but with fangs and preternatural strength. Also, the vampire must adopt the pose of individual rebellion, a rebellion that is centred on making the self spectacular in its nonconformity. The appeal of this blend of characteristics – glamorous rebelliousness combined with vampirism being against ones' will – is summed up in the following fan comment, by Lea, on *The Lost Boys*:

> I really love that film, not so much the story – I really love the vampires in it. It was the whole idea of their gang and where they lived and trying to get Michael to join. The Michael character was my favourite 'cause he didn't want to kill ... But then I really didn't want them to live happily ever after. I wanted him to be a vampire and for it to just go on.

The sympathetic vampire-as-star moves back and forth between texts and fannish interpretations. Texts that produce this 'vampire star' quickly become favourites, ones that do not produce it are often read through this lens anyway, and sometimes, a vampire who starts out with the rebellious glamour but not pathos of the 'vampire star' soon develops along these lines. This happened to Lestat in the *Vampire Chronicles*, a vampire who transforms from fiend to friend in the second novel; it is also the case for the most recent vampire rebel, Spike from *Buffy the Vampire Slayer*.

HOW SPIKE BECAME A VAMPIRE STAR

A recent addition to the vampire-as-glamorous-outsider is also a punk-rock biker figure – the vampire Spike from *Buffy the Vampire Slayer*. The published academic writing on this phenomenally successful cult television series has tended to concentrate on the character of Buffy, perhaps not surprisingly; as the series protagonist and a powerful young female heroine who 'kicks demon ass', she occupies an interesting role in contemporary depictions of femininity, and this will be discussed in the following chapter. However, a great deal of the fandom for the series, including fan fiction, websites, convention attendances and so on, centres on the vampire Spike. Spike's character actually began as a parody of the bad-boy, and a foil for the more 'manly' vampire with a soul, Angel, and in the original script Spike was written to be killed off. But the fan culture took to Spike with great enthusiasm in Britain and America, for he seemed to potentially fulfil the requirements of the meta-interpretation of the 'vampire star'. Spike mixes elements from the vampire gang from *The Lost Boys* – themselves a mix of 1980s punk and 1950s biker gang, but Spike is a peculiarly American interpretation of the 1980s English punk, and in fact pulls directly on the image of Billy Idol. He looks and dresses like Billy Idol, and affects the same self-conscious irony of camp. He even speaks like Billy Idol in a put-on mock cockney accent, or 'mockney', that plays up to American perceptions of the English bad-boy. This image was deliberately cultivated by the series; the official *Buffy the Vampire Slayer* fanzine asks 'Spike' in an interview in 1999:

> Interviewer: *Spike, has anyone told you that you look a lot like Billy Idol?*
> Spike: Has anyone ever told you that you'd taste like prime beef? Of course they've told me that. It's a look, okay?

Fig. 12 Merchandise for the vampire Spike in *Buffy the Vampire Slayer*

This choice of image is a canny one on the part of series creator Joss Whedon, because Billy Idol was one of the very few punks to make it big in the US. In this sense, as Stacey Abbott puts it, Spike lives 'in the now' (2001: 6). Spike also partially acquires the Byronic idea of the vampire bohemian, as the series takes us to his past in the (again mock) streets of nineteenth-century England, where he is shown to be a tortured soul as a failed Romantic poet turned-evilvampire, William the Bloody. Like Louis and Lestat, Spike is irreverent towards outdated vampire lore; but it is Spike's humour, rather than the sorrow of Louis or the glamour of Lestat, that reveals his pathos. From his first appearance, Spike's joking language sets him apart from the other vampires and links him to the Scooby Gang.[2] For example, Spike uses humorous asides to distinguish himself from the vampires of the Brethren of Aurelius, and he even calls the 'Anointed One' the 'Annoying One'.

With the growth in Spike's popularity amongst fans, his character arc over the seven series moves from almost a send-up of a punk evil vampire out to kill Buffy, to a far more complex figure, who comes to love Buffy and is crucially bound up in Buffy's fate. Pastiche turns to genuine pathos as his character develops, and at least one commentator has suggested that the humour surrounding Spike's predicament is an important component to the sympathy he increasingly garners (Boyette 2001). Michelle Boyette argues that Spike transforms from a 'figure of fun, a buffoon', into a 'comic anti-hero' and is significantly redeemed by his humour (2001: 1–2). Crucially, however, Spike is a figure of sympathy. Indeed, on the AllAboutSpike.com website, a regular contributor, Laura, explains Spike's appeal:

> As a human, he was incredibly sensitive ... as a vampire, Spike is still 'tainted' by humanity ... Spike is capable of love and selflessness. Spike loves more completely and powerfully than any other character on the show ... Why relate to Spike? Spike is the ultimate outcast. He does not fit in anywhere, and is struggling to find his place in the world.

This description of Spike and his appeal clearly aligns Spike with the tradition of the sympathetic vampire from Ruthven to Lestat; sensitivity, reluctance, the 'taint' of humanity and outsiderdom are characteristics that Spike shares with each incarnation of the sympathetic vampire.

However, there continues to be a dangerous and unpleasant edge to Spike. He becomes Buffy's lover, but in the episode 'Seeing Red' in the penultimate season (cut for British terrestrial television), he attempts to rape Buffy, thus confounding all fannish expectations of a sympathetic vampire star (despite having suffered months of physical, sexual and mental abuse at Buffy's hands). However, at this point the actor, James Marsters, crucially intervenes, for he has also learned the meta-interpretation of the 'vampire star' (and perhaps knows that his livelihood is dependent on Spike retaining this interpretation). His personal appearances following the rape scene bolstered the fannish interpretation of Spike as a sympathetic character; the sympathy for the screen character had become bound up with the off-screen persona. On his web site and in appearances, Marsters plays the tortured soul to perfection. In one of numerous interviews in 2003 he comments:

> That was the hardest day of my life ... It's something I don't even want to watch ... What you see on that screen is just my terror at having to do that scene ... They show it sometimes and I'm always like, 'Oh, God'. I hope that since Spike has a soul he's not capable anymore of doing anything like that. That's what I really hope. That they won't bring him back in that state of mind ... The writers are fabulous, but when I showed up on set that day I told them: 'Sometimes you guys just don't know what you do. You just do not know what you're asking us' ... I'm proud of it artistically, but as a human being I never, never, never want to do a scene like that again and I will always refuse because I know what it does to me. (Butler 2003)

Marsters has not only 'suffered' at the hands of the writers (and this sentiment chimes with many fans; the notion of series writers ruining favoured characters is a characteristic of fan discourse), he also overtly confuses his own emotions with 'what he hopes' for Spike, thus inviting a simultaneous reading of the two. In discussing the character-as-star, Gwenllian Jones has suggested that 'an important aspect of Lawless's off-screen role in relation to fans is that she can seem to provide a measure of authenticity to fans' interpretations of Xena by sanctioning them either directly, by explicitly endorsing certain readings of the character, or indirectly, by refraining from contradiction such readings' (2000: 15). In the case of sustaining a sympathetic reading of Spike, Marsters' intervention was explicit. The sympathetic response from fans to Marsters' emotional disclosure fed directly into their understanding of Spike's screen vampire persona. Gwenllian Jones has commented in relation to Xena, that 'the cult star status of Xena puts Lawless in a curious position in relation to her character and, in particular, in relation to her character's fans. She is not expected to "be" Xena, but she is frequently expected to function as Xena's earthly representative' (2000: 14). We can see this process at work in relation to Marsters intervention in fannish interpretations of Spike – it was not really 'Spike', it was the series writers. Marsters here can be seen to be Spike's 'earthly representative'.

The fannish meta-interpretation of the 'vampire star' as sympathetic and suffering, steeped in images of glamorous renown and imbued with personal rebellion, exceeds any single depiction of the vampire or any specific actor who plays the vampire. The 'vampire star' is produced not only through the fans' engagement with a text (subtextual or otherwise), but by their engagement with an intertextual vampire, and this interpretation is bolstered by actors like Marsters who play along and act as the 'vampire star's earthly representative' in their dealings with fandom and with the media. If, as Gwenllian Jones suggests, 'the Xenaverse effectively takes stardom to its logical conclusion, abolishing altogether the need for an obvious referent in the form of a "real" person' (2000: 12), then the sympathetic 'vampire star' who resides across a variety of texts and through a number of actors, takes this process even further. Joss Whedon, who is a well-known 'lurker' on *Buffy* Internet newsgroups, was surprised by the fan response to Spike, but he responded to it by developing Spike's character and story arc in line with the more complex 'vampire star' that engages fans. At the end of the final series, Spike's suffering is genuinely heroic as he sacrifices his own life to save the world. The fact that he comes back to life as the only *Buffy* character to regularly reappear on *Angel* after *Buffy* came off the air is further evidence of Spike's increased importance to the imaginative universe know as the 'Buffyverse'.

The sympathetic and pathos-filled meta-interpretation of the vampire continues in *Buffy the Vampire Slayer*. *Buffy* has deployed the 'vampire star' in its depiction of the sympathetic vampire, but also, significantly, the show infuses its female human characters with melodramatic pathos and preternatural strength and thus produces a number of important textual transformations to produce a *fin-de-siècle* vampire tale very different to its predecessors.

CHAPTER 4

THE PREDICAMENT OF THE VAMPIRE AND THE SLAYER: GOTHIC MELODRAMA IN MODERN AMERICA

Such has been the popularity of *Buffy the Vampire Slayer* that, according to J. Gordon Melton, it was 'able to move Anne Rice's novels, which had dominated the vampire world for a decade, off centre-stage' (2002: 1). *Buffy* seems to have turned the tale of the vampire upside down. In this television series, it is neither a patriarchal vampire hunter like Dr Van Helsing, nor is it the vampires themselves who possess the power and who dominate the screen, but a slightly built, blonde, teenage American girl named Buffy Summers, a vampire slayer who possesses supernatural strength. The series creator, Joss Whedon, has claimed feminist intentions for *Buffy*: 'The idea for the film came from seeing too many blondes walking into dark alleyways and being killed. I wanted, just once, for her to fight back when the monster attacked, and kick his ass' (quoted in Havens 2003: 21). However, as a number of critics have noted, Buffy draws on a long lineage of young female heroines. Jenny Bavidge considers Buffy to be the 'latest incarnation of a specific tradition of teenage heroine in popular and literary culture: the figure of the "Anglo-American Girl"' (2004: 42). Bill Osgerby suggests that Buffy is not an 'abrupt "quantum shift" in popular representations of teenage femininity', but developed out of 'a longer "teen-girl" TV tradition' (2004: 83) that did not 'simply construct young women as passive and submissive' (2004: 71). However, the combination of pathos and strength found in Buffy's character and the depiction of sympathetic vampires to whom Buffy is persistently drawn, marks a shift from the more playful and hedonistic depictions of female figures in shows like *Gidgit* (1965), instead drawing on melodramatic codes and conventions. The empowered femininity depicted in this series and the moral complexity of its sympathetic vampires has provoked debates about its feminist politics and progressive credentials amongst academics, and these will be examined here.

However, while many critics have recognised that *Buffy*'s 'emotional structures have more in common with soap opera relationships than with most genre series' (Kaveny 2002: 5), the significance of this melodramatic structure has not been discussed, despite the enormous interest in the cultural politics of soap opera and melodrama among feminist academics. This chapter will argue that melodrama is as central to the appeal of *Buffy* as it has been to previous vampire tales, despite the important updating of conventions and its pick-n-mix use of genres. *Buffy* rearticulates the dilemma of the self at the heart of the

Gothic and melodramatic vampire tale in the context of the paradoxes of contemporary Anglo-American culture. These paradoxes are particularly inflected
with issues of gender and race in our time, because the twentieth century witnessed huge changes wrought by the civil rights and women's movements and
society promised us an equality which it did not deliver. *Buffy* is shot through
with these tensions and speaks directly to them, and also to the problematic
experiences of the self these conditions give rise to.

Buffy is thus part of a broader context. It struck a cord with a certain *fin-
de-siècle* mood in Anglo-American culture at least, when the questions of what
it means to be human are closer to the surface than at other times. This is not
to suggest that *Buffy* expressed the *zeitgeist* of the cultural moment at the end
of the twentieth and beginning of the twenty-first centuries, for I have already
suggested what may be some of the problems in designating a cultural moment
in such sweeping terms (see chapter one) and supposing that a single work
might then embody it. Also, as we shall see, despite its enormous popularity,
Buffy did not attract a 'mass audience', and thus while it speaks to the wider
experience of the self in cultural modernity, it does so in a manner that appeals
to specific audiences, rather than general ones.

Buffy is part of the broader context, however, in another important aspect.
Many of the official *Buffy* guides credit the success of *Buffy* to the 'genius' of the
series creator, Joss Whedon. Without wishing to diminish his accomplishment,
it is important to recognise the variety of factors that have shaped the fortunes
of *Buffy* (not least, the team of writers, actors and production staff who helped
to make the programme). As Rhonda Wilcox and David Lavery have suggested,
the original vision for a television show 'grows within a press of forces – both
social and artistic expectations, conventions of the business and the art' (2002:
xvii). I would add to this the current state of the television industry and the
changing formations of its audiences in the US (and to a lesser extent Britain).
While Wilcox and Lavery suggest that *Buffy* 'fights the forces' that 'bad' television yields to, I will argue in this chapter that *Buffy*'s prospects were instead
situated in the increasingly vertically integrated, niche-marketed television
industry in the US, aimed at affluent, educated, female and mostly white consumers. I will also examine the role of *Buffy* fandom in this context, and will
suggest that it is caught up in the logic and the struggle over meaning and
legitimacy that marks the field of culture; from anti-censorship campaigns, to
the consumption of merchandise and celebrity, *Buffy* fandom demonstrates the
operation of contrasting cultural values and cultural capital at work in designating cultural worth. Also *Buffy*, with its multilayered and knowing meanings,
is a model text for such activity, as we shall see, for it invites interpretation.

VAMPIRES, BUFFY AND YOUTH CULTURE: MELODRAMA AND FEMALE SELF-MANAGEMENT

Buffy the Vampire Slayer is, as the opening voice-over declares, about a seemingly
typical Californian high-school girl who is 'the chosen one', the latest in a long

line of female demon-slayers who fight 'the forces of darkness'. The series is set in Sunnydale, a typical southern Californian town – 'So Cal' as Boyd Tonkin dubs it (2002: 40) – except that it is also the Hellmouth, a magnet for the gathering of evil, which Buffy and her friends ceaselessly combat in its various incarnations.

Commentators have noted that the series deploys Gothic fantasy as a metaphor for the problems associated with contemporary adolescence. For instance, Roz Kaveny comments that the series' 'central conceit' is 'a bunch of high-school kids who fight supernatural evils that often map metaphorically over teenage preoccupations' (2002: 2), while Susan Owen argues that the show has much in common with other 'popular dramatic teen series such as *Dawson's Creek*, *Felicity*, and *Party of Five*' (1999: 25), and like them, deals with the

> reconstructed problems of middle-class, Anglo, heteronormative, North American teenage socialisation: shifting gender scripts, sexual matura-tion, sexual violence, drug use, the numbing banality of educational sys-tems, the fragmented heterosexual, middle-class family unit. (1999: 27)

Rhonda Wilcox suggests that in *Buffy*,

> the problems teenagers face become literal monsters. Internet predators are demons; drink-doctoring frat-boys have sold their souls for success in the business world; a girl who has sex with even the nicest-seeming boy discovers that he afterwards becomes a monster. (1999: 16)

In this sense *Buffy* shares a great deal with the melodramatic structure and quo-tidian concerns more usually associated with soap opera, but set in the realm of the supernatural. Even the Gothic deployment of monsters as metaphors for everyday problems is comparable to soap operas' uses of exaggerated plot lines, and has been deployed in at least one previous American television Gothic soap opera, *Dark Shadows*. Ien Ang pointed out in the early 1980s that 'personal life in soap operas is dominated by conflict and catastrophe, which are blown up to improbable proportions ... [an] endless piling up of appalling crises' (1982: 60). *Buffy*'s world is regularly threatened with apocalypse and mayhem, but it functions, like the exaggerated plots of soap opera, to address the problems and conflicts in the personal sphere. However, the significance of this melodra-matic structuring has not been pursued in the extensive academic discussion of *Buffy*. I want to examine the programme's melodramatic structuring, because, despite the programme's genre blend of action, comedy, horror, it is melodrama that provides the show with its core.

The programme actually blends two forms of melodrama. The Manichaean-style melodrama (usually found in action films), in which good and evil are easily-named characters that battle it out, is the outer skin of the programme, its action orientation. But the inner skin is the morally ambiguous melodrama discussed in chapter two, which is usually associated with women's fiction, the continual serial and soap opera. This form of melodrama, as many feminists have argued, is built around emotional attachment and emotional realism (Ang 1982; Modleski 1982; Gledhill 1985; Brown 1990; Geraghty 1991; Brunsdon 2000). Joss Whedon himself remarks that emotions are at the heart of the series and that emotional investment with the characters forms the centre of the programme; he stresses the importance of the developing character arcs for the protagonists (cf. Havens 2003: 41–51). *Buffy*'s melodrama is Gothic, not only in its use of the supernatural as a metaphor for the problems the protagonists encounter, but also, as in the vampire narratives examined in chapter two, it presents vampirism as misrecognised innocence in the figure of two sympathetic vampires with souls – Angel and Spike. Indeed, all of the core characters suffer the pathos of their predicament, the human and the demons, and this links the suffering of the 'self' to the suffering of the 'other'. Also, the youthful world of adolescent humans and sympathetic monsters is contrasted to the monstrousness of the adult world.

Sarah E. Skwire considers *Buffy* to be a modern-day fairytale turned upside down. For Skwire, *Buffy* is 'a brilliant inversion of the generally accepted dynamic of fairytales both as tales and as pedagogical devices' (2002: 196) where sage-like adults instruct the young. Sunnydale, however, is populated by 'uncomprehending adults who are blind to, and foolishly trapped by, demonic dangers' in contrast to 'wise children who see what adults cannot see and who understand the reality of these "imaginary" evils' (ibid.).

In this respect, *Buffy* also draws on an evolving set of narrative conventions in the vampire tale which Ken Gelder identified in the early 1990s, concerning the management of troublesome youth culture and dysfunctional families. The vampire has actually been heading for the young for some time, upending the world of adult morality. For instance, when Terrence Fisher produced *The Brides of Dracula* for Hammer in 1960, vampirism was overtly depicted as a troublesome youth cult. *The Brides of Dracula* replaced Dracula with Baron Meinster, an attractive youthful vampire who even sports a trendy quiff (for the time) and who preys on the young female inhabitants of a girl's academy. The Baron's vampiric waywardness is connected to his own incomplete family and bad parenting. He has no father (no discipline), only an 'overindulgent mother' who first spoils him to the point of 'madness' (Gelder 1994: 100) and then in despair locks him in a room with a golden chain, from which he inevitably escapes with the help of a naïve young female school teacher.

The father figure of the Academy is depicted as overly strict and ogre-like, and thus ineffectual in the management of youth – 'the cause of youthful waywardness rather than the solution' (ibid.). In contrast, Dr Van Helsing is introduced as a good father figure who demonstrates paternal understanding and is thus able to resolve the family crisis; he shows 'both concern about the growing 'cult' and understanding for those who would be drawn to it' (ibid.). This is in stark contrast to Van Helsing's role in Stoker's novel which is to disconnect the young members of the Crew of Light from their understanding of, and empathy for, the vampirised Lucy. Gelder suggests that Van Helsing's role in Fisher's film is to mediate between the strictness of the parents (which does not work) and the loose morals of the young (which get them into trouble); his role ... is one of *management*' (1994: 101). In this case, the management of troublesome youth cults is handled from above, that is, from a parental authority figure. The girls of the Academy are shown to be 'prematurely independent' (ibid.) and brought back into the parental fold.

Buffy the Vampire Slayer overturns this narrative structure while retaining an emphasis on the troubles of adolescence (at least in the early seasons), and not only because Buffy and her friends ('the Scooby Gang') manage both the trouble of vampire cults and their own problems; there is now no adult authority and adults are often depicted as woefully blind to the monstrous problems that plague Sunnydale, or are the source of monstrousness itself – school principles transform into gigantic serpents, and the city's civil authority is shown to be in league with dark forces. In *Buffy*, we are treated to *management from below*, that is, from a community of friends who shun authoritarian intervention. Even Giles, Buffy's adult watcher, must develop a relationship with her which is a conversation, rather than instruction, because of Buffy's obstinate questioning of his authority. When he informs her in the first episode that his role is to 'prepare' her as the Slayer, she replies,

> 'prepare me for what? For getting kicked out of school? For losing all my friends? For having to spend all of my time fighting for my life and never getting to tell anyone because I might endanger them? Go ahead – prepare me.' ('Welcome to Hellmouth', 1.1)

Buffy regularly questions Giles' judgment, makes her own decisions and looks to her group of friends for moral guidance. This scene also underlines the melodramatic pathos of Buffy's situation. Like melodramatic heroines of old, Buffy is locked into circumstances not of her own choosing, and thus the programme contains what Ang terms 'emotional realism', that is, the depiction of unacknowledged suffering in everyday life. *Buffy* brings hidden suffering to the surface, but usually through the deployment of supernatural occurrence,[1] filling everyday suffering with greater resonance. *Buffy* therefore shares the 'tragic structure of feeling' with the sympathetic vampire narratives that preceded it. Ien Ang coined this term in relation to soap opera, and by it she is referring to the core impulse of the melodramatic form, 'a refusal, or inability, to accept insignificant everyday life as banal and meaningless, and ... a vague, inarticulate dissatisfaction with existence here and now' (1982: 79). However, *Buffy* updates the pathos of the melodramatic heroine, because Buffy has superhuman strength with which to intervene in the circumstances she did not choose, and in this way the show speaks more directly to the experience of circumscribed choices found in a culture which tells young women that they can 'have it all'.

Furthermore, the inversion of adult/adolescent relations adds to the melodrama of the programme as the adolescent protagonists have to struggle with problems that the adult world will not acknowledge exists. As we have seen in chapter two, melodrama emerges in relation to cultural disavowal, and deals with anxieties that have no name. Gothic melodrama deploys the supernatural to make meaningful those submerged anxieties and injustices while at the same time foregrounding culturally marginalised experiences. *Buffy* may not have been the first vampire fiction to use adult disavowal as a metaphor for the powerlessness of the young, but the show develops this convention delightfully.

Two films, both from 1987, also link vampirism with the trials of adolescence, and advocate youth self-management; it is the conventions developed in these films which *Buffy* draws on and expands. *Near Dark* and *The Lost Boys* depict a link between troublesome youth and vampirism, the vulnerability of the family and the need for managing adolescence. In both films, the family is incomplete; Caleb in the former film has no mother, while Michael in the latter film has no father. Both films focus on the transformation of the central male protagonist and on his trauma at becoming a vampire, which involves moving away from the respectable (if incomplete) family and towards the lawlessness of the cult, figured as 'vampire gangs with a certain cool glamour' (Gelder 1994: 103). However, Gelder argues that what is advocated in these films is not 'management from above' in the figure of an adult (as in the Hammer film) but 'self-management' from the teenage boys themselves. Indeed, the adult world is depicted as particularly inept as spotting supernatural evil, particularly in the case of *The Lost Boys*, where Michael's mother unwittingly dates the king vampire who is posing as a local video store owner, and she thus invites evil into the home. Gelder argues that 'youth is now asked to be, or shown to be, capable of handling its own problems' (ibid.). The gender shift in this move to self-management is also significant, for *The Brides of Dracula* depicts *female* adolescents in need of kindly adult authority, whereas the latter films centre on the growing autonomy of *male* adolescents as they enter adulthood. Meanwhile, the boys' girlfriends in both *Near Dark* and *The Lost Boys* are depicted as male-dependent. The vampirised boys eventually reject the alluring lawlessness of the vampire cult (although as we have seen, vampire fans do not) and return to their proper masculine roles, both in terms of their sexuality and in terms of heading now 'complete' families.

Buffy draws on and reworks these narrative conventions in a number of ways, particularly in its depiction of adolescents managing troubles in the context of incomplete families. Buffy also comes from an incomplete family, as do many of her 'Scooby Gang' friends. But *Buffy* significantly inverts the gender dynamics associated with vampire films dealing with the troubles of adolescence, as we shall see. *Buffy* even sets the (incomplete) family dynamics in the same southern Californian terrain found in *The Lost Boys*. This setting is highly appropriate for depicting the duality of adolescent life, the 'normality' of daytime high-school life contrasting with the dangers and temptations of the night time shadows; as Tonkin suggests, 'in "So Cal" shines the blinding light that hides sinister secrets ... this phoney paradise (and paradise for phoneys) may mutate, at any moment, into a sudden inferno' (2002: 28).

Buffy Summers comes to Sunnydale after expulsion from her previous school, with her divorced mother, Joyce, so that Buffy's family, like Michael and Caleb's, is also incomplete. Like Michael's mother in *The Lost Boys*, Buffy's mother is blissfully unaware of the demons that populate this white Californian suburban town and is unable to comprehend the problems that her teenage child faces. In an early episode, Joyce Summers grounds Buffy for cutting class just as Buffy is about to leave the house to save the world from the hundreds of vampires who are trying to raise the Vampire Master and open the mouth of hell. When Buffy appeals to her mother, 'Mom, this is really, really important', Joyce responds, 'I know – if you don't go out it will be the end of the world' – and, of course, we, the audience know (with Buffy) that it will be. Buffy and the Scooby Gang are repeatedly shown to be more aware of what is happening in the world and more able to tackle it, than the adults who populate Sunnydale, and this generation inversion is a central device in the first season of the programme.

Buffy, as in *The Lost Boys* and *Near Dark*, also advocates the self-management of youth. However, Buffy actually takes this narrative convention one step further. While *Near Dark* and *The Lost Boys* advocate self-management in order for wayward boys to re-enter patriarchal social relations, *Buffy* advocates the self-management of youth as *management from below*, that is, as a critique of patriarchal authority. Like the protagonists in *The Lost Boys* and *Near Dark*, Buffy grows into adulthood over the course of the series, but it is not a process that resolves her back into the patriarchal fold. This is most clearly highlighted by Buffy's anti-authoritarian and anti-hierarchical stance. Early in the series, for instance, Buffy not only refuses the authority of her own Watcher, but is depicted in opposition to the hierarchical nature of the Watchers Council. This theme persists throughout Buffy, even as its characters move from adolescence into adulthood. In the penultimate episode, Buffy throws herself into a mystical vortex to gain the strength she needs to fight the evil of the First Evil. The ancient men who set up the idea of the single girl watcher destined to fight to save humanity from evil (the original watchers) now want Buffy to imbibe an extra-human force to aid her in this deadliest of tasks, but she refuses and escapes. An alternative matriarchy is discovered by Buffy, who long ago created an Arthurian-style weapon that can only be removed by a slayer who feels its power. This weapon is importantly wielded by Buffy in the final episode of the show demonstrating that patriarchal power is undermined by matriarchal power.

Another aspect of the way that *Buffy* advocates 'management from below' stems from the existence of the 'Scooby Gang' – her group of friends that help in her fight against evil. Wilcox suggests that the notion of lone heroism, which Buffy's chosen status might invite, is consistently undermined by Buffy's reliance on the Scooby Gang, whose intervention time and again 'saves the day when Buffy could not have triumphed alone' (1999: 4). The Scooby Gang also insistently undermine the individualism of the single hero and this is carried through out to the end of the series. In the final dénouement, Buffy, who has been becoming increasingly authoritarian as a result of the pressure of her leadership role and her fear that the gang will not be strong enough to overturn the First Evil and its army, is kicked out of the leadership role, to be replaced by another slayer, Faith, who has been depicted as Buffy's rival, and who was only activated when Buffy temporarily died. This triggers the final collective moment of the series; Buffy returns to the gang after a time of loneliness and self-reflection to ask them to use Willow's Wiccan magic to turn all of the potential girl slayers in the world into actual slayers. This act overturns the patriarchal insistence of the Watchers Council that there should only be a single 'chosen one' at any moment and it is the collective strength of the girls-turned-slayers who have been flocking to Sunnydale (along with the sacrifice of the sympathetic vampire Spike) that vanquishes The First Evil.

The make up of the Scooby Gang is also significant, for as Kaveny has pointed out, they are all 'refugees from hierarchy of one sort or another' (2002: 7). Populated by high-school geeks, fallen vengeance demons, lesbian Wicca's, werewolves and conscience-tortured vampires, Buffy's friendship circle not only complicates the issue of monstrousness, but embraces socially marginal identities, speaking from and for the experience of outsiderdom. Gina Wisker suggests that *Buffy* occupies a space between 'radical contemporary women's vampire fiction' and the 'condemnation of the vampire and all forms of Otherness, or difference'. In this sense, it attracts 'a wider audience, more used to teen soaps, and can cause them to think about the nature of conformity and transgression, of hypocrisy and power relations, or of recognising the Other we abject, in ourselves.' (2001: 9)

The sense of the Scooby Gang as outsiders is reinforced by the official *Buffy the Vampire Slayer* fan magazine, one of the many instances in which the personalities of the celebrity actors is brought to bear on our understanding of the programme characters. In December 1999, an article entitled 'High School Hell' by Matt Springer overtly links the shows angst with that of the writers, director and actors. Even the actor Sarah Michelle Gellar is depicted as an outsider with the comment, 'Kids were hard on me. I was always excluded from everything because I was different' (1999: 7). Springer even quotes the co-executive producer David Greenwalt's comment that, 'if Joss Whedon had had one good day in high school, we wouldn't be here' (ibid.). The cast and producers reinforce the sense that *Buffy* speaks directly to the experience of outsiderdom; it is an intertextual theme that informs our understanding of the characters and the actors who play them.

PATHOS AND OUTSIDERDOM IN BUFFY'S AMERICA

Outsiderdom is a theme that spans the entire series and it is also taken up in specific episodes such as 'Out of Sight, Out of Mind [aka Invisible girl]' (1:11). This episode contrasts the popularity of Cordelia who is running for the May Queen, with Marcie, a girl so unpopular that she physically disappears and no one can remember her. When Marcie's isolation drives her mad, she manages to capture Buffy and Cordelia and then she binds them to chairs in the basement of the high-school hangout, the Bronze. Her intention is to disfigure Cordelia and slashes at her face with a knife, but she is finally subdued by Buffy who has managed to escape her bonds. However, the theme of outsiderdom is underlined in a scene in this episode in Ms Jackson's English class where the students are studying 'the anger of the outcast' through *The Merchant of Venice*. Here we see the use of supernatural elements to depict one of the many submerged miseries in everyday experience tackled by *Buffy*. *Buffy* uses monsters and magic to address that which is usually not acknowledged as suffering at all, suffering that is therefore difficult to communicate. This theme is taken up again in the episode 'Earshot' (3:18). Buffy has acquired the power to read minds and can hear someone in the school threatening to kill the students. She assumes that it is the alienated outcast Jonathan who is planning the shooting, but in fact he is planning suicide. Buffy manages to dissuade him and the Scooby Gang discover that the voice Buffy hears belongs to the cook and Buffy manages to avert the disaster. This is one of two episodes of *Buffy* that were postponed by Warner Bros. (the WB network) a month after the murders at Columbine High School in Littleton, Colorado. That it might be American society itself that produces such severe alienation in its youth is not generally acknowledged, except by left-of-centre critics such as Michael Moore (2003). Instead, as Lisa Parks points out, ironically programmes like *Buffy* are held responsible 'for violence in American high schools' (2003: 121), in order to avoid confronting the difficult issues of alienation that trigger such tragedies. Parks also comments that 'the WB network became a temporary apologist for button-pushing content and then raced to capitalise upon it once Columbine faded from the news headlines' (2003: 122), noting the way that television networks 'regulate the meanings of TV violence for maximum financial gain' (ibid.). However, for Parks, the real offence of *Buffy* is not its depiction of violence of the 'visible blood and gore' variety; 'what truly assaults dominant logic is a woman (well, not really a woman, a girl) who occupies a place in the field of vision with physical strength and has narrative agency and who is allowed to be weak/abject as well' (2003: 124). Parks makes a convincing case for the idea that Buffy upsets the sensibilities of family values groups and Christian moral guardians in the US. Buffy herself is presented in opposition to these social values and through 'Buffy speak' constantly digs at presumed adult authority. For example, Buffy comments in the episode 'Gingerbread':

> 'Maybe the next time that the world is getting sucked into Hell, I won't be able to stop it because the anti-Hell-sucking book isn't on the Approved Reading List' (3:11).

Buffy has regularly been praised for its quick and witty dialogue and Rhonda Wilcox has persuasively argued that the teenagers' fight against social and personal problems (which is translated into Gothic symbolism) is 'a mediation of meaning that parallels the mediation of the teen language' (1999: 23). Buffy-speak also provides the basis of the show's humour, perfectly understating the peril of the character's predicament. The combination of humour and poignancy can be found in the finale for season five, when Buffy sacrifices her own life to save the world, rather than see the death of her younger sister Dawn, who is actually a mystical key. At one moment Buffy asks Giles, 'This is how many apocalypses for us?' Giles replies, 'six at least, but if feels like a hundred'. However, just as Buffy is about to leap from the tower to her death, her teen register does not change, but her tone does and her words are very moving:

> 'Dawn, listen to me. I will *always* love you. But this is work that I have to do. Tell Giles I figured it all out. And I'm OK. Give my love to my fiends. You have to take care of them now ... you have to be strong. The hardest thing in this world is to live in it. Be brave. Live for me' ('The Gift', 5:22)

THE CULTURAL POLITICS OF BUFFY THE VAMPIRE SLAYER

Given the themes of female empowerment, anti-authoritarian collective activity, and in the later seasons, an exploration of sexuality (particularly in the relationships between Willow and Tara and Buffy and Spike), it is not surprising that *Buffy* has generated as much academic interest as it has fannish interest. It is also hardly surprising that much of this interest has focused on the feminist politics of the programme. Many critics have written approvingly of Buffy's character; as Susan Owen puts it, she is a 'California valley girl who kicks ass, literally' (1999: 25). For Owen, the show's transgression is rooted in its disruption of the traditional action-adventure genre – it is 'a female controlling the narrative and delivering the punches' – but it also offers us a challenging view of the adolescent female body, 'signifying toughness, resilience, strength and confidence' (ibid.). Owen argues that Buffy's 'embodied strength, power, and assertiveness destabilise the traditional masculinist power' (ibid.).

A number of critics have made similar comments about Buffy's female-centred empowerment. Anne Millard Daugherty suggests that 'Buffy is a symbol of female empowerment' (2002: 149). Daugherty argues that Buffy is 'not the object of the traditional male gaze ... she kicks butt and so can we all' (2002: 164). Zoe-Jane Playden argues that 'Buffy's particular combination of knowledge and power places her outside the mainstream of super-heroes and leads to particular ideas of learning, of spirituality, and of citizenship, which challenge the dominant discourses of Western patriarchy' (2002: 120). For Playden, *Buffy the Vampire Slayer* offers emancipatory readings of women in each of these spheres because for a slayer 'there is no division between being and knowing: they are born Slayers and simultaneously they learn to slay' (2002: 127). Thus the all-female world of slayers is seen to disrupt the Western distinction between 'being' and 'knowing' which are widely considered to be fundamental to the subjugation of women. Playden accounts for Buffy's transgressive ontological status by contrasting her to another girl slayer, Kendra. Buffy is considered to provide a more transgressive and progressive approach to her ontological unity than Kendra because of her rebelliousness. Playden, like other critics, point to Buffy's refusal of the patriarchal authority of the Watchers Council in favour of the guidance of her friends. Thus for Buffy 'learning' is not about accepting the dictates of the Watcher's Council, it is about developing understanding. Buffy's rebelliousness is once again underlined by the fact that Giles has not bothered to show her the Slayer's handbook. After discovering from Kendra the existence of a slayer handbook, Buffy asks Giles about it and he replies: 'After meeting you, Buffy, I was quite sure the handbook would be of no use in your case' ('What's My Line, Part 2'). This is in marked contrast to Kendra who informs Buffy: 'I study it because it is required. The Slayer's handbook insists on it.' Unlike Buffy, Kendra does not question the traditional wisdom of her calling and her preparation is understood as 'training', rather than Buffy's more progressive 'education'. Playden argues that this difference points to Buffy's alternative politics 'which refuse a mind/body split and insist on alternative readings of what it is to be human' (2002: 143).

There are, however, feminist readings of *Buffy* that are less celebratory, including Owen, who argues that while the show offers a 're-imagining [of] gendered relations and Modernist American ideologies', it also, 'reifies mainstream commitments to hetero-normative relationships, American commodity culture, and a predominantly Anglo perspective' (1999: 25). Furthermore, there are feminist critics who read the Kendra/Buffy split less progressively; it is considered to be endorsing an Anglo perspective. Elyce Rae Helford critiques Kendra's role in performing the 'insider/outsider dichotomy based on race and culture' (2002: 27). She argues that Buffy seems to champion difference in order to reinforce standards of normalcy (2002: 28). Lynne Edwards reads the opposition between Buffy and Kendra as an updated version of the 'tragic mulatto myth' in American screen culture. The 'tragic mulatto' is traditionally portrayed as a beautiful, young, mixed-race female who is trying to pass as white. The contemporary version of the myth finds characters not trying to pass as white, but trying to be accepted by white society. In either case, the quest is doomed because she 'threatens the balance of power between whites and blacks by gaining legitimacy through acceptance by the white community' (2002: 88). Today's 'tragic mulatta' character appears to be accepted into her white peer group, but this is 'contingent on her assimilation into the dominant group' (2002: 90). Thus while she is formally accepted by whites, this is only an appearance of acceptance that is, 'in reality, a denial of her race by whites' so that whites can 'deny her "otherness"' (ibid.). Edwards argues that this is the narrative trajectory of the character of Kendra. Her racial identity is marked as 'ethnic' (that is, not 'white') by her physical appearance, her sartorial style, her Jamaican patios, her lack of understanding of 'Buffy-speak', even her name. Helford concurs that Kendra is marked as different linguistically – 'a girl of colour with too much hostility and too little sense of humour' (2002: 29). Buffy first rejects Kendra and even mocks her lack of understanding of Buffy-speak in a manner which underlines the issue of race. Buffy tells Kendra not to go 'wiggy' and Kendra does not understand. Buffy explains:

'You know, no kicko, no fighto.' Buffy later grows to accept her, but Edwards argues that 'the acceptance comes only when Kendra begins to accept Buffy's way of slaying, when Kendra is assimilated' (2002: 93). But Kendra threatens Buffy with her quest for legitimacy in the role of Slayer because it challenges Buffy's position as *the* Slayer. When Kendra is finally killed by Drusilla in her attempt to help Buffy save Angel, her death is, according to Edwards, 'symbolic of the new mulatta tragedy, the ultimate loss of identity in order to gain acceptance' (2002: 94). Edwards argues that like other 'tragic mulatta' figures, 'her quest for legitimacy is doomed to fail; her destiny is to remain in her place' (2002: 95).

However, season five of *Buffy* extends the death-as-sacrifice trope to Buffy herself and, as we have seen, the finale season of *Buffy* does indeed result in Buffy giving up her status as *the* Slayer. Yet this does not undermine Edwards' argument vis-à-vis race, because, although some of the would-be slayers are black, they are not central characters in this series dénouement and the slayer Buffy does share power with is also white. Faith, who temporarily steps into Buffy's leadership role when her friends have banished her, has had her working-class difference previously marked. Faith's working-class anger and rebellion had been shown in season three to be spiralling out of control after she oversteps the line and accidentally kills a human in a rage ('Bad Girls' (3:14)). Showing no outward remorse, Faith does not accept appropriate middle-class standards of propriety and 'once a playmate who helped Buffy take risks and challenge boundaries, Faith becomes a renegade whose example now easily pushes Buffy back to middle-class normalcy' (Helford 2002: 31). Helford argues that Faith's character, 'teaches, blatantly, that girls' anger, when allowed free reign, is not only harmful to others but is entirely self-destructive' (2002: 33). However, Faith is rehabilitated in the final season, and her working-class character position contributes to the censure of Buffy's growing authoritarianism which provides Buffy (and the audience) with her final lesson in collectivity when she gives up the status as *the* slayer. But the fact that there is no equivalent female black presence seems to add weight to Edward's arguments about race.

Tania Modleski, writing about melodrama in the early 1980s, suggested that melodrama functions in a 'highly contradictory manner ... such art simultaneously challenges and reaffirms traditional values, behaviour and attitudes (1982: 112). *Buffy*, it seems, is also marked by contradictions, empowered femininity is served up, but to a white, middle-class sensibility. Thus *Buffy*, like all Gothic melodrama, is contradictory, and its contradictoriness is rooted in the moment, in which racism no longer 'officially' exists, although it *actually* does, even in the most progressive of popular narratives.

BUFFY, GENDER AND THE DILEMMA OF THE FEMALE SELF

Helford points out that Buffy's justified anger about being 'chained to a lifestyle over which she has little choice' is a metaphor for girls who experience justified feminist anger at having their lives directed by circumstances or individuals beyond their control' (2002: 24). I want now to consider what these circumstances are in the context of early twenty-first-century Anglo-American culture. For I would like to suggest that *Buffy*'s use of Gothic melodrama speaks not only to the issue of empowerment identified by many feminist critics, but also to the persistent, yet hidden impositions on femininity and the female experience today. As we have seen, melodrama has long addressed 'what cannot be said' (Brooks 1995: 11). Today, 'what cannot be said', along with the continuing existence of racism, is that women are not equal; the formal (but non-enforced) equality in some areas of the law has evacuated from the language the means of naming women's experience of discrimination and oppression. Anglo-American culture promised the equality demanded by the civil rights and women's movements, but it did not deliver that equality, although we are told that it did. *Buffy*, like many popular narratives, expresses the contradictions in experience produced by this situation. The show is written at a time of shifting gender relations, the opening up of opportunities for women *and* at a time which denies that there are limits to feminine freedom even though it produces them. *Buffy* speaks directly to this dilemma and expresses the contradictoriness of the female experience. It does so, however, in a manner which foregrounds the experience of white, middle-class American women.

One of the consequences of the official non-existence of discrimination is that discrimination has been re-privatised. It is no longer seen primarily as a social ill, but as a personal failing. Young women are told that there are no longer any restraints to their ability to achieve, and if they are not successful, many feel that it must be their own fault. *Buffy*, in contradictory ways, speaks to that experience, by presenting a powerful female protagonist who is, nonetheless, a victim of her circumstances, despite her rebellious nature. As Jenny Bavidge comments, Buffy as the contemporary television depiction of the Anglo-American Girl is both 'symbol of optimism' and a 'point of weakness', she is both the 'ass-kicking Girl' and the Maybelline 'lipstick lovely' (2004: 46).

Underlying the promise of equality for black women and men and white women, is a much broader cultural promise issued to all, which links equality to the rights associated with personal fulfilment. In fact, Anglo-American culture does not just promise fulfilment, it demands it. As Chris Rojek has argued, 'cultures built around the ethic of individualism' inevitably insists on the 'desire to be recognised as special or unique' (2001: 97). But as the cultures which insist on this heightened individualism also ensure that this kind of achievement is closed to the majority, 'most ordinary people suffer from *achievement famine*, a psychological condition that results from frustrated desires for material and romantic achievement of the sort the rich and famous enjoy. The democratic ideal of being recognised as extraordinary, special or unique collides with the bureaucratic tendency to standardise and routinise existence' (2001: 149).

Whether one considers *Buffy* to be dealing with the meta-issues of rationality, freedom and the (Anglo-)American dream, or the so-called mundane problems of everyday life, the promises that our culture offers have been altered by the liberation movements of the 1960s. The way that *Buffy* speaks to these conditions, then, reflects the manner in which contemporary cultural promises are phrased and crucial to this is the way that the post-1960s concept of 'equality' now includes black men and women and white women in its official discourse. Today 'equality' is officially extended to all, and so there are no longer any 'official' fetters on a citizen's ability to achieve fulfilment. It is here that the dilemma of the self is rooted in contemporary Anglo-American culture, because hidden inequality and injustice persists and Anglo-American culture therefore creates the very conditions which ensure that its promise of personal fulfilment is not achievable. The everyday experience of fetters that no longer *officially* exist is the experience at the heart of today's Gothic-influenced vampire tales, including *Buffy the Vampire Slayer*. Like the pre-twentieth-century Gothic, the appeal of today's 'new' vampire tale is to do with its ability to represent what is disavowed, to speak to anxieties and desires that are difficult to name. As David Punter argues, 'contemporary manifestations of the Gothic open up deeply wounded and wounding questions about how fulfilment is to be achieved' (1996: 189). In *Buffy*, however, this takes on the contours of the white female experience of gender impositions. Buffy is a white middle-class girl with all of the privileges of her race and class. But she represents the dissatisfaction of this position through her melodramatic structuring, for she is also a heroine caught in circumstances outside of her control. Indeed, Buffy also shares certain features with contemporary 'chick-lit' such as *Bridget Jones' Diary* and the television series *Sex and the City* and *Ally Mcbeal*. What all of these fictions have in common is the expression of the lack of fulfilment of young, white, middle-class women in today's post-second wave American society. Young women today are told that, unlike their mothers, they can have it all – careers *and* family, happiness *and* personal significance in the world. Yet for many young women this promise is not achievable and the personal fulfilment that is supposed to accompany 'having it all' is still elusive. Chick-lit deals with this dilemma of the (female) self in very different ways. While Ally McBeal and Bridget Jones search for fulfilment through the rather conservative and old-fashioned notion that self-completion comes through a monogamous relationship with a man, *Buffy* handles the dilemma of the self for young, white, middle-class women in a far more complex fashion. This is because *Buffy* starts from the (melodramatic) premise that one is not going to be allowed to live the life one chooses, that fulfilment is not an option, nor is romantic love. All that Buffy faces, as she herself explains at the very start of the series, is difficulty, duty and an early death. Her attraction to the sympathetic vampires may be, as Linda Williams has suggested more generally in relation to monsters and women, 'a flash of sympathetic identification' (1984: 87), with fellow creatures of pathos, who, like mirrors to the self, give expression to her powers, but also to her limits and the impositions she faces. In the end, the only chance that Buffy has to change her destiny is collective. She learns to fight alongside her peers, rather than lead them. She learns to give up her status as special, and become just one slayer among many. She eschews the very values of uniqueness that her culture insists on in favour of collective endeavour, and this is an admirable version of 'ass-kicking', but one that is nonetheless marred by its privileging of a white, middle-class perspective.

Buffy Fandom and the Television Industry

It is not only *Buffy*'s progressive message that is couched in terms of middle-class white sensibilities; it is also *Buffy*'s target audience. *Buffy* ran for seven series between 1997 and 2003 on new networks in the US that were attempting to build a brand image in quality, young, adult drama. The television critic James Poniewozik notes that when the two new networks that aired *Buffy* first went on air in the mid-1990s they 'started with a schedule heavy on African-American stars, built an instant following among minority audiences, then largely spurned them with new programming that went after young white viewers' (2001: 1). In the US, *Buffy* aired on the Warner Bros. network initially as a mid-season replacement in March 1997 (in Britain it aired on Sky One in January 1998 and on terrestrial BBC2 from December 1998), until it was poached by UPN in 2001. Both networks were set up in 1995 by 'studio-based conglomerates in the throes of deregulation' (Holt 2003: 12). The combined force of the repeal of the Financial and Syndication rules in the US in 1995 (which had prevented networks from having an ownership stake in their prime-time programming), and the Telecommunications Act of 1996 (which abolished network ownership caps on stations and increased the audience reach limitation for networks from 25 per cent to 35 per cent) led to a 'phase of frenzied merger and acquisitions activity' (ibid.) from which the new networks that aired *Buffy* were born. Warner Bros. is owned by AOL Time Warner, a result of the largest merger in media history, and UPN is owned by Viacom-CBS.[2] Yet *Buffy* did not reach a mass audience. According to *USA Today*, *Buffy* had an audience figure of about 4.5 million viewers per episode at its highest.[3] This is actually rather a small audience figure and one that might have seen other shows cancelled. Compare these figures to *ER*'s 22.5 million viewers per episode or *Friends*' 24 million viewers per episode, both aired on NBC.[4] Poniewozik comments that *Buffy* is 'a big hit by the standards of a little network. But it's a niche show nonetheless: it would never go to NBC, ABC or CBS' (2001: 2). However, *Buffy* had a high concentration of the Warner Bros.'s target audience – 18–34-year-old, educated, white and affluent viewers – a demographic that advertisers are keen to reach. That UPN were prepared to offer a reported $2.3 million per episode, as opposed to the Warner Bros.' $1 million is evidence that the programme was reaching the young, white, educated audience that both networks were keen to establish a foothold amongst. UPN had struggled to get a solid hold in primetime television and Buffy was a 'bargain' at any price because it guaranteed a substantial increase in viewers who made up the station's key demographic target.

Mark Jancovich and James Lyons suggest that the emergence of programmes like *Buffy*, which are considered to be quality 'must see' television, happened at a time when network television was 'going through a crisis in audience demographics not dissimilar to that which resulted in the production strategies of "post-classical" Hollywood filmmaking' (2003: 2). These programmes were emerging at a time when network television audiences overall were declining in competition with cable and satellite channels.[5] Jancovich and Lyons argue that networks thus became less concerned with attracting mass audiences, in favour of 'retaining the most valuable audiences: affluent viewers that advertisers were prepared to pay the highest rates to address' (2003: 3). *Buffy* came about at a time when networks were looking for lucrative niche markets through programming intended to appeal to young, affluent and 'highly educated consumers who value the literary qualities' of 'quality' television (ibid.), and its fortunes were enhanced by this climate.

Buffy also emerged at a time when television was gaining greater cultural legitimacy. Indeed Jancovich and Lyons argue that television's shift to attract these niche audiences has been 'instrumental in television's acquisition of greater cultural legitimacy' (ibid.). Television, according to Jancovich and Lyons, is open to the 'appropriation and legitimation by the middle classes' now, just as the cinema became appropriated by the middle classes in the 1960s and 1970s after the 'dramatic decline in cinema audiences' (ibid.); in both cases the decline in audiences is indicative of 'formal features' of texts that 'exclude sections of the viewing public' and a shift in perception from 'debased popular entertainment to respected art form' (ibid.). This may also go some way to explaining the establishment of fan scholarship as an academic discipline in the 1990s, just as Film Studies became one in the 1970s, a theme we shall return to in the following chapter. *Buffy* is considered by the academic and the television world alike to be 'quality' television. The programme has generated scores of academic articles, texts, anthology contributions and even a few academic websites. Joss Whedon won an Emmy award for the episode of *Buffy* entitled 'Hush' and a Saturn award for Best Genre Network Series. *Buffy* was ranked among the top ten shows by *USA Today*; it was ranked as number five by *TV Guide* and *Entertainment Weekly* called it 'the best drama on television'. *Buffy* was Warner Bros.'s second rated show and it's most prestigious – the one that 'consistently lands on the critics' best lists' (Poniewozik 2001: 1). These plaudits contribute to the networks brand image as 'quality', and thus (indirectly) help viewer ratings among the desired demographic.

The demographics of Warner Bros. and UPN are also a sign of the demographic character of the large fan culture that surrounds *Buffy* and its spin-off programme *Angel*. *Buffy*'s rich, intertextual narrative was designed to attract a large, literate and educated fandom. Sara Gwenllian Jones argues that the 'wide open, producerly texts of these series appeal not so much to their audiences' desire to be entertained as to its need to be imaginatively involved' (2003: 166). It is well known that Joss Whedon courted fandom, through the inter-textual references, the invitation to bring your own subtext (in one episode Giles even remarks 'I think the text is quickly becoming the subtext'), and through his interaction with fans on the Internet. Jancovich and Lyons have pointed out that fandom is increasingly important to networks, not only because of their demographic status, but also because 'fans generate a loyal audience base that might help a show avoid cancellation in its vulnerable early days' and also 'act as a source of additional revenue through merchandising' (2003: 2). This is one of the reasons for the emergence of the cult television text. As Gwenllian Jones argues, 'from 1990 onward, a number of televisions series have been produced and marketed precisely in order to attract particular microcultures and to foster within them not just regular viewers but also a high proportion of fans' (2003: 166).

Fans are no longer considered to be 'oddities or nuisances' (Jancovich and Lyons 2003: 2). This shift is clear in the attitudes towards fans shown by the creative team and cast of *Buffy*. We have seen previously how Whedon responded to fannish interest in the character of Spike, as did the actor who plays him, James Marsters. The star of *Buffy*, Sarah Michele Gellar is equally complimentary about fandom. Gellar's comment, 'I don't think we'd be here if it wasn't for the Net. It was the Internet that really kicked us off, because that's where this loyal fan base could get together and spread the word', (quoted in Havens 2003: 45) is in marked contrast to William Shatner's famous rebuke to *Star Trek* fans to 'get a life'. This phrase is used as part of the first chapter title for Henry Jenkins' 1992 book on media fans, and points towards Jenkins' defence of fandom and the celebratory model of fandom-as-resistance that the book advocates. But attitudes towards fandom have changed considerably in the past ten years, as they have towards the television text, and fan culture has taken a far more accepted place in the field of cultural legitimation and the struggle over cultural values, but it has *always* taken a place in that field. Today, however, well-known producers proclaim their own fandom. This is certainly the case with Joss Whedon, who considers himself to be a fan, not just of his own programme, but more or less as a subject position. Commenting directly on the Shatner 'get a life' comment, Whedon responds 'I have never had any particular life of my own, so I don't see why anyone should run out and get one' (quoted in Havens 2003: 44), thus this successful, wealthy and influential producer is clearly aligning himself with fandom.

The increasing cultural legitimacy of the television text, and evidence of its middle-class appeal and fan base, suggests a need to thoroughly rethink the models of fandom that emerged in the early 1990s which constructed fans as members of subordinate social formations resisting the 'sanctioned interpreters' of the dominant classes' (Jenkins 1992: 25). Jenkins has since explained that his celebration of fandom was a tactical move which accented the positive because academic discourse on fandom was predominantly negative (see Jenkins 2001). Jenkins has, since his 1992 book, discussed the increased visibility of fandom, but he continues to characterise it as 'a participatory culture through which fans explore and question the ideologies of mass culture' and empower 'popular creativity' (1998: n.p.). Jenkins is still celebrating 'popular readings' in his latest discussion of fans in *Hop on Pop* (2002). A number of critics have offered critiques of this model of fandom and have begun to rethink fan culture (Brower 1992; Barker 1993; MacDonald 1998; Jancovich 2000; Hills 2001; Thomas 2002; Gwenllian Jones 2003), but Jenkins' well-known model of fans as 'textual poachers' was very influential amongst scholars of fandom in the late 1990s (Merrick 1997; Watson 1997; Baym 1998; Cartmell *et al.* 1998; Classen 1998; Dell 1998; Gillilan 1998; Harris 1998; Tankel and Murphy 1998) and marks an entire approach to fan culture which continues to be influential in fan scholarship today, evidenced in the manifesto introduction to *Hop on Pop* and the numerous celebratory contributions on fandom that the anthology contains. In the following chapter I will argue that it is not only recent changes that have undermined this model, but that it *never* adequately defined or explained fandom. Jenkins argued that the fan 'constitutes a scandalous category in contemporary culture, one alternately the target of ridicule and anxiety, of dread and desire' (1992: 17). For Jenkins, the manner in which fans are stereotyped 'amounts to a projection of anxieties about the violation of dominant cultural hierarchies' (ibid.). However, Jenkins' assessment of the social characterisation of fandom needs to be questioned.

Matt Hills has convincingly argued that Jenkins has created a 'moral dualism' around fan culture, which pits the 'good' fan against the 'bad' non-fan who is responsible 'for reproducing negative stereotypes of fandom' (2001: 9). Hills argues that fans are academics' imagined others (and vice versa) in order that academia can regulate 'who has the power over cultural representations and cultural claims to legitimacy' (2001: 5). This is important for the academic sphere, because so much of fan activity is like academic activity – close readings of canonised texts, interpretations and counter-interpretations of those texts, attendance at conferences where works are discussed, and so on. Equally though, Jenkins' approach of writing 'as a fan' has inaugurated a certain cache in academics proclaiming their fandom. Jenkins, Tara McPherson and Jane Shattuc turn to Bourdieu to support this point:

> If 'immediacy' is what, according to Pierre Bourdieu, distinguishes the popular from the bourgeois aesthetic, then we should be suspicious of attempts to write about popular culture from a distance ... The challenge for our emergent perspective is to write about our own multiple (and often contradictory) involvements, participations, engagements, and identifications with popular culture – without denying, rationalising or distorting them. (2002: 7)

However, Jenkins *et al.* wrongly designate the cultural field as dominated by a struggle between the popular and the bourgeois aesthetic. As we shall see in more detail in the following chapter, Bourdieu argues that the central struggle in culture is between two dominant bourgeois sets of values: art-for-art's-sake versus art-for-profit, who continuously struggle with each other in an endlessly thwarted attempt to establish their own domination – thwarted due to the very struggle between them. These two opposing sets of cultural values influence the entire field of fandom, some fan clubs tending towards fandom-for-fandom's-sake and the other towards fandom-for-profit. Rather than recognising that the cultural field is marked by struggle between these different factions, Jenkins reproduces the moral dualism identified by Hills above, in order to place 'good' fannish academic practice on the opposite side of a monolithic bourgeois culture. Today in fan scholarship it is *de rigueur* to write as a fan first and an academic second because of the problems that are seen to inhere in preserving the 'status of the outside observer, the objective and impersonal Ethnographer' (Jenkins 1998: 263) and most studies of fandom give an account of the author's own fandom (Hunter 1996; Kermode 1997; Cavicchi 1998; Jancovich 2000; Hills 2001; Thomas 2002).[6] I have avoided giving an account of my own fandom in this volume, not because I wish to preserve my status as an academic against the fan; I was a vampire fan long before I joined academia at a relatively late age, but I have avoided giving a personal account because I do not entirely accept the critique of 'distance' and 'objectivity' that such a strategy implies. I am not suggesting a return to the practice of using the label of objectivity to mask a reactionary and conservative position, but that there is value in attempting to objectively understand the dynamics and logics of phenomena. Terry Eagleton reminds us that while establishing the truth of something is a 'taxing and messy business' (2003: 106), and that 'all truths are established from specific viewpoints ... it does not make sense to say that there is a tiger in the bathroom from my viewpoint but not from yours. You and I may contend fiercely about whether there is a tiger in the bathroom or not' (ibib.), but in the end, one of us has to be wrong and if I am going into the bathroom, I would like to know which one. Eagleton suggests that distance, or

> disinterestedness does not mean being magically resolved from inter-ests, but recognising that some of your interests are doing you no good, or that it is in the interests of doing an effective job to set certain of them apart for the moment. (2003: 134)

With this in mind, I will now offer a personalised account in order to demonstrate that 'distance' *can* be a necessary component to an understanding of a phenomenon.

When I first began to interview vampire fans in 1997, I started with my friends and members of various vampire fan clubs across Britain. I share a great deal of cultural capital, dispositions and political orientations with the many of the people that I interviewed, often including the same gender. the same occupation as a teacher, and the same labour and trade union affiliations. I have learned a great deal from these fans and friends. However, the prevalent view of fandom as an inclusive and democratic space could not have been investi-gated from this insider's position; from 'within' as it were. My proximity to the phenomena that I was studying actually restricted my ability to fully observe the dynamics at work amongst people with whom I had so much in common. It was actually only when I travelled to New Orleans to interview members of the Anne Rice Vampire Lestat Fan Club (ARVLFC) in 1998, that I was able to identify the tensions, hierarchies and differing cultural values that make up a large part of fan culture. I also encountered the ARVLFC at a particular moment when the club was in process of transition which highlighted the processes at work and I will discuss this in more detail in chapter six. My point, however, is that it was my *distance* from this fandom rather than proximity and affinity, which enabled me to engage with these processes, or even to identify them. It is not the case either, that US vampire fandom is rife with tensions and British vampire fandom is not; my experience in New Orleans enabled me to iden-tify similar tensions in British vampire fandom that were right under my nose (people being expelled from groups, court cases and the like), but that I had ignored because of my affinity with other fans. Thus writing from a 'position of proximity or closeness ... from a position of ... [one's] own lived subjectivity' as Jenkins (1998: 263) advocates, can only really tell us about that subjectivity. I am not suggesting that it is therefore an unacceptable practice, for there is a rich tradition of work which writes from the subordinated position of female, gay, lesbian, black and working class in order to bring to the public domain voices and experiences that had hitherto been neglected.[7] But fandom is not a subordinated social position in the way that these other positions are, and so this rationale does not hold. Writing as a fan is not the same as writing as a lesbian, an African American and so on (although both are sometimes fans, it is inadequate to collapse the two subject positions together) as fandom is a cultural choice. Writing from within the fan position has incorrectly produced a view of fandom as subversive *per se* because the political orientations of the academic/fan writing about this terrain has been overlaid on the terrain itself. Fandom was constructed as a subordinate social formation and a resistant one, 'modern-day Robin Hoods ... busily snatching back "our" popular cultural texts from the greedy global conglomerates', as Gwenllian Jones puts it (2003: 163), as part of the logic of the practice of speaking from 'within' and of collaps-ing distance. Yet many vampire fans and many other media fans share more with academics than with the working class and poor that populate Britain and America, whose voices are genuinely neglected.[8]

The correspondence between fan and academic is only being intensified by the 'niche' market changes in the television industry's address to middle-class, educated, affluent audiences. Much of *Buffy* fandom shares cultural disposi-tions and cultural capital with the academic (and, as it happens, with the televi-sion critic). *Buffy* fans construct web pages and engage in Internet discussions about character and story arcs, they debate the politics of the show, and inter-pret subtexts. In this sense fan activity is not dissimilar to the academic activity surrounding *Buffy* (including, of course, this chapter).

The middle-class orientation of media fandom does not mean that fans are not also targeted as consumers; just the opposite, for it is the middle-class pocket book that makes this group a key demographic. The profit-oriented section of the media bourgeoisie have long addressed fans as consumers and potential sources of profit through merchandising and the consumption of stardom and celebrity. And this is an instance where the media conglomerates that dominate global cultural production cannot lose – *Buffy* merchandising is a prime example of this. *Buffy* is owned by Twentieth Century Fox. Fox sells *Buffy* to either Warner Bros. for a cool $1 million or UPN for a $2 million price tag per episode. But another enormous source of revenue that Fox makes from *Buffy* comes from its merchandising empire. I have not been able to acquire the gross merchandising revenue figures for *Buffy* alone because Fox does not release them. However, the website Leading Licensors rates Twentieth Century Fox as number twenty of the top merchandising licensors and have stated (based on 2002 retail figures) that its merchandising revenues jumped from $770 million in 2001 to $1 billion in 2002 and it lists *Buffy* as the fourth-largest money maker via merchandising just below *The Simpsons*, *Robots* and *Mad Max*. From these figure we can see that *Buffy* merchandising is highly profitable, and it is a source of revenue that will continue after *Buffy* has gone off air. Some *Buffy* websites are entangled in this commercialism because their websites have links to merchandising outlets that provide them with a source of revenue. Other websites refuse to provide such links, with an insistence that fandom should be non-profit and independent. We can begin to see in this one example the way that the two dominant but conflicting sets of cultural value impact on the values of fandom. By this I am not suggesting that buying *Buffy* merchandise makes a fan a dupe of the capitalist system, but neither are these purchasing acts fannish challenges to the capitalist media. Instead I am suggesting that fans have always been influenced by either set of the competing sets of values whose struggle forms the field of cultural production. The following chapter will examine and critique the way that fandom has been theorised and will outline in greater detail the manner in which Bourdieu's ideas – which feature in a partial way in most accounts of fandom – might be reassessed to provide a model for understanding fandom in contemporary culture.

CHAPTER 5

VAMPIRE FANDOM: REBELS WITHOUT A CAUSE? THEORISING FANDOM IN THE FIELD OF CULTURAL PRODUCTION

This chapter begins the second part of this book which moves away from a close analysis of vampire texts and fans' interpretation of those texts in order to examine the practices of vampire fandom and to offer a theoretical context for understanding these practices. The following chapters will be concerned with issues related to the concepts of rebellion and resistance, not least because vampire fans articulate some of their activities in these terms. I will consider these claims of rebellion (including their limitations) and will examine the consequences of this understanding of the self to vampire fans' identities.

It is also the case, as we began to see in the previous chapter, that theories of fandom have been concerned with issues to do with rebellion and resistance. Much fan scholarship has reproduced fannish claims of resistance and has produced models of fandom on this basis. I will assess these accounts of fandom, as well as examining the work of a small but growing number of scholars who challenge this view.

Most scholarship on fandom draws on concepts from Pierre Bourdieu, either from the perspective that sees fandom as resistance, or from those who contest this view. However, in this chapter I will argue that the use of Bourdieu in fan scholarship has been partial, and has not focused on the most essential part of Bourdieu's analysis of culture – the struggle between two opposing but powerful poles of culture which provide the dynamic of cultural production. I will argue that this has led to an overly monolithic view of 'dominant' culture, and thus to both overly grandiose claims about fannish resistance and to overly pessimistic claims about fannish incorporation into consumer capitalism.

READING AS RESISTANCE

Most accounts of fandom in the 1990s theorised fan culture as a mode of resistance (Bacon-Smith 1992; Fiske 1992; Jenkins 1992; Chibnall 1997; Merrick 1997; Watson, 1997; Baym 1998; Classen 1998; Dell 1998; Gillilan 1998; Harris 1998; Tankel and Murphy 1998). Academics have drawn on Michael de Certeau (Jenkins 1992; Merrick 1997; Classen 1998) or Bourdieu (Fiske 1992; Watson 1997; Baym 1998; Dell 1998) and often a mixture of both (Jenkins 1992; Fiske 1992; Dell 1998; Harris 1998) to theorise the subversive character of fandom.

Probably the most influential account of fandom comes from Henry Jenkins. For Jenkins, media fans are 'nomads' and 'poachers' of popular texts, re-working them and re-writing them to suit their own needs. Drawing on de Certeau, Jenkins argues in his 1992 book, *Textual Poachers*, that authorial meaning is a major agent of social control, where sanctioned interpreters restrain the 'multiple voices of popular orality', and where the 'reader is supposed to serve as a more-or-less passive recipient of authorial meaning' (1992: 25). Furthermore, Jenkins argues that respect for authorial integrity of the message has 'the effect of silencing or marginalising oppositional voices' (ibid.). Jenkins compares this form of reading to the way that fans engage with texts; they creatively appropriate the texts of mass culture and rewrite them without any respect for authorial integrity. Fans are likened to guerrilla fighters, making tactical raids on the structures of the powerful by poaching from their texts. Jenkins thus theorises fandom as 'the various tactics of popular resistance' (1992: 26) to authorial control and therefore to the dominant power that is upheld by it. We saw in the previous chapter that Jenkins (2001) suggested that he was accentuating the positive side of fandom in *Textual Poachers* because of the ridicule that fandom faced, but his characterisation of fandom-as-resistance has not significantly altered. Jenkins continues to assert that fan creativity

> rejects the idea of a definitive version produced, authorised and regulated by some media conglomerate. Instead [fan fiction] pushes towards a world where all of us can participate in the creation and circulation of cultural myths. (1998: n.p.)

Yet Jenkins' claims about the subversive character of fandom do not just stem from his use of de Certeau, he has also drawn on the ideas of Bourdieu. Jenkins claims:

> From the perspective of dominant taste, fans appear to be frighteningly out of control, undisciplined and unrepentant, rogue readers. Rejecting the aesthetic distance Bourdieu suggests is a corner stone of bourgeois aesthetics, fans enthusiastically embrace favoured texts and attempt to integrate media representations into their own social experience. (1992: 18)

Jenkins, however, is wrong to suggest that 'dominant taste' fears the fans' 'undisciplined' readings. He has since referred directly to the quotation above to suggest that a 'non-fan reader had little basis for understanding this account of an active subculture' (1998: n.p.). However, it is not the taking of a fan subject position (or not taking one) that leads one to reject this account; it is that it was not accurate at the time, is not accurate now, and is a misreading of Bourdieu. For Bourdieu, aesthetic distance is not the 'corner stone' of bourgeois aesthetics as a whole, but rather, it is the corner stone of the artistic elite fraction (or 'autonomous pole') of the bourgeoisie, who struggle with the profit-oriented bourgeoisie ('heteronomous pole') over the designation of cultural worth. It is this struggle between these two powerful poles in the field of cultural production that provides it with its dynamic, according to Bourdieu (1984; 1993). This is important to note, because Jenkins (and Fiske 1992) misinterpret Bourdieu to suggest that fans operate against a single monolithic dominant taste. That 'dominant taste' is characterised by a struggle between competing values disrupts the resistant construction of the fan, and begins to suggest the different ways that the fan may be addressed by different sections of the bourgeoisie that dominate the media and cultural industries. Furthermore, even if fan readings are out of control, undisciplined and enthusiastic, this will hardly 'frighten' that fraction of the bourgeoisie who distinguish themselves from these dispositions as the basis of their greater cultural legitimacy. According to Bourdieu, those at the autonomous pole of the field of cultural production expect popular taste to reject aesthetic distance, to be enthusiastic and to be undisciplined. Rather than frightening autonomous bourgeois taste, it reinforces the very taste distinction upon which the autonomous (elitist) disposition bases its claims to legitimacy and greater cultural dominance. Thus, even if this characterisation of fannish reading practices is correct (and this is debatable) embracing media texts and integrating them into one's social experience is not a 'direct and vocal affront to the legitimacy of traditional hierarchies' (Jenkins 1992: 18), according to Bourdieu's scheme of taste distinctions (1993: 237).

However, Jenkins continues to retain a utopian view of fandom, now vested in fandom's preferred terrain – the Internet. For Jenkins the 'digital revolution' is a 'cultural revolution' (1998: n.p.), with the web containing 'enormous potential for the creation of a more diverse and democratic popular culture – one which allows much broader opportunities for grassroots participation' (ibid.):

> Even in a climate where the web is increasingly commercialised, its decentralised structure can support the creation of viable alternatives to the now-dominant media and expand the diversity of our existing popular culture. (Ibid.)

However, such a view ignores the fact that the Internet is still primarily a resource for the Western educated middle-classes which has tended to reflect existing social inequalities rather than undermine them. Andrea MacDonald has conducted participant observation with *Quantum Leap* fans that use computer-mediated communication (CMC), and she questions the celebratory claims about on-line science fiction fandom:

> Science fiction fandom is predominantly a white, middle-class phenomenon. Given the expense of computers and computing time, the group of fans I am talking about narrows considerably. (1998: 150)

MacDonald argues that CMC users are an 'elite group': 'They are either academics or work for companies with connections to the Internet ... or have the necessary finances to purchase computing equipment and pay for on-line time charges' (ibid.). Thus, according to MacDonald, rather than CMC opening up a democratic space for the equality of expression, 'computing norms emerge, old social practices merge with new creating a different but not radically new discursive space' (1998: 133). This is an important alternative view to the perspective that Internet fandom presents a challenge to dominant culture from below, and one that I will examine more closely in chapter eight, which examines vampire fans' writing practices.

THE FAN AS SOCIAL SUBORDINATE

The radical claims about the character of fandom are related to the view of the fan as socially subordinate. For instance, as part of his original claims of resistance, Jenkins argued that all fans 'operate from a position of cultural marginality and social weakness' (1992: 26). Jenkins conceives of fandom as an alternative community 'whose values may be more humane and democratic than those held by mundane society' (1992: 281). He argues that fans react against 'unsatisfying situations, trying to establish a "weekend-only world" more open to creativity and accepting of differences' (1992: 282). However, at least one other scholar of fandom writing in the early 1990s contested the view of fans as oppressed rebels. Susan Brower's analysis of Viewers for Quality Television (VQT) proposed that this organisation is made up of 'mature, middle-class, well-educated women and men' (1992: 163). Rather than subordinate groups making tactical raids, Brower argues that 'these devotees of primetime network television have ... fashioned themselves as a rational, well-organised group engaging in aesthetic criticism (defining and discriminating "quality television") and social activism (advocating the continuance of "quality television")' (1992: 164). This is in contrast to the more familiar approach to fans that can be found in Cheryl Harris's analysis of Viewers for Quality Television in the US, which suggests that while these fans are not involved in 'some kind of populist overthrow of the television industry' (1998: 51), their immersion in fan practices constitutes a form of 'empowerment' which she defines as the ability to 'resist and challenge the hegemonic forces ... of a monolithic industry' (ibid.). However, rather than resisting the television industry, Brower argues that these fans have produced a, 'philosophy of broadcasting [that] increasingly replicates the networks it attempts to challenge' (1992: 176). Furthermore she argues that 'this "democratic" organisation seeks to create a position of privilege – *clout* – in relation to the networks, based on its status as an elite minority, an association of tastemakers' (ibid.). This analysis puts a rather different emphasis on the 'empowerment' that VQT members may gain from their participation.

Yet, despite the changes in the structure of the television audiences and the increasingly middle-class character of fandom, Jenkins continues to assert that fandom is a subordinate social formation, populated by the oppressed. Fans both threaten 'corporate power', and 'remain outside [its] clubhouse'

(1998: n.p.). Jenkins, McPherson and Shattuc liken fandom to racial, sexual and gender oppression with the claim that

> For many of us, being a fan represents a collective cultural and political identity that links us to other cultural communities. Our cultural preferences, no less than our racial, sexual and political identities, are difficult to shed when we write. (2002: 7)

Mark Jancovich has recently demonstrated that cult movie fans, far from inhabiting a rebellious subordinate social position, tend to be middle-class, educated men, who are often academics adopting oppositional rhetoric: 'If cult fans usually make claims to oppositionality, they are largely middle class and male, and their oppositionality often works to reaffirm rather than challenge bourgeois taste and masculine dispositions' (2002: 3). Jancovich also suggests that there is a historical link between academic film studies and cult film fandom, both of which rely on a set of values that distinguish them from the 'ordinary viewer'. He argues that:

> Cult movie fandom and academic film studies may have historically diverged into relatively independent scenes, but the both emerged through the arts cinemas, college film societies and repertory theatres of the post-war period, and hence employ similar discourses and reading strategies. (2002: 308)

These are reading strategies that both academics and fans employ in order that they may present themselves 'in clear distinction to a conformist mass of viewers' (2002: 310).

Similarly, Joanne Hollows has demonstrated that 'cult has been culturally constructed as masculine ... based on a rejection of the feminine [which] may also work to exclude "real" women from some of the practices associated with cult fandom' (2003: 39). Hollows suggests, following Sarah Thornton's analysis of club culture, that cult fandom is only open to women who 'opt to be "culturally one of the boys"' (ibid.). Crucially, as Jacinda Read points out, it is not only fans who articulate masculinist positions; it is also the male academic 'fan boy'. Read argues that, with the institutionalisation of feminism within the academy, 'academic discussions of cult are ... characterised by a desire to identify the cult critic or fan with an oppressed, "feminine" position' (2003: 56). However, Read suggests that these discussions also assert the 'masculinity of cult [and] function also to reassert the cult of masculinity' (2003: 57). The adoption of a 'feminine', subordinate reading position is simultaneous in this academic milieu, with manoeuvring the 'straight white male academic into the position of a deviant, resisting "disempowered" minority, and feminism ... into the position of the conformist, dominant mainstream' (2003: 60). Furthermore, Read suggests that this counter-aesthetic amounts to a 'celebration of the kind of laddish political incorrectness made famous in the 1990s by publications such as *Loaded* (2003: 62). Read argues that in the UK context, the ironic reading of politically incorrect texts by 'fan boy' academics 'intersects in specific ways with a historically and nationally specific cult of masculinity'(2003: 63) that was made 'hip' and 'cool' by magazines like *Loaded*. The claims for ironic readings made by such critics

> make such political incorrectness very difficult to engage with seriously, since to do so is to risk the accusation of 'not getting the joke', and therefore of being uncool and unhip. In this way, irony functions not only to deflect accusations of sexism and prevent serious engagement with the issues, but to exclude anyone who is unable or unwilling to read texts in this way. (Ibid.)

I am not suggesting that Henry Jenkins is 'one of the lads' (and Read is aiming her criticism elsewhere), but his view of fans as 'grassroots activists' (1998: n.p.) campaigning against the commercial cultural industry *does* similarly transform the middle-class, white, educated fan into an oppressed rebel, and ignores the elitist distinctions that fans make. Jenkins actually slides between different terms to denote what it is that fans are resisting. At one point he is 'discussing ways that subordinate classes elude or escape institutional control' and thus 'analysing locations where popular meanings are produced outside of official interpretative practices' (1998: 26). Later it is 'patriarchal authority' which is being resisted and it is women fans who are doing the resisting of 'masculine interpretive strategies' (1992: 113–15). By the conclusion of *Textual Poachers* though, it is 'mundane life' which is being resisted (1992: 282). It is worth considering this slippage in terms for a moment. These three terms all signal 'bad authority' in Jenkins' scheme of fandom and who would disagree that domination and patriarchy are bad? But resisting 'mundania' is not as unproblematically progressive. For what is this mundane world, the resistance to which Jenkins can only approve? At one level it is the drudgery of work-a-day life. But that is not all there is to it. When Jenkins supports the distinction fans make between 'fan culture and the mundane world' (1992: 262) he is applauding distinctions which have derogatory connotations regarding class and gender. For example, a 'filk' song describes mundane life as a

> 'Barbie and Ken' existence in suburbia, watching soap operas, discussing *Readers Digest* articles, eating Big Macs, gossiping about the neighbours, and engaging in quick sex at a single's bar before settling down to raise their 2.3 children. (quoted in Jenkins 1992: 263)

Jenkins congratulates the author for a 'biting satire of American consumer society' (ibid.). But the target is not the powerful corporations of American consumer society. Instead it is the 'mundane' consumers. Looked at more closely, one can identify two sets of distinctions being made that seem to be in line with some of the values at the autonomous pole of the field. First there are a set of class-biased distinctions being made. References to eating Big Macs and living in suburbia are not empty of value, but signify working-class, or lower-middle-class, America. Gender is also marked, because the remaining descriptions draw distinctions that have derogatory inferences of femininity. Barbie and Ken are girls' toys, and soap opera 'gossiping', reading *Readers Digest* and raising children are all considered (and devalued) as female occupations and interests (cf. Huyssen 1986). The fannish descriptions of 'mundania', such as the one quoted above, reveal a great deal about contradictions in fannish opposition to the 'mainstream' and the distinctions being drawn and should be unpacked rather than celebrated. As Bourdieu argues, taste 'unites and separates' (1984: 56) and these distinctions share important characteristics with the autonomous aesthetic disposition, namely 'distinguishing oneself from the common people' (1984: 31).

Jenkins at times acknowledges the contradictory elements of fandom, but he does not investigate this aspect of fandom. He chooses instead to focus on the group of fans who can be seen to be defiant. He admits that 'the solutions fans propose are not ideologically consistent and coherent' (1992: 283). He endorses the view that male fandom can be exclusive and that straight fandom can be homophobic, yet he concentrates on the 'radicalism' of the slash fan or female fan. However, the following chapter will demonstrate that *female* fans, some of whom are lesbians, also engage in elitist distinctions between themselves and other (often female) fans. Jenkins does not incorporate this insight into his model of fandom. Instead, he argues that 'fandom remains a space where a commitment to more democratic values may be renewed and fostered' (1992: 282), and then that it 'contains enormous potential for the creation of a more diverse and democratic popular culture' (1998: n.p.). Thus despite his cursory nod in the other direction, the thrust of Jenkins' approach is to make celebratory claims about the defiant and progressive nature of fandom. But how would the celebratory model of fandom-as-resistance (including the notions of fandom as democratic, inclusive and accepting) stand up to a systematic examination of those fans who display racism, sexism or homophobia? I encountered a number of white (female) vampire fans who displayed racist attitudes in the course of my research (and who expected me, as a white researcher, to be unprovoked by such views). At least once, such an encounter resulted in an acrimonious severing of further contact. Yet often (as in the case just mentioned) these female fans were in favour of gay and lesbian rights at the same time. It is important to recognise that such contradictory ideas exist within fandom and the people who populate it. But I think this adds another dimension to the argument against considering fandom as an all-inclusive space, which is not to say that all white vampire fans are racist; rather that fandom and racism can coexist. Fandom as a cultural formation does not, in the US or Britain, lead to a questioning of racism, one of the major social divisions in both countries that keep the marginalised separated, and the system of domination in place.

Also, Jenkins, McPherson and Shattuc cast their own writing on fandom as a form of activism. They liken themselves, as scholars of fandom and popular culture, to organic intellectuals 'able to articulate the knowledge, interests or experiences of their own class or social group within wider social and political fields' (2002: 12). They compare their own position as organic intellectuals speaking for fandom, to 'bell hooks, Michael Eric Dyson, Gerald Early, Henry Louis Gates Jr., Patricia Williams, Cornel West, Todd Boyd and Tricia Rose' (ibid.) who speak for the African American population, a population not only with a history of enslavement, but one that continues to suffer systematic oppression and discrimination in the US (and Britain). Media fans, on the other hand, do not make up a disproportionate percentage of the prison population; they do not suffer systematic discrimination in the education system, employment and housing, at the hands of the police, or in the criminal justice system. To liken the way that a fan scholar speaks from within 'a skin' of experience to the way that an African American scholar does, is untenable. Fan scholars who position themselves as intellectual activists and fans as subordinate rebels achieve these claims by ignoring the hierarchies that exist in fandom, and by inadequately characterising 'dominant' culture.

While many scholars of fandom draw on Bourdieu to theorise 'mainstream' or dominant culture, it is John Fiske (1992) who produced the first systematic (and influential) attempt to apply Bourdieu's cultural model to the sphere of fandom. However, Fiske also misinterprets Bourdieu's work significantly in a number of ways, and this misinterpretation has had a problematic effect on fan scholarship, as we shall see, for it culminates in an inaccurate account of 'mainstream' or 'dominant' culture.

Fiske draws on Bourdieu to discuss the 'cultural economy of fandom'. He proposes that the cultural system 'works like the economic system to distribute its resources unequally and thus distinguish between the privileged and the deprived' (1992: 31). This produces a legitimate culture or 'high' culture which is sanctioned in institutions such as education, art galleries, museums and so on. Fiske suggests that the sum of these sanctioned cultural values constitutes a single 'official culture' (ibid.). One can acquire official cultural capital just as one can acquire economic capital, but the acquisition of this capital is limited, excluding those who are subordinate within the social formation. Fiske argues that 'official culture, like money, distinguishes between those who possess it, and those who do not' and he suggests that cultural capital 'works hand in hand with economic capital to produce social privilege and distinction' (ibid.).

Fiske argues that fandom is an 'appropriate culture for those in subordinated formations of the people who feel themselves unfairly excluded from the socio-economic or status-enhancing rewards that official culture can offer' (1992: 45). He argues that participation in fan culture produces different forms of productivity which leads to 'empowerment' (1992: 35) through the accumulation of unofficial or subcultural capital. Fiske then likens fan culture to Bourdieu's notion of proletarian culture by arguing that like proletarian culture, 'fan culture is functional – it must be for something' (ibid.); it empowers the socially subordinate by allowing them to accumulate subcultural capital in the shadow economy of fandom. I have already argued that fans are often educated and privileged, and Brower's analysis of VQT demonstrates that even in the early 1990s fandom was not by its nature a subordinate social formation, and thus while fans may be accruing a form of cultural capital through their fandom, it is neither *sub*ordinate nor *sub*cultural. It is not possible to possess 'sub'cultural capital in Bourdieu's schema, there is no such thing. Subcultural capital is simply the cultural capital that is jockeying for position with more traditional and established forms of cultural capital, what Bourdieu terms the non-consecrated avant-garde. At any rate, when Bourdieu argues that the popular aesthetic must be *for* something he is referring to the way that proletarian taste focuses not on subcultural capital but on *content*, whereas 'pure taste' focuses on *form*.

Bourdieu argues that popular taste embraces *content* and emotional investment because it is *excluded* from cultural capital, not because it possesses an alternative form. It is a response to being refused access to cultural capital – that is, to participate in this (autonomous) aesthetic. The reluctance of ordinary working-class audiences to participate in the game of cultural capital stems from a recognition that the logic of this system is based precisely on excluding them: 'Formal experimentation – which, in literature or the theatre, leads to *obscurity* – is, in the eyes of the working-class public, one sign of what is sometimes felt to be a desire to keep the uninitiated at arms' length' (1993: 238). The proletarian aesthetic, then, is one of investment in content rather than form, the refusal of the logic of cultural capital, not the participation in it, and this is not the dominant aesthetic of fandom. I am not suggesting that there are no working-class media fans, but I am suggesting that working-class and middle-class fans do not share the same aesthetic disposition, or if they do, then it is because working-class fans have decided to engage in the game of cultural capital, rather like those women who, as Hollows has demonstrated, opt to be 'culturally one of the boys'. Class differences in fan culture are as marked as in any other avenue of social life and fan culture has a minority of participants who will join the ranks either of elite cultural producers or commentators, a sizable number of middle-class participants who have the appropriate habitus to participate at an amateur or semi-professional level (either economic or symbolic), and a sizable number of working-class participants who either feel excluded from many fan practices (particularly in the area of writing) or learn to adopt an appropriate disposition.

Fiske (like Jenkins), however, produces another important misreading of Bourdieu when he suggests that there is a single 'official culture, in distinction from popular culture' (1992: 31).[1] Fiske's notion that there is a 'popular culture' made up of subordinate social formations 'whose politics lie in its opposition to the official dominant one' (1992: 34), is both an inaccurate characterisation of fandom and is an important misconstruction of Bourdieu. Bourdieu argues that the field of cultural production is dominated by two opposing sets of values which are in constant conflict with each other, and it is this conflict which provides the dynamic of the field. This is not the conflict between bourgeois aesthetics and proletarian aesthetics, but between the commercial bourgeoisie and the cultural elite. It is worth examining Bourdieu's account in some detail because of the way, as Jim McGuigan puts it, his work has been 'raided and sanitised' (1992: 72) in order to suggest that any engagement with popular culture is subversive. Indeed, McGuigan has produced an influential critique of cultural populism, including a critique of Fiske. He argues that Fiske produces 'a kind of subjective idealism, focused more or less exclusively on "popular readings", which are applauded with no evident reservations at all, never countenancing the possibility that a popular reading could be anything other than "progressive"' (ibid.). For McGuigan, although Fiske presents an 'ostensibly critical' look at the power relations in the cultural arena, in effect, 'the gap between "popular" and "mass" culture is finally closed with no residual tension' (1992: 73). We can see in those who follow on from Fiske that the gap has indeed closed. For example, the introduction to a volume of fan studies, *Trash Aesthetics: Popular Culture and its Audience* (Cartmell, Hunter, Kaye and Whelehan 1997), produces a populist celebration of commodity culture. It begins with a manifesto-style proclamation about fandom. It celebrates shifting attention away from 'what ideal audiences should be reading and viewing to what real people actually enjoy' (1). It discovers the 'unexpected complexity in "trash culture"' and argues that the 'most vibrant research is committed to taking audiences and their pleasures seriously' (ibid.). Cartmell *et al.* have produced what James Curran (1990) characterises as 'the new revisionism' which really amounts to a reworking of traditional liberal pluralism. It is a liberal pluralist celebration of commodity culture, for instance, that informs their argument that:

> Academics are learning what advertising agencies have always known: the power of consumer sovereignty. One of the many pleasures of consumer capitalism is that it so perfectly services this fragmented, postmodern individual. Out there in the global pick-n-mix is a text just for you; or a text you can customise to your desires. (Cartmell *et al.* 1997: 3)

This venerates the very commodity culture whose organisation and practices play a role in the maintenance of unequal power relations. Yet, however popular Bourdieu's work has become in fan scholarship, the cultural populism that runs through this terrain did not emanate from Bourdieu.

BOURDIEU AND THE STRUGGLE IN THE FIELD OF CULTURAL PRODUCTION

Bourdieu proposes that the field of cultural production should be analysed in a way which emphasises the specificity of the field's genesis as a set of relations. For Bourdieu this means 'constructing the space of positions' available in the cultural field and also 'the space of position-takings [*prises de position*][2] in which they are expressed' (1993: 39). Bourdieu argues:

Every position, even the dominant one, depends for its very existence, and for the determinations it imposes on its occupants, on the other positions constituting the field; and that the structure of the field, i.e. of the space of positions, is nothing more than the structure of the distribution of the capital of specific properties which governs success in the field and the winning of external [i.e. commercial] or specific profits (such as literary prestige) which are at stake in the field. (Ibid.)

For Bourdieu, the space of possible positions is thus a result not only of the internal differences between the positions available, but also of the history of positions that have made up the field (and into the structure of which new positions necessarily enter) and that these positions are linked to the uneven distribution of different forms of capital. This leads to the second point: that the field is not just made up of positions, but also of position-takings. By this Bourdieu means that positions only become positions when taken up and occupied by a social agent, and that the taking up of positions can alter the structure of available positions, as did Flaubert when he wrote Madame Bovary.[3]

Further, Bourdieu proposes that the dynamic of the cultural field (resulting from this structure) is struggle. For Bourdieu, the cultural field is 'a *field of forces*, but it is also a *field of struggles* tending to transform or conserve this field of forces' (1993: 30). This is because those groups or individuals who hold positions which accrue to them capital (symbolic or economic) attempt to hold their positions against those who struggle to establish the dominance of their own positions. Thus, for Bourdieu, the direction of movement in the field of cultural production depends on the struggles therein. This is concretely shaped by the given state of the system (which is the range of possible positions given by the history of positions and position-takings that make it up at any given moment). But also, it is the actual positions that agents take up in any given moment and the balance of forces between these social agents, 'who have entirely real interest in the different possibilities available to them as stakes and who deploy every sort of strategy to make one set or other prevail' (1993: 34). For Bourdieu, this system is not the result therefore of 'coherence seeking intention' but is the product of permanent conflict (ibid.).

Bourdieu proposes that the struggle of the two groupings at the dominant end of the field is between those who see cultural value based on the profit motive and those for whom cultural production should be for its own sake. The former makes up the dominant set of positions. These are the 'heteronomous' positions which see their own success in economic terms. High in economic capital, these groups want to reproduce their economic capital *and* to reproduce commercial values and the profit motive as the *raison d'être* for cultural production (1993: 40). Thus the dominant positions in the field are engaged in large-scale production which reproduces economic capital (1993: 53).

Still situated within the dominant end of the field of cultural production are what Bourdieu calls the 'dominated' (1993: 30), whose principles of cultural legitimacy are opposed to the bourgeoisie. This is the artistic pole which bases its claim for legitimacy, not on large-scale production and the reproduction of economic capital, but on the recognition of one's peers (who are those who also occupy positions high in cultural capital, but sometimes low in economic capital). Bourdieu argues that there is an inversion of the fundamental principles of the economies in other fields so that artists consider economic success a sign that one has 'sold out' (1993: 39).

Thus for Bourdieu, the field of cultural production is fundamentally a field of conflict between the economic bourgeoisie and cultural elite; principles of legitimacy in accord with the logic of profit versus principles of legitimacy autonomous from the logic of economics. Furthermore, he argues that both sets of principles are principles of 'hierachisation' (1993: 40) because both are involved in struggles for dominance over what genres and forms are considered most valid and also who is legitimately entitled to designate what is legitimate:

> The struggle in the field of cultural production over the imposition of the legitimate mode of cultural production is inseparable from the struggle within the dominant class (with the opposition between 'artists' and 'bourgeois') to impose the dominant principle of domination (that is to say – ultimately – the definition of human accomplishment). (1993: 41)

This struggle therefore produces two opposing principles of hierarchisation which correspond to each sub-field: the dominant end produces a 'heteronomous principle' of hierarchisation (1993: 40) which is a struggle for cultural dominance linked to economic and political domination and thus to the profit motive. Their struggle for legitimacy and dominance is a struggle *against* the autonomy of the cultural field and *for* its integration into the value systems of economic, political and class power. It is heteronomous in the sense that it is linked to the logic and interests of other fields.

In opposition to this is the 'autonomous principle' of domination (ibid.) which, despite its opposition to bourgeois values and interest and its demand that the profit motive be denied in the cultural field, also tries 'to impose the dominant definition of the writer and therefore limit the population of those entitled to take part in the struggle to define the writer' (1993: 42). Bourdieu characterises this pole as the art-for-art's-sake disposition with its own drive to monopolise the power to 'consecrate producers and products' (ibid.). Also, this set of positions is not without its own drive to accumulate capital. But rather than the accumulation of economic capital, this group are accumulating symbolic capital, or cultural capital. This is what Bourdieu characterises as accumulation in the long run. Unlike the bourgeoisie who want a rapid return of profits through rapid circulation of products (1993: 97), those at the 'autonomous pole' will eschew short-term popularity in favour of becoming a long-term classic and the winning of the symbolic capital that is conferred from this sort of recognition.

Furthermore, while the autonomous pole seems to be in a position to liber-ate 'their products from all external constraints', this cannot happen due to the specific historical conditions under which the 'process of autonomisation' took place (1993: 113).[4] Instead, it creates its own hierarchy which not only distin-guishes it from the bourgeoisie, but also the 'commoners', and thus the art-for-art's-sake position creates its own form of elitism in the process of distinguish-ing itself from the values of the bourgeoisie because it must also distinguish itself from the ordinary population. Thus the autonomous position, in order to distinguish itself from the wealthier bourgeoisie, demands that an object be appreciated in terms of its internal characteristics (rather than its content) and also demands knowledge of the specific history of the transformations in the internal form of art. It developed the principles of formal detachment and disinterestedness, which precludes any displays of emotional investment in the object *and* which also excludes the uninitiated.[5] The opposition of the 'autono-mous pole' to bourgeois values is thus contradictory because it is saturated with concepts of 'the pure', 'the abstract' and 'the esoteric' (1993: 20) which necessitate exclusion. Bourdieu argues that this is the basis for the 'quest for distinction' (1993: 119) found in the autonomous disposition. Fan culture, as a sub-field of the field of cultural production is influenced by either of these two sets of opposing cultural values.

One of the most innovative and original aspects of this analysis is Bourdieu's emphasis on the struggle between the two principles of legitimacy. There is no single homogenous 'dominant culture' or 'mainstream', with one set of values; Bourdieu demonstrates that the competition between the two dominant sets of positions produce contradictory and conflicting values of cultural worth. Rather than being a hermetically sealed system, the struggles for dominance create the space (potentially) for new positions within the cultural field. Cultural value and 'dominant tastes' are not fixed, but are in a process of con-tinual conflict. Bourdieu argues that both the heteronomous and autonomous principles of hierarchisation would 'reign unchallenged' (1993: 38) were it not for the struggle between them. It is this struggle to impose dominant systems of values (which are diametrically opposed to each other) which produces the shape of the field of cultural production. However, Bourdieu himself pays too little attention to the importance of this insight. Instead he concentrates on the struggles between various dispositions of the cultural elite and says less about the impact on the cultural field of the instability in its core dynamic. He set himself the task of unpacking the 'pure gaze' and its historic role in the development of cultural distinction which offers only the privileged few a role in the claims for a non-commercial culture. This emphasis means that he says very little about the production and consumption of the ordinary public and that he concentrates on regressive (or elitist) aspects of the cultural pole's opposition to economic cultural values. He offers no systematic consideration of the destabilising effect of the struggle which is at the heart of the field, nor does he consider the impact this might have on those who are dominated and the possibilities opened up by the fact of this struggle between the two poles.

The fact that the field of culture is not ideologically hermetically sealed raises the possibility for the existence of ideas of cultural value based on opposition to the logic of economic profit beyond the narrow confines of artistic specialisms. Bourdieu alludes to this issue when he discusses left-wing or 'social art', but he does not draw the conclusion that there is another set of values at the dominated end of the field of cultural production that also circulate, influence and result in possible positions. Bourdieu argues that significant changes in the structure of the space of possible positions is generally a result of the impact on the cultural field from the overarching fields of politics and class power, and he offers the example of the 1848 revolutions in France as one such example of when artists moved to the left, 'towards social art' (1993: 58). Bourdieu considers the impact, however, to be short lived, and here I would like to take issue with his analysis to suggest that 'social art' has its own history of possible positions which contributes to the struggle to define cultural worth. This space of possible positions is distinctive because, unlike heteronomous culture, it does not subordinate human experience to the profit motive, and unlike the abstract formalism of high modernism, it has attempted historically to produce cultural objects (sometimes using modernist techniques) which do not abstract from the hopes and pains of ordinary people, but which have tried to give expression to them. In the twentieth century there seem to have been at least three such movements in the field of politics whose impact on the cultural field has changed the space of possible positions: the women's movement, the civil rights movement and the anti-imperialist movements of the 1960s and 70s, each of which have forced their way on to the cultural agenda. These momentous challenges to traditional ways of seeing (both economic and autonomous) are enabled by the contradictions that shape the cultural field and the surrounding fields of power. To ignore these challenges (and to accept an uncritical acceptance of Bourdieu's own application of his schema) can lead to cultural pessimism, despite Bourdieu's enormous achievement in unlocking for us the key to understanding the dynamics of the field of culture.

FAN SCHOLARSHIP AND THE CONCEPT OF THE MAINSTREAM

Fan scholarship which draws on Bourdieu also underestimates the potential raised by the struggle that structures and destabilises the field. Fan scholars have either posited a homogenous 'mainstream' culture, or have concentrated their analysis on only one set of cultural values; either on the economic influences in fandom, or on the non-commercial but elitist influences in fandom. We have seen how academic accounts of fandom can deploy under-theorised conceptualisations of dominant culture to denote the power which fans are said to resist, and thus to rationalise fandom-as-rebellion as a necessary condition of this social formation. Sometimes this is called the 'mainstream' or 'official culture' (Fiske 1992; Jenkins 1992), sometimes it is called 'patriarchal culture' or 'masculinist culture' (Bacon-Smith 1992; Jenkins 1992; Penley 1992) and other times it is termed 'mundania' (Jenkins 1992). These terms pose a one-dimensional notion of dominant culture in order to stand-in for a thorough discussion of that which fans are said to resist. In this instance, the oversimplification of the concept of the 'mainstream' has led to triumphalist claims about the scope of fannish resistance. But it can also lead in the opposite direction, to pessimistic claims about the scale of incorporation into dominant culture. Jenkins *et al.* criticise the work of Michael Budd, Robert M. Entman and Clay Steinman for reinforcing the idea that 'production becomes the realm of politics, while the site of consumption only speaks for pleasure' (2002: 21). This is not actually their point. Their point is that all media-generated cultural objects and audiences are subordinated to economic imperatives, and this perspective too is not entirely accurate. They rightly argue that cultural studies can offer an 'incomplete and in some respects misleading view of the political role of the media in the United States' (1990: 170). But they go on to insist that 'those heterogeneous fragments' that make up the flow of television 'start to sound and look a lot more alike once you consider their economic purpose' and that all audiences are 'spending their "leisure" time as work, learning to buy and to be bought' (1990: 172). This view not only misses the opposing autonomous cultural values that circulate and influence audiences, it also returns us to the 'audience as dupe' formula. Advertisers want to reach affluent audiences in broadcast television, certainly, but this does not mean that audiences are fools – what it does mean is that much of the population are not addressed, as we saw in the case of the changing target audience of Warner Bros. and UPN. It has long been established that the act of reading or viewing is an act of interpretation, not signal recognition. But, in fact, the monolithic 'dominant culture' that Budd *et al.* consider to dupe the audience into compulsive consumption is exactly the same monolithic industry which the Jenkins *et al.* insist that audiences are subverting. They share a monolithic view of the cultural field, but only diverge in their assessment of audiences' ability to resist it.

Despite criticising the populist mode of fan scholarship, non-celebratory studies of fandom and subcultures have tended to focus exclusively on the economic pole of the field or else to focus exclusively on the elitist autonomous pole. It was Sarah Thornton's work on club culture which first pointed out both the way that so-called radical subcultures used elitist distinctions, and the way that academics inadequately theorised the 'mainstream' and paid little attention to the hierarchies that exist within subcultures. Thornton's analysis drew on Bourdieu's *Distinctions* (1984) to propose that club cultures are 'taste cultures', and are 'riddled with cultural hierarchies' (1995: 3). These hierarchies are based on drawing distinctions between themselves and the 'mainstream' media. Thornton likens the ideologies of clubbers to those of the elite art world:

> Both criticise the mainstream/masses for being derivative, superficial and *femme* [and] conspicuously admire innovative artists, but show disdain for those who have too high a profile as being charlatans or overrated media-sluts. (1995: 5)

Thornton has identified the way that clubbers share the aesthetic disposition of the autonomous pole of the field of cultural production, despite the difference in the cultural objects they value.

For Thornton, clubbers are accumulating 'subcultural capital' which confers 'status on its owner' and produces 'distinctions' (1995: 11) and she argues that 'distinctions are never just assertions of equal difference; they usually entail some claim to authority and presume the inferiority of others' (1995: 10). This in turn produces hierarchies, and in club culture the top of this hierarchy is populated by the 'alternative', 'hip', 'authentic', male 'insider'. At the bottom of the hierarchy we find the 'mainstream', 'naff', 'commercial', female ('Sharon and Tracy dancing around their handbags') majority (1995: 115). The insight that subculture participants (including fans) make taste distinctions between themselves and others, through the accumulation of 'symbolic capital' resulting in hierarchies within the subculture has been an important challenge to academic celebrations of subcultures. However, as I have argued elsewhere (2001), Thornton also misconstrues Bourdieu's analysis of the dominant pole of culture, by ignoring the struggle between dispositions that make it up. Thornton, like those she is challenging, collapses together the concept of the 'mainstream' and the concept of 'commercial culture'. But these two concepts are different and need to be separated, for the concept of 'commercial culture' is crucial to understanding, as Bourdieu argues, the values of the dominant group at the dominant pole of the field of cultural production. This concept is not simply a fantasy in the subcultural service of 'us' and 'them', it plays a major legitimating role for the dominant pole's designation of cultural worth and refers to concrete practices and positions within the field. Therefore, Thornton misses (as does the resistance-to-mainstream position) the way that Bourdieu defines the cultural field as not made up of a monolithic 'dominant', but of two opposing sets of dominant positions who struggle with each other for power in the field. Those who dominate the dominant end of the field of cultural production would have it that commercial imperatives were accepted as the *raison d'être* of cultural output. This is particularly evident in the increasingly commercial climate in Britain and the US where deregulation and privatisation are the key phrases of the broadcasting policy makers (cf. Freedman 1998; Holt 2003). The fact that there is another (less powerful) elite who dispute these values means that 'dominance' is not monolithic or incontestable, and the idea that cultural production should be for profit does not reign unchallenged. These differing values have influence beyond the differing poles of the bourgeoisie who espouse them, and both sets of values influence fandom.

Thornton's suggestion that values within club culture (or dispositions) are *only* ideologies to legitimise the distinctions being made and the elitist agenda of 'us' and 'them', then, is as one-sided as those who claim that 'popular cultural capital' is never 'discrimination' and always 'democratic participation' (Fiske 1992: 45). It is true that adopting a position of opposition to the commercialism of culture does entail entering a concrete space of positions which are saturated with elitist concepts. Yet, however flawed, this is still a form of limited opposition to the increasing commercialism of cultural life, although it is constrained by its very ideology of autonomy from other fields of power. This is not the resistance of the socially subordinate to something called the 'mainstream'; it is part of the struggle to define cultural worth. But as I have argued, this struggle enables pressure from other fields of power to impact on the cultural field and potentially radicalise the claims for a non-profit culture.

For critics still interested in understanding the processes of opposition within an increasingly commercialised, deregulated cultural field and the relationship between conflict in the cultural field and the field of politics and economics, it is neither adequate to cast all interactions with the products of the culture industries as acts of subversion, nor to view any (sub)cultural attachments to values which oppose the dominant commercial imperatives in the field, *only* as acts of elitist distinction. One approach sees resistance everywhere and can end up celebrating consumer capitalism. The other refuses to recognise resistance where it actually exists. This can be seen in Thornton's disparaging remarks about those 'ravers' who took to the streets to fight the introduction of the Criminal Justice Act in the early 1990s in Britain (1995: 168) – an instance when politics entered the cultural field and radicalised some of the participants. It did not radicalise those of an economic disposition who set up lucrative legal clubs (cf. Osgerby 1998). Instead it radicalised those of autonomous dispositions who began to make links with political radical organisations. In the end Thornton seems to deny even the existence of 'cultural dominations of some ruling class' (1995: 163).

Recently, Mark Jancovich has drawn on Bourdieu and Thornton to provide an excellent examination of the cultural distinctions at work in cult movie fandom. Jancovich demonstrates the way that cult cinema fans (and film academics) deploy discourses which pit cult cinema in 'opposition to 'mainstream, commercial cinema' (2002: 309). He argues that

> this shared opposition to the 'commercial mainstream' is necessary to both camps [academics and fans] because it presents them as standing in clear distinction to a conformist mass of viewers, and allows them to present their own favoured films as defamiliarisations of the 'signifying practices' associated with the mainstream. (2002: 310)

For Jancovich, as for Thornton, the 'image of mass culture as the inauthentic other, and as the consumer of mass culture as the simple conformist dupe' (2002: 312) is a process of engaging in cultural distinction. Jancovich points out that the dispositions through which cult movie fans 'celebrate these films and define their distinction from, and superiority to, the consumers of "mass culture"' are based on economic and social privilege and that 'these dispositions are not natural but are themselves the products of economic investments, investments in books, magazines, cinema-going, etc' (2002: 318).

Jancovich actually follows Bourdieu more closely than Thornton when he suggests that the oppositional taste in cult movie fandom is part of a struggle within the bourgeoisie, rather than against it. For Jancovich, 'it is the very ideology which insists that these markets are free from economic criteria which needs to be criticised' (ibid.). However, I would suggest that it is the ideology and practice of producing culture for profit that first and foremost needs to be challenged, whilst recognising the problems with the existing elitist critique of commercial culture. After all, it is important to remember that it is these profit-oriented values that are our dominant cultural values – not the art-for-art's-sake values. A concentration on the elitist pole of cultural production can skew a view of the relations of power in the field by implying that the autonomous pole dominates. Jancovich argues that both Bourdieu and Nicholas Garnham (1977) have shown that 'it is the very sense of art as something which exists as outside of economic relations that needs to be challenged because the values through which art is legitimated and mass culture is rejected' (ibid.) are linked to unequal distribution of access to society's resources. While Bourdieu does emphasise the process of elitist legitimation (and I have offered a criticism of it above), my reading of Garnham, at least, is different. While Garnham demonstrates that the role of the tradition of Matthew Arnold and L. R. Leavis in cultural analysis propagates privilege, he argues for our recognition of the economic logic of culture *the better to contest it*. The article to which Jancovich is referring demonstrates the increasing, and in Garnham's view, problematic encroachment of the profit motive into larger and larger areas of human endeavour. Garnham recognised early that 'the field of information, of which cultural production in the narrow sense, including mass media and education, are a part, is now one of the economic leading edges of developing multi-national capitalism' (1977: 342). He argued that the debate about 'private or public control of the tertiary sector [was] assuming increasing strategic importance within the cultural sphere' (1977: 344) and one that was worth intervening in. For Garnham, the traditional academic neglect of the economic face of culture would disable its ability to critique the 'the invasion by exchange values of ever widening areas of human activity' (1977: 351) and would lead to ignoring the way that the increasing incorporation of 'culture' 'into the sphere of exchange value would help capitalism solve its current crisis' (1977: 349). Sadly, Garnham's predictions proved correct, and the economic imperative now penetrates even more areas of life than thirty years ago, while the media and information sectors of the economy are now central to capitalism. But this does not mean that politically-engaged academia now, as then, should not ask itself 'whether it wishes to be a party to that cultural infiltration' (1997: 356). Instead, this indicates that it is this economic pole that is winning the struggle for cultural legitimation and thus that it is this pole that must be our primary target, holding onto Garnham's insight that cultural elitism will hamper rather than aid this aim.

In the subfield of fandom, it is crucial to remember that fans are not only influenced by the autonomous pole of cultural production; they are also influenced by the heteronomous pole. Again, fans may be excluded from actual possession of economic capital, but not from the *idea* of economic pursuit as a legitimating principle for cultural production. Those fans who occupy positions in line with the dominant commercial principles tend to reproduce the legitimacy of economic values and accept commercial imperatives for culture and adopt positions in their own fandom in line with this. These fans do not even engage in the limited and compromised opposition to the culture-for-profit values which dominate. Fans who accept the view that cultural production should be an economic activity accept the cultural values of capitalism. Gwenllian Jones suggests that media fans are 'media consumers *par excellence*' (2003: 167) and that the imaginative world building of fandom is 'world-building for profit' (2003: 166). The culture industry produces cult texts and merchandising objects in order to 'cater to and capitalise upon fans' hunger for immersion in the imaginary world of the text' and even imitates the 'text-producing practices of fans' (2003: 167) in order to 'sell fans shinier versions of their own texts, all stamped with an official seal of approval' (2003: 168). Yet Gwenllian Jones' conclusion that 'fans, as the culture industry's most voracious consumers, are complicit in the very processes they are supposedly resisting' (2003: 171), once again views fandom from the perspective of only one set of the conflicting cultural values that make up the cultural field. While Jancovich and Thornton focus their analysis on the autonomous disposition, and say little about the commercial aspects of fandom, Gwenllian Jones focuses hers on the heteronomous one.

However, as I have suggested, the problem with focusing on one or other disposition is the tendency to produce an overly deterministic view of the population's relationship with cultural production. Thus Gwenllian Jones casts fandom *per se* as, 'already co-opted from the moment it comes into being' because 'fandom is an effect of the culture industry' (2003: 173). *Some* fan clubs are co-opted into commercialism, and are an effect of the industry – this is certainly the case for official fan clubs set up or endorsed by a media conglomerate – but not *all* fan practices are 'an effect' of commercialism. To suggest such returns us to the notion of the passive audience who are duped by consumer capitalism. It also ignores the way that a core impulse of a great deal of fandom is to oppose the values of the 'commercial mainstream', from however an elitist point of view. Furthermore, to see *all* fans as *only* engaged in a process of elitist cultural distinction is equally one-sided; it ignores the heteronomous side of fandom and underplays the opposition to culture-for-profit to be found there, despite the tendency towards elitism. It is worth pointing out that fans who oppose commercial values do really oppose them, it is not *just* a game of cultural distinction but it is constrained by the processes of distinction. It is the existence of these differing cultural values in fandom that produce the conflict and struggles to be found there.

The problems of one-sided approaches to the cultural field can be found in scholars recent discussion of the issue of intellectual property rights which has become a focus of much attention because of the way that fandom exists in large part on the Internet (but not exclusively), and because of the ease with which fans can poach official sounds, words and images and rework them. For instance, Jenkins offers a predictably overly radical view of the opposition fans are engaged in. For Jenkins, the 'cultural revolution' is to be fought on the 'bloody battle ground of intellectual property rights'; he wants to 'believe that the net has a transformative potential in culture, society and politics' (1998: n.p.) and sees fans at the front of exploring this. Gwenllian Jones offers a very important and detailed critique of this hyperbolic perspective. She analyses the way that the appeal of the cult text lies in its invitation to an interactive response from viewers and comments that Hollywood studios are beginning to recognise this and incorporate it into their marketing strategies. But she concludes that there is nothing oppositional in fan struggles against 'cease and desist' orders from big Hollywood studios. She considers it 'as much a boardroom negotiation as it is a civil liberties debate' (2003: 174) and one that will work out in fandom's favour because online fandom 'encourages and participates in its [capitalism's] commercial operations' (2003: 172). It is for this reason that she considers 'cease and desist' letters to be ambiguously worded. One example Gwenllian Jones offers is that of a letter from Twentieth Century Fox's lawyers to a webmaster of a *Buffy the Vampire Slayer* fan site. The letter begins by unambiguously instructing the webmaster to 'remove all wallpaper, screensavers, desktop themes, fonts, skins, audio and video clips and the image galleries relating to *Buffy the Vampire Slayer*' (2003: 173). Gwenllian Jones suggests that this blow is, 'softened by a statement of limited tolerance':

> We note that your site contains *Buffy the Vampire Slayer* stationary-frame images on other images of the web site besides the images galleries. We must inform you that the unauthorised display and distribution constitutes a copyright violation. While we are not asking you to remove these at this time, we nonetheless request that you revise your legal notice and disclaimer and prominently display the following on every page of your site exhibiting any *Buffy the Vampire Slayer* images. (Ibid.)

The reader must make up her own mind, but I fail to see this as anything other than a heavy-handed attempt to control the circulation and display of images and to protect Fox's claims to ownership of these images. This is particularly significant, for as we saw in the previous chapter, the *Buffy* team are an especially fan-friendly one, and the fan role in launching the success of the series is acknowledged. This seems to be a case when a studio would like the fandom for one if its shows to be a mere adjunct to its marketing strategy, but the fandom itself has other ideas. Gwenllian Jones is right to critique Jenkins' view that putting up unauthorised images on the Internet amounts to an overthrow of the capitalist machinery, but she is mistaken to imply that total Hollywood control of Internet imaging will have no impact on our cultural freedom. The fact that some media conglomerates tolerate some fan poaching in order to promote their own merchandising does not mean they would not like to have greater control and it does not take away the oppositionality that fans are engaged in on this front – instead it reminds us of its limits. The struggle over the use of

Hollywood images on the net is facilitated by the existence of anti-commercial values in fan culture which in turn is enabled by the struggle between the two dominant values in the cultural sphere that make either pole unstable. It does not constitute a revolutionary challenge to the logic of the cultural field, but it does demonstrate that many fans are not taken in by the commercial ideologies of the cultural industries.

FANDOM IN THE FIELD OF CULTURAL PRODUCTION

So what does all of this mean for fandom? Fan culture is influenced by the two opposing sets of values that dominate the cultural field and fans take positions in line with either set of values. Therefore fandom is shot through with conflicts that emanate from this struggle and it has its own drive towards hierarchisation based either on heteronomous or autonomous cultural values. There are important class differences in fan culture too that are linked to other forms of social discrimination. A white, middle-class female fan who posts her own fan fiction, or who runs a fan website, does not possess the same established cultural capital as the university lecturer or professor who has built a reputation through scholarship in this subfield, nor that of the professional media producer/writer – because in each of these latter cases cultural capital is a part of a professional occupation and financially rewarded. But the former fan is likely to possess cultural capital (via a university education) that her working-class counterpart is excluded from. This fan may well police the borders to her fandom, by weeding out material she considers to be inappropriate, or by inculcating the appropriate values in the uninitiated, deploying her amateur or semi-professional cultural capital. However, even those fans who are excluded from specific symbolic capital are not excluded from the concepts of legitimacy that it is based on. In other words they are not excluded from the *concept* of cultural production for other than economic gain, for this idea has to circulate widely in order to assert dominance. The circulation of anti-commercial ideas about culture contributes to the inability of the profit motive to reign supreme. Those fans who adopt positions influenced by autonomous cultural values tend to reject commercialism and this *does* constitute opposition to the commercial domination in the field. However, the more a fandom is influenced by the autonomous pole, the more likely are the fans who run the fandom to demand the possession of appropriate cultural capital and to see their fan practices in 'pure' terms – fandom-for-fandom's-sake – rather than related to wider culture, or to other fields of power. This tends to limit the scale and scope of opposition, because opposition to commercialism also involves a rejection of the social connections of culture. Where fans bring pre-existing political dispositions or socially-engaged ideas to fan culture, instauration into fandom tends towards focusing ones attention and energies in these area into the limited space of the fandom.

However, opposition to commercialism in cultural production is a prerequisite for any serious challenge to the power of the cultural industries. As a cultural value, it will be a precondition to any future resistance to the dominance of Western media conglomerates, but only if it is detached from the myopic elitism that insists that culture is disconnected from the rest of the world. The process of detaching anti-commercial values from cultural elitism, however, is less likely to come from within the cultural field itself (never mind fandom), as it is to come from broader social movements that will transform the field of culture. The opposition that exists in fandom is genuine opposition, but it is severely limited by the values that support it, or else it is limited to the realm of the self, and thus some fan practices can be part of the way some people have of not accepting 'things as they are'. But mostly, fandom is a way for many people to engage with cultural objects and the character of that engagement will depend on the cultural values held by the participant. The following chapter will demonstrate how these opposing sets of cultural values operate in practice in vampire fan clubs.

VAMPIRE FANDOM IN THE FIELD OF CULTURAL PRODUCTION: A VAMPIRE FAN CLUB CASE STUDY

This chapter will apply Pierre Bourdieu's analysis of the cultural field to discuss vampire fandom as it exists in clubs and societies. This analysis is based on an in-depth case study analysis of the operations and attitudes that surround the Anne Rice Vampire Lestat Fan Club (ARVLFC) in New Orleans, although I will also discuss a number of other fans clubs that I participated in and conducted research upon. I am focusing on the ARVLFC because it highlights many of the processes found in fandom. The accounts offered in this chapter mainly come from women vampire fans surrounding this club as well as numerous discussions with female and male fan club personnel, as well as my own observation of club practices. I visited New Orleans in March 1998 with a friend, Susie Coggles, who helped me interview a number of vampire fans and fan club personnel. I will demonstrate below that there were significant tensions between the fan club and other fans at the time of our visit. I have since understood that these tensions were particularly highlighted at the time because the fan club was in a state of transition and was becoming more formally tied to Rice financially. I have argued in the previous chapter that fandom is influenced by one or other sets of cultural values that dominate the field of cultural production and I will suggest that this can produce a split in fandom, which in the case of this fan club exists between 'official vampire fandom' and 'unofficial vampire fandom'. I will argue that this split is explicable through competing values as outlined in Bourdieu's model. The ARVLFC 'official fandom' is influenced by the economic ideas at the dominant pole (some fan clubs adhere more to the economic principles that emanate from the dominant end of the dominant pole and some adhere to the autonomous ideas of the dominated end of the dominant pole which, rather than 'art-for-art's-sake', may be understood as 'fandom-for-fandom's-sake').

Bourdieu argues that the direction of artistic movements is dependent upon 'the system of possibilities ... that is offered by history and that determines what is possible and impossible at a given moment within a particular field' (1993: 183). I will suggest that this applies also to fan culture where there are specific spaces of possible positions to adopt for those wishing to enter the fandom, and which delimit the practices of the fandom, depending on which of the dominant set of values influence the particular fan organisation. This chapter will show how the ARVLFC enters into and produces a space of pos-

sible positions to do with the particular emergence of the club and its concrete history of position takings. This history leads towards the adoption of
commercial values in the 'official' fan club and I will demonstrate how these
values jar with other vampire fans outside of the 'official' sphere. I will demonstrate the importance of key position-takers for establishing the positions
that other fans encounter as the space of possible positions on their entry into
the fandom. I will demonstrate that there is a conflict in attitudes between
the official fans who police the fandom in various ways and the unofficial fans
whose expectations of vampire fandom were at odds with their encounters
with the fan club, resulting in disillusionment and cancelled memberships. I
will suggest that the space of possible positions open to fans was often one
that many fans were not prepared to adopt and this led fans to retreat from the
fandom and set up smaller networks elsewhere rather than struggle against such
organisations.

This chapter will then examine the role of Anne Rice herself and her
company, Kith and Kin, in the development of official vampire fandom in New
Orleans in relation to the economic values at work in this fan club. The principle of hierarchisation (which Bourdieu suggests is key element of the cultural field) will be shown to be in operation by those jockeying for position in
vampire fandom. I will argue that vampire fandom is not operating outside 'the
mainstream', but is influenced by the ideas and practices of the two antagonistic groups who vie with each other to dominate the values of cultural worth. It
will be proposed that the influence of these conflicting sets of principles can be
found in the differing attitudes that fans have towards fan clubs and organisations, the objects of fandom and each other.

OFFICIAL AND UNOFFICIAL VAMPIRE FANDOM IN NEW ORLEANS: THE MEMNOCH BALL

The examination of fan attitudes towards fandom in New Orleans begins
with a discussion of the Memnoch Ball for a variety of reasons. The ARVLFC,
unlike other fan clubs, has no regular activities. The only event hosted by the
club is the annual 'Gathering of the Coven of ARVLFC'. Usually, the ball is
held in a local night-club called Tipitina's, but in October 1995 Anne Rice took
over the organisation of the Ball and hosted it in St Elizabeth's Orphanage
in the Garden District of New Orleans. The ball's title came from Rice's
fourth *Vampire Chronicle*, *Memnoch the Devil* (1995). The venue, St Elizabeth's
Orphanage, is the setting for significant action in the novel and is owned by
Anne Rice. This ball was a very big event in the calendar of vampire fandom
in the US (and to an extent in Britain, as members of British vampire fan clubs
flew to New Orleans to attend) and it was anticipated with great excitement,
some fans working on their costumes for up to a year. The attitudes of unofficial fans (fans who are not club personnel or aspiring club personnel) demonstrate their expectations of fandom and the frustration of those expectations.
For instance, Melinda comments:

I went to the Memnoch Ball but I was so terribly disappointed I stayed twenty minutes and I left. You've seen how big St Elizabeth's is, but it has the capacity for 4,000 people, there were 7,000 people there that night ... The spirit of the books or the spirit that drives me or rather draws me, was so utterly lacking ... The spirit was gone, there was nothing that I recognised from her books or wanted to be a part of ... it was a lot of people getting drunk and it was very cold ... as I understand it there were 4,000 people who paid for tickets and 3,000 people who were invited guests and they were treated so much better than the people who actually paid and stood in the line – and the victim beer? No! And Anne and all of her 3,000 invited guests up on a pedestal? No! This is my world, she should have paid more attention to the fans ... If you were not one of the elite; they had little passes for the elevator and stuff like that so they could go up and down quickly as opposed to the rest of the unwashed, we had to climb the stairs and things of that nature. Didn't need that at all, no. Caused a lot of resentment. I wasn't the only one to leave early. I was with a tremendous group who went early. I was with a tremendous group who said 'forget this, let's go'. We went, um, this really meant a lot to me, I had a gown commissioned ... working nine months on that costume and leaving after twenty minutes you had to do something, so I went to Bourbon Street and got drunk, boy did I get drunk. I was so depressed. And everyone cancelled their membership immediately.

Melinda's criticism of this event combines a sense autonomous discrimination (the crassness of the victim beer and plastic rats) with a sense of disappointment at the hierarchy in the fandom. Her available position as 'fan' (that is, included, insider) was denied. These sentiments were echoed by all of the 'unofficial' fans that I met in New Orleans in 1998. Both Andrea and Shirin thought the ball was horrible and commented that they will not attend in the future. Andrea states:

It was something I started planning for in July, the problem is that, that one was horrible ... they were the rudest crowd I've ever seen, they were very rude ... usually it has been rather pleasant, but this one was horrible, I don't know if I'll go next year.

These accounts of the Memnoch Ball challenge Henry Jenkins' notion that fandom allows the fan to 'speak from a position of collective identity' (1992: 23), for vampire fandom in New Orleans does not automatically confer a sense of collectivity or a shared identity. The unofficial fans felt badly treated and rather than have a common identity with the fan club, felt as if they were put in a subordinate position in the hierarchy of vampire fandom. Furthermore, when confronted with a fan club which is operating hierarchically, the unofficial fans did not fight, but withdrew, bitterly disappointed, and attempted to re-establish a sense of common purpose and community elsewhere. This tendency in fandom leads to the formation of restricted networks rather than expansive cultural communities. For instance, Melinda, having left the ARVLFC, joined a small Internet e-mail group consisting of a handful of fans.

The unofficial fan attitudes found above are in stark contrast with official fans, many of whom were employed at the ball. For instance, an 'official fan' Diane comments:

> Everything is growing so much, I mean these are just average people who volunteer their time to run this stuff, they're not professional. So, Anne kind of took over for Memnoch and she had it at St Elizabeth's Orphanage which has got 50,000 square feet and she spent several thousand dollars and opened up that house and let everyone come. There was about 4,000 people there and she had dancers and she gave away ... Mardis Gras beads and cups you know, there was entertainment, she gave out wine and beer free. Anne does things on a grand scale, we always laugh, don't just order one for her, order ten ... and she had a local brewery brew this stuff called 'victim beer', you know the beer label, it was just a huge extravaganza.

Diane was the assistant manager of the Garden District Bookshop which has very close links with Anne Rice. For instance, the bookstore was the only outlet for tickets to the Memnoch Ball other than directly though the fan club. Both Diane and the other employee, Max, were employed by Rice's company to work at the ball. The bookstore organises book-signing events for Anne Rice at the book store and occasionally in other venues. The employees from the bookstore go back and forth to Rice's residence with boxes of books to be signed, and to drop deliveries and so on. They also order specialist books for Rice, and will spend considerable time tracking books down to help Rice with her research. Diane comments on this close link:

> I'm the assistant manager of the bookstore and what happens is we work very closely with Anne and she comes up with the ideas for the signing, she decides what she wants to do and where she wants to have it and then we kind of do what she wants to do, that's basically the thing. And so we work with the publisher and with Anne and then however we can set it up to where it's practical, you know we work very closely with her staff too, and we talk almost every day ... we're just kind of always right there and people call from all over – reporters – and we're just involved and it's fun.

Although Diane is an ordinary member of the fan club rather than officer, I have counted her part of the official set up because of her close links with the fan hierarchy due to her role in the bookstore. When I asked her if the ARVLFC was identified with the bookstore she responded 'oh yeah, because we're so close to her and a lot of the times it is the only way people can get in

Anne Rice's Vampire Lestat Fan Club

Newsletter

• • • • • • • • • • March, 1996 • • • • • • • • •

The Memnoch Ball ....

They came, they saw, they partied! The Seventh Annual Gathering of the Coven of Anne Rice's Vampire Lestat Fan Club, otherwise known as The Memnoch Ball, was a stupendous success. Sure, there were problems, there always are. For the most part, a splendid time was had by all. The music, the food, the drink (especially Abita's Ice Cold Victim beer), the building itself - everything was enchanting. Here, presented in your words and photographs, is The Memnoch Ball, held in New Orleans at St. Elizabeth's Orphanage on October 28, 1995.

Ball a few nights ago. It was apparent at every turn (and there were turns aplenty in that massive structure) that you folks performed superbly a monstrous undertaking - it succeeded on every level in my opinion. Thank you so much for a most memorable excursion into the fantastic!   Mike Costello #

Bravo! The Memnoch Ball was well worth the wait. This was the best ever!! Thank you for making it "an affair to remember."
                                    Sal DiStefano #294

It was well worth traveling 1000 plus miles to attend. I am impressed at the great job the club officers do on a volunteer basis. I know it is an awesome task. Hang in there - we love you for it!
                                    Kathy Sanders #3307

Thank you, thank you, thank you! My wife and I had what was probably the best evening of our lives! We love New Orleans, the Quarter, the zoo, Anne and Stan, Lestat, Ex-Voto, the Blacksmith Shop, and all of you!   Valerie & Simon
         Becerra #3517 & 3518

I don't know where to begin with my sincerest thanks for the incredible Memnoch

I loved it! Anne and you guys made the party a fantasy come true. I can't remember the last time I saw such beauty. St. Elizabeth's, the people, the food, the music... it was all perfection. The visit from Kirsten Dunst was more than a surprise (I got her autograph!). The only downfall, if there was one, was that it was not possible to see everything. That place is vast! And the people - how many were there? It makes me very proud to be an admirer of not only a great story teller, but such a sweet, genuine, generous person. Can you imagine opening your home to thousands of strangers?
                                    DeaconBankes #

It's a week later and my head is still spinning. Saturday night was a complete sensory overload! I loved it!
                                    Cheryl CoeyKrummen #4359

The party was fabulous!!! I was simply stunned the whole evening! My congratulations to the fan club for a wonderful night (and to Anne)! I tried to describe it to my friends when I came home and the only word that fit was carnival. Greg and I had a great time. Peabody really made a fan out of Greg. By the end of the night, unfortunately, we had NO

Fig. 13 The Memnoch Ball. Coven gathering of the Anne Rice Vampire Lestat Fan Club held at St Elizabeth's Orphanage in New Orleans USA, October 1995

touch'. Diane was not only supportive of Rice's handling of the ball (in contrast to the 'unofficial fans') she also considers herself to be close to the fan club personnel and to Rice's staff. The differences between the attitudes of the officials and the 'ordinary' vampire fans is further revealed in their attitudes towards each other, as we shall see below.

VAMPIRE FANS TALKING ABOUT EACH OTHER

Bourdieu argues that the space of possible positions in each area of the field of cultural production exists prior to agents taking up those positions and that in adopting positions, agents are also demonstrating their predispositions; that is, revealing their 'habitus'. He argues that there is an 'extraordinary correspondence between the hierarchy of positions' and the 'associated dispositions' (1993: 189). The attitudes demonstrated by official fans towards ordinary fans reveal that part of the process of occupying the position of 'official fan' is adopting the correct, or associated disposition which is achieved by drawing distinctions between one's own practices, attitudes and positions and those of the ordinary fan. Diane, for instance, regales us with numerous stories of the 'ridiculous' behaviour of the fans. She says that the fans 'will take anything, they will take a leaf off a tree, they steal the dog's collars all the time ... they'll ring the buzzer and say, "can I take a leaf off a tree?"' Ordinary fans are characterised as undiscerning in their activities and overly invested in their fandom. Another example is Diana telling a story about handing out colour-coded cards at one of the book-signings, to organise the fans:

> ...and the day after it was over we threw them away and somebody came in and said they were selling these things on the Internet ... and right here where we are sitting, we put the trash outside in boxes and sometimes her boxes come with her name on them, you know on the side – I was coming down here to use the bathroom and there was somebody with an Anne Rice box going through the trash at one of the tables and I said *'is that our trash?'* They even come dressed up to the store, its like they're on a pilgrimage.

A significant proportion of the interview with Diane involved similar anecdotes about fan behaviour. She distinguishes herself continuously from those fans who collect Anne Rice items indiscriminately. She comments that 'they get themselves all whooped up on the Internet ... that's how serious they are, like every single thing you say is being read by so many people and they think about it all the time and so you just have to be careful about what you say'. Despite the fact that Diane is a fan herself, her comments about ordinary fans are strikingly similar to the distinctions that Joli Jensen proposes 'aficionados' make between themselves and fans. He argues that fans are 'believed to be obsessed with their objects, in love with celebrity figures' in contrast to the 'affinity' of the aficionado which is deemed to involve 'rational evaluation, and is displayed in more measured ways' (1992: 20). Diane seems to be drawing just such a distinction. Furthermore, Jensen suggests that it is acceptable to be attached to 'prestige-conferring objects' but not to be attached to 'popular, mass-mediated objects' (ibid). But there are mass-produced items that have the 'prestige' of commercial value if one is of this disposition, and it is these kinds of things that Diana collects. For example she collects pre-publication material and all of Rice's first editions and tries to get Rice to sign them to make them more valuable. She told me that a Rice first edition hardback from Alfred A. Knopf, the publishers, was worth $100–$150 in 1998 and that the first editions from the British publisher, Chatto and Windus, were worth even more. Diane told me that she buys these books as an investment but she does not read them. She reads the cheap paperback copies and keeps the first editions in 'mint condition'. Two of the official fan club officers also spoke of having Anne Rice sign first editions for them, but they ask her to leave their own names out of the inscription as it makes the volumes more valuable still. Diane confirms this:

> Anne will sign, you know, she's very gracious. She will sign anything. Some authors are very particular about what they sign and she'll just sign anything ... I gave her a galley one time and I said 'could you sign this for me' and she said 'did you want it personalised' and I said 'no just sign your name' and she said 'that makes it more valuable doesn't it?' And I said 'yeah, [laughter] just put your name so it'll be more valuable'. And you know we were both laughing about it ... anything we get at the bookstore, that just booksellers get, you know, we always put aside. We always ask the sales reps to send us extra things for us ... they'll send us covers of books before the books are actually out.

Diane and other fan club personnel also told me of taking great pains in deciding which bits of memorabilia from the Coven Gatherings may become valuable and then collecting these items in as large quantities as possible. One fan club official had managed to 'hang onto' four cases of 'Victim Beer' and several plastic rats from the Memnoch Ball. These attitudes toward collecting demonstrate that the official fans are drawing a distinction between themselves and the 'ordinary' fan who will simply 'collect anything'. What is interesting is that these fans are producing distinctions on the basis of economic values rather than autonomous ones and seems to indicate that the process of distinction emanates from both poles but attached to different values. The official fans seem to be adopting values in line with the principles of the dominant heteronomous pole of the field and are using their official position to maximise the commercial worth of their items.

The collecting habits of the unofficial fans seem to be more in-line with the autonomous values of cultural production. The fans do not, in fact, collect 'just anything'. They are very selective about what they collect and see it as a form of preservation. Hannah comments:

> The incredible thing about news-groups is that you put it out there and it stays there for a month and then it disappears ... and the one thing I hate watching is a good piece of work disappear or go to waste ... and I'd seen other people make archives of fan fiction out there and I thought, 'you know we really ought to do this because there is good work that people are putting out, out there'.

Here is a display of a more autonomous disposition which depends on the possession of the cultural capital needed to judge worthy work. The vampire fans connected with this Internet group are not interested in collecting for economic gain, in contrast with the official ARVLFC fans. Both Hannah and Melinda thought that the plastic rats and the 'Victim Beer' collectibles from the Memnoch Ball were 'tacky' and not at all in keeping with the 'romance' of the *Vampire Chronicles*. In general, the unofficial fans were less interested in collecting 'official' memorabilia and more concerned with collecting 'valuable' material produced by other fans, whether this takes the form of 'specs' (speculative stories based on Rice's characters) or hand-made items of clothing, alongside the commercially-produced favourite films on video and books. The items collected were deemed to have aesthetic worth which did not translate into commercial value, but into cultural capital. Hannah even comments that Rice 'has gone completely over to commercialism' while Melinda suggests that 'she would sell Lestat's sperm if she thought she could get away with it'. Melinda and Hannah are adopting the language of fandom-for-fandom's-sake that shuns 'crass' commercialism, just as the artistic avant-garde shun material success as evidence of selling out.

Furthermore, while the official fans have a tendency to pathologise ordinary fans, unofficial fans in New Orleans are quite clear about their dislike for the fan club hierarchy. They feel 'snubbed' and their own positions in fandom are undermined by the success of the ARVLFC as the following comments demonstrate:

Andrea: I joined the fan club really to get tickets to the ball, 'cause I tell you those people are none too friendly.

Shirin: At one point I was organising some meetings, but Anne Rice, you know, has grown so much in popularity here that everybody has got Anne Rice *on the brain* and the Anne Rice fan club got started and they've just like, stolen everybody away. And we attended a meeting or two and we were not impressed. They were just like, very cliquish. They just kept themselves to themselves, you know?

Hannah: the fan club should be by the fans, for the fans, or 'of' the fans, and it's not, it really isn't.

Melinda: I disassociated myself with the group. I'm not currently associated with nor have knowledge of any one that is a member or would recommend it ... this is clannish, this is cliquey on a grand scale, this is exclusivity to the point of paranoia and I honestly wish that it were different ... these are your fans, these are the people you take care of, you know? I'll get off my high horse now [laughs]. But they don't take it at all seriously, they figure, 'we've got the product, we don't have to'. They have Anne, and they're the only ones who do, they've got the coven ball, they've got New Orleans – and well [pause] I don't think they treat the fans well at all.

These comments demonstrate the frustration with the fan club. But it is not only that the fans feel excluded by the club (although that is certainly the case), there is in the comments a sense of being at odds with the commercial values (they've got 'the product') and also that the official fan club impinges on the activities of other fan clubs ('they've stolen everybody'). The unofficial fans experience the ARVLFC in terms of the limits and the impositions that the fan club puts on their own possible positions as vampire fans. The official fan club were clearly winning the game of position-taking in New Orleans in the late 1990s. However, positions in fandom are not secure and the official fan club has now come into difficulties of its own.

OFFICIAL FANS: GATE KEEPERS AT THE BOUNDARIES OF FANDOM

Jenkins argues that fans come up against powerful media organisations on the Internet who use lawyers to 'shut down grass roots activities that cannot be so readily incorporated' (1998: n.p.). He further argues that media producers also 'police what can and cannot be said within the fan community' (ibid.) under the instruction from corporate lawyers. However, he tends to ignore the conflict between fans on the Internet which complicates the terrain of fandom. In New Orleans, the open conflict is between the fan club personnel and other fans, it is not a case of fans versus a powerful media corporation, but fans versus fans. This becomes very clear in Hannah's account of a series of 'flame wars' that broke out on an Internet fan newsgroup. Hannah, who keeps the archives of 'spec' stories for this group, describes how official fan club members came on-line to try to stop the speculative stories. She comments that Random House (Rice's publisher) could 'slap' them with a 'cease and desist order', but that they had not done so to date. Rather, they wrote to congratulate her on her archive (this supports Gwenllian Jones' point that some companies do tolerate fan appropriation, 2003). Instead, according to Hannah, it was official fan club personnel who tried to stop the 'specs' being posted:

There were like three of them directly in a row [flame wars], started all by the same group ... and you know, they actually were Anne fans. You know, they were the Anne Rice Vampire Lestat Fan Club, but their protest was that it was <Alt.books.Anne_Rice>, and we should only be talking about Anne Rice and what the hell were the specs doing on here anyways. So they attacked the spec writers personally and ... they kept bringing up the fact that 'well, you're infringing on her copyright', you know, 'it's unlawful, she could slap you with a lawsuit', you know, 'you're all gonna get sued', and that's why we started printing the disclaimers at the top, 'this is non-profit amateur fiction', you know, and 'no infringement intended'. And you know, that was where we actually started doing research into getting another newsgroup or listserv or something to pull the specs off the newsgroup but to this date it hasn't happened. The specs are still there.

Here is evidence of fans jockeying for position in the sub-field of fandom and are doing so in accordance with the conflicting cultural values in the field. If Hannah's story is correct, the official fans positioned themselves as policing Rice's interests, and we shall see other examples of this below. It was a shock to Hannah who was young and new to vampire fandom and not versed in the position-taking practices of fandom:

> We suddenly got inundated with people who, you know, swore that they knew how to run it and everyone, you know, it's an unmoderated newsgroup. No one can tell you what you can or can't post, and suddenly there are all these people who thought they could and caused this huge fuss, you know, threatened to like slap legal action on the spec writers. You know, just everything else, and just nasty, nasty posts flying everywhere and everybody was really upset and it just stopped being a good place to hang around in. I didn't like it very much.

Hannah's account of the fan club attitude is supported by my own discussions with fan club personnel. I was told a number of times by fan club personnel and bookstore fans that Anne Rice does not like fans writing about her characters and that others have 'no right' to write their own stories about them. But it is not only in the Internet newsgroup that fans feel the fan club bearing down on them. Melinda explains that she had a law suit threat hanging over her head at the time of our interview which was worrying her. She explains:

> Way back when before we grew wise in the ways of lawyers ... a group of friends and I got together and decided that we wanted to give tours about the works of Anne Rice, and we were fan club members and so we came together and started this ... almost three years ago really ... and we weren't in it for profit, you've got to understand ... it started out as 'well, damn it, somebody's gotta organise it, it might as well be us' ... And so we tried and unfortunately we did run foul of business and lawyers, and without being able to say too much specifically about it.
> *Milly: Was it because somebody else – is it because Warner Bros. owns the characters?*
> Melinda: No, and if there was just you and me and a conversation, I could tell you a lot more, but unfortunately I can't name too many names because already there is the threat of law suits hanging over our heads ... I wish I could, but they certainly do give us a new perspective on how certain companies and organisations are run, and we went into it very naïvely, certainly no way to deny that. We just thought that it would be fun. It would be fun, we wanted to meet people who thought like us and

everybody who comes to New Orleans thinking of this as Mecca, this way they have a resource. We would be able to meet with them and show them and explore and share the joy that we found when we thought ... 'I can't believe it. Look, this is where they lived for sixty-five years'! You know, I mean, I've seen so many people do that, and it just gives me a kick every time ... So anyway, unfortunately – I don't know how to put this without getting too specific – I'm now not associated with the fan club as a direct fallout of what happened with the tours.

Melinda's implication is clear. As a member of the fan club, she and others set up non-profit-making tours of the world of Rice's vampires and in some way the fan club and Rice's company were involved in shutting the tours down and (successfully) threatening Melinda with legal action. What I did not know at the time was that while Warner Bros. retained the visual options for the first four *Vampire Chronicles*, the merchandising rights on the characters had recently reverted to Rice. While it is impossible to check the facts of Melinda's account, it is worth pointing out that later that year (1998) Anne Rice's family management company Kith and Kin began their own tours of New Orleans: 'Anne Rice's Garden District Tour' at $30 per ticket, 'Inside the World of Anne Rice' at $98 per ticket and 'Anne Rice's Lost New Orleans' at $48 per ticket (the cheapest ticket price being considerably higher than other local tour companies with a standard price for an hour-long tour at $20 per ticket in 1998).[1] The implication of the unofficial fan accounts is that the ARVLFC act as 'gate keepers' in the kingdom of Rice, and this is supported by my own observation of the club and numerous conversations with fan club personnel.

COMMERCIALISM IN VAMPIRE FAN CULTURE

Vampire fan culture in New Orleans is at odds with the suggestion made by John Fiske that fandom always operates as a 'shadow cultural economy' (1992: 30). His notion that fandom can be seen as 'a sort of "moonlighting" in the cultural rather than economic sphere' (1992: 33) makes little sense in the context of Melinda and Hannah's experiences of the fan club. Fiske argues that fan organisations 'begin to produce equivalents of the formal institutions of official culture' but under 'popular control' (ibid.). It is on the basis of this perspective that Fiske sees fandom 'outside and often against official culture' expropriating and reworking 'certain values and characteristics of that official culture to which it is opposed' (1992: 34). The relationship of the ARVLFC to Rice and her commercial concerns demonstrates the inaccuracy of this perspective. Instead, what is significant about this fan club is the way that it is implicated in the 'official' commercial imperatives of Rice's empire which was expanding at the turn of the century. It is not under popular control, nor is it moonlighting in Rice's empire. Instead, it operates in line with the values at the dominant commercial pole of culture. It has relinquished its autonomy to such values and has benefited by subordinating the needs of fandom to those of Rice.

The ARVLFC is the only Anne Rice fan club officially endorsed by Anne Rice. Some of the founding members are now employed by Rice's company, Kith and Kin. The original president (who had established the club in 1988) had become Rice's personal assistant by 1998. The second president is employed as an assistant to one of Rice's key personnel and works in the offices in Rice's home. The current president (who was not a founding member and the first male president) held the post of vice-president during my visit to New Orleans. His offices are in St Elizabeth's Orphanage. He was also hoping to be taken on as a paid employee. The fan club has a further nine staff, two of whom are related to the president. It seems then, that the name of the company, Kith and Kin, is rather apt. Further, both the fan club and Rice have very close links with the Garden District Book Shop and at least two of the employees are fan club members. Alongside the close collaborations with Rice's book-signing events, this store is also used as a distribution centre for Rice publications as well as other merchandise from the fan club and is a ticket outlet for the fan clubs' annual event.

It is clear from this sketch that the fan club is very closely linked to Rice and depends upon her for resources and also that the 'official fans' are embroiled in the commercial aspects of the vampire fandom in New Orleans. Such a set up limits the space of possible positions that fans may adopt in official vampire fandom. The fan club's close association with Rice confines the potential positions that fans may adopt to ways of being useful to Rice.

THE SPACE OF POSSIBLE POSITIONS IN THE HIERARCHY OF OFFICIAL VAMPIRE FANDOM

The forms of fandom engaged in by the official fans are primarily to do with working *for* their object of fandom, Anne Rice. There is an emphasis on being 'helpful' to Rice and showing that you will put yourself out for her, in order to achieve an 'insider' status which is denied to most fans. In other words, the space of positions is delimited to 'useful functionary' with the promise of a future position as 'well-regarded insider'. The evidence that the former position may transform into the latter is held out to the official fans in the person of the original president of the fan club who is now Rice's personal assistant and who travels the world with her. The official fans are keen to establish both their usefulness to Rice and their level of 'insider-hood'. For example Diane, who, as has been established, positions the ordinary fans as 'they', seems to spend less time helping the fans and more time servicing Anne Rice. This is not limited to her role as the assistant bookshop manager. For instance she takes great delight in telling me of her role at the heart of disseminating information regarding Rice:

> I had a girl call the other day that ... She called from Canada on a pay phone ... saying 'I heard that something, that Anne was sick or that she's not doing well and something might happen to the next book and

I just wanted to make sure that she was OK'. And I said 'I just talked to her, she's fine. The book has already been written. It's gonna come out' ... Anne had an MRI done. She had sinus problems and she just had an MRI so they could check everything out. And so she said 'oh, let's make a T-shirt out of it' ... Course they made thousands – no hundreds. And they were very popular. Well, it was on the Internet, you know, about the T-shirts. Well then this one girl came in ... and she said 'an MRI is so serious and it costs so much money and something's really wrong with Anne and does she have a brain tumour. Does she?' – 'No', I said 'let me' — I said 'wait a minute'. And I went in there and I called Sandra [Anne Rice's personal assistant and fan club ex-president]. I said, 'Sandra – you know all these people on the Internet are really worried', I said, 'what do you want me to say?' I said, 'What's the official word so I can tell these people that it's nothing?' And she said, 'just tell them it was for sinuses'.

It seems to me that through telling me this story, Diane is trying to establish herself in a number of ways; that her status is one of an 'insider' as evidenced by the fact that she spoke to 'Anne' the day of the first phone call, and that she can simply pick up the phone and speak to Anne's personal assistant. (It is not easy getting an interview with this individual. I had to wait to be invited to a special event to have an audience with her and she was guarded and clear that her comments were 'off the record'). Diane also demonstrates her willingness to 'give the official line'; showing that she is part of the hierarchy and that she is trusted as such. I am also guessing that her shift from indicating 'thousands' to 'hundreds' of T-shirts was another example of following the 'official' line – hundreds of T-shirts are more valuable to those who purchased them than thousands. In other words she occupies the 'useful to Anne' position at the same time as trying to position herself as 'well-regarded insider'. It is also interesting that the commercial imperative surfaces in the middle of this account as it seemed to in all of my discussions with club personnel. Many fans would make a sarcastic joke about a celebrity selling T-shirts printed with said celebrity's MRI scan. For example, members of the London Vampire Group (LVG) travelled to New Orleans in October 1997 to go to the ball. One fan wrote about the trip for the LVG's journal *The Chronicles*:

Thus we entered (deep breath) 'The Ninth Annual Gathering of the Coven of Anne Rice's Vampire Lestat Fan Club'. Ms Rice, never being one to miss out on the merchandise angle, there were a selection of T-shirt designs and signed posters to mark the event.

This comment begins to indicate the LVG's own sets of positions are in line with 'autonomous' cultural principles.

There seems to be little acknowledgement in the versions of fandom-as-resistance that popular writers like Anne Rice (and more recently Joss Whedon) are both the producers of fans' preferred cultural products and objects of fandom themselves. Diane completely accepts Rice's commercialism because the space of positions in this official fandom necessitates accord with Rice's values. Throughout the interview Diane is keen to tell me stories about her interactions with Rice, both as helper and as friend. For instance she tells me how much time she spends tracking down books for 'Anne':

> ...like for the *Servant of the Bones* she just rings me and says, 'get me everything there is on this or that' ... and I can spend eight hours on the phone to like, Hasidic booksellers in New York finding out what there is ... So I know, you know, I know what she ordered. I know what I found for her ... She called one day and she said 'get me something on banking in Vienna'. Or she'll say 'get me picture books of opera houses'...

From the outset, this fan is establishing herself in a position of close association with Anne. Later she says:

> ...and now that I'm working where I am now, she's more part of my life, you know, 'cause I'm right here and we talk to them almost every day.

Employment at the bookstore has given Diane the opportunity to strengthen her position in the fandom. Her attitude towards her own position and other fans is in considerable contrast to 'Dot' the bookstore employee discussed in Janice Radway's (1984) study of American female romance readers. Dot spent substantial amounts of time writing reviews for the other women readers and giving them advice about stories that would match their requirements. This 'official' fan, on the other hand, sees her role as helping 'Anne' rather than the 'unofficial' fans.

On my second visit to the bookstore, there was an arrangement for me to meet the ARVLFC vice-president (now the president), who in the course of our conversation demonstrated similar attitudes. Without prompting, he told me about his relationship to 'Anne', 'I don't get in her face you know? When she needs me I'm there, but I don't *bother* her.' The implication is that these fans understand the rules of their fandom as quite different to the rules for 'ordinary' fans and these are expressed in the adoption of an appropriate position. The reward for adopting such positions is the achievement of 'insider status' and an actual position in the kingdom of Rice.

An important aspect of position-taking in vampire fandom involves knowing how to behave appropriately in relation to the space of positions. As Bourdieu argues, the space of position-taking is inseparable from the space of positions which is defined by the possession of the appropriate capital and 'by occupation of a determinate position in the structure of distribution of this specific capital' (1993: 30). In dominant circles, that specific capital may be the appropriate knowledge of the sub-field and its history as well as the ability to designate the canon, or the clout that comes with economic capital. In the sub-field of official vampire fandom, capital is still defined as such, in the case of positioning oneself as an 'insider' though, it is the ability to internalise the correct behaviour, to adopt the appropriate disposition. That this 'capital' is not evenly distributed was demonstrated to Susie and I on one of our visits to the bookstore. We witnessed the fan club vice-president teasing Max, one of the part-time bookstore employees (and fellow fan club member) in a cruel manner. The comments revolved around the way this fan too openly demonstrated his awe of Anne Rice. He could always be seen 'hovering in the background' of photos of Rice. He spent too much time acting like a 'love-sick puppy'. Max responded by going bright red in the face as the other fan club members present had a good laugh at his expense. When Max discovered a few days later that Rice's personal assistant had offered Susie and I a tour of St Elizabeth's Orphanage he commented that 'some people would crawl butt-naked over broken glass' for such an opportunity. When Susie suggested (in earshot of the vice-president) that he come with us, he looked so eager that the vice-president relented and said 'okay, why not'. Later, as Susie and I were leaving the bookstore, Anne Rice and her entourage were spotted by Max walking up the steps of the small shopping mall which houses the bookstore. Like a shot, he ran to open the door for Rice and genuflected as she entered. This 'trainee' official fan had obviously not yet internalised the appropriate protocol of an 'insider' and 'functionary' and his apprenticeship seemed to chiefly involve being ridiculed when his behaviour was deemed inappropriate. He was still behaving too much like an 'ordinary' fan and those who possessed the appropriate disposition soon let him know his place.

Max eventually does seem to learn the rules of the position of 'official fan'. In a late 1998 edition of the ARVLFC newsletter he is introduced to us by the very fan club president (and newsletter editor) who had teased him so mercilessly the previous April, as a new regular columnist for the newsletter.[2] This column consists of advice about collecting the valuable editions of Anne Rice's works and is entitled 'Interview With the Collector'. The column finishes with a section called 'What are they worth?' – listing each of the values of Rice first editions and ends with the statement 'Information gathered from the Garden District Bookshop. Most first editions are in stock.' This is followed by the store's telephone number. This new column not only underlines once again the close links between the bookstore and the fan club, but also demonstrates that Max has adopted an appropriate (heteronomous) disposition and is on the road to achieving the desired 'insider status'.

These official fans' conception of their practice as working *for* the object of their fandom in order to establish themselves as 'insiders' is significantly at odds with Jenkins' characterisation of fandom as a 'democratic' space for those who share a subordinate position in the cultural hierarchy; nor does it fit with the notion that fans see themselves as part of a more expansive and inclusive cultural community. Indeed the map of vampire fandom in New Orleans is a hierarchical terrain in which official fans jockey for position within a hierarchy which they embrace rather than subvert. This poses serious questions about Jenkins' contention that 'fandom's very existence represents a critique of conventional forms of consumer culture' (1992: 283). Rather than being at odds with a powerful producer (as Jenkins suggests is often the case), in this case the 'powerful producer' is both object of fandom and source of income.

Jenkins claims that active media fandom has a tendency to have a distant relationship to textual producers. He argues that this is due to the predominantly female nature of media fandom where women 'discovered that the close ties between male fans and male writers created a barrier to female fans' (1992: 48). Yet in the case of vampire fandom in New Orleans it is four female fans who establish a close relationship with Rice and set up the ARVLFC, thus establishing 'official' vampire fandom in New Orleans, and to an extent, the space of possible positions which subsequent fans must adapt themselves to. Jenkins' argument that there is a regressive 'traditionally male-dominated literary fan' as opposed to a progressive 'fan culture more open to women' (ibid.) does not fit the vampire fan culture in New Orleans. In this primarily female fandom, the split between fans here cannot be discovered along the lines of gender, but between official positions (occupied by women and men) which offer access to Rice and unofficial ones that do not. This is not to dispute the view that some fandoms are male-dominated and that these fandoms can be exclusive of women. However, female vampire fans in New Orleans are not sharing common problems and common interests within vampire fandom, nor are they empowering themselves through the expression of a collective identity with other fans in fan culture.

The fan club has a material interest in continuing its relations with Rice and thus finds it useful to police the boundaries of that fandom, both in terms of reiteration of Rice's intellectual property rights over her characters, and in terms of distinguishing between 'endorsed' activities and those that are not. This not only further demonstrates their usefulness to Rice, but also ensures the continued dominant position of the fan club. The newsletter of the fan club reminds fans in July 1996:

> As stated many times before, there are no other official Anne Rice fan clubs, nor are their any official branches of the ARVLFC. Anyone claiming to be part of such an organisation other than this New Orleans-based club is fully unauthorised and is not recognised by Anne Rice, her publishers, or Anne Rice's Vampire Lestat Fan Club.

The implication of this 'warning' is that the ARVLFC is not only the only 'official' fan club, but also the only 'authentic' club because of its access to Rice and its recognition by her publishers. The fan club makes great use of their official links with Rice and her organisation in terms of the prestige and 'authenticity' of the club's position in the field of vampire fandom. Earlier that year (March 1996) the newsletter carried the following warning in its pages:

Beware! There are two organisations that are claiming to have endorsements or recommendations from the Anne Rice Vampire Lestat Fan Club. They are Walking Tours here in New Orleans and Penny Lane Productions Inc.'s Darkside Weekends. We are not saying their product is bad. The point is we were never invited to participate in these events. We cannot recommend them to you if we haven't experienced them ourselves.

It is impossible to establish the 'truth' about these claims and it is possible that 'Walking Tours' might be referring to Melinda and her friends. What is of interest is that the fan club finds that it is able to make these statements and necessary to do so, in order to maintain its position and to keep poachers out of the grounds of Rice's fandom. The fan club newsletter claims the authority to 'recommend' or not on the basis of its insider status. On the same page of the newsletter was an advert for a video produced and sold by the vice-president:

The Memnoch Ball ON VIDEO! The official video of the Memnoch Ball has arrived. Do not be fooled by imitations...

Below this advert, the vice-president endorses a new book *Haunted City: An Unauthorized Guide to the Magical, Magnificent New Orleans of Anne Rice*. These are symptomatic of the fan club's attempt to patrol the (commercial) borders of vampire fandom in New Orleans in relation to Rice and to promote and protect their own merchandise and position by way of official association with Rice. This kind of 'gate keeping' is combined with vocally reproducing certain attitudes held by Rice herself regarding the activities of fans. At the time, Warner Bros. owned the movie rights for many of Rice's vampire characters and she was by her own admission (and still is) protective about her intellectual property rights. On her own home page Rice comments:

Remember guys, I love your feedback on everybody from Azriel to Louis and Armand, but when it comes to ideas about plots and things of that nature, those are things you should really use to create your own wonderful literary world. (1996: n.p.)

These sentiments are defended by the official fans in New Orleans who disparage the fan fiction and comment that the characters are 'Anne's creations' and should remain so. One can only assume that the fan club is unaware of how central fan fiction is to fandom in the US or that they are unprepared to assimilate it into the fandom of Rice, due to the conflicting interests of Rice and their connection to her. For it is also the proximity of Rice to this fandom that delimits the space of possible positions in the fan club to those in line with her interests. The following section will discuss Rice's own position-taking in this sub-field of fandom.

ANNE RICE IN THE SUB-FIELD OF VAMPIRE FANDOM

Ken Gelder draws on Bourdieu's concept of 'positions' and 'position-takings' to argue that Rice herself adopts more than one position in the cultural field. In particular, he suggests that Anne Rice attempted to occupy more than one position in the field of cultural production during the making of *Interview With the Vampire* (Geffen Pictures/Warner Bros., 1994). He suggests that she refused her place in the relatively 'restricted' field of the 'author' by making public statements about the casting of the film. For example, in an interview in the *Los Angeles Times* she voices her disapproval of Tom Cruise in the role of the Vampire Lestat, 'Cruise is no more my vampire Lestat than Edward G. Robinson is Rhett Butler' (quoted in Gelder 1996: 30). Later, she also takes out a full page advert in *Vanity Fair* to repeat these claims. Rice refuses to be simply the 'author' of the book which is to become a film. She attempts to place herself in the field of large-scale movie production by these public pronouncements. She also insists that the screenplay is attributed to her even though it was written by the film's director, Neil Jordan. Thus Rice is attempting to occupy more than one 'available position' in relation to the making of the film.

However, it was not only during the making of *Interview With the Vampire* that Rice attempted to occupy more than one available position. Rice occupies the multiple positions of writer, cultural critic, star personality, 'accessible' object of fandom, property developer, famous recluse and head of a dynasty. But crucial in terms of the fans' confusion about their 'included' status as fans, is Rice's simultaneous self-positioning as 'top-ranking fan' and 'object' of fandom. There is a strict hierarchy in the official vampire fan culture in New Orleans and Rice is at the apex of it both in terms of occupying the position of the object of fandom and of the 'top fan'.

Rice positions herself as *object* of fandom in a number of ways; she has a fan hotline with a personal message from her to the fans which changes every few days and fans can leave messages for her on this number; she attends book-signings at various locations; the publication of *Commotion Strange* which is a newsletter and a website where she writes directly to her fans which has an intimate and accessible tone. These are conventional avenues by which fans may gain access to the object of their fandom. However, Rice also positions herself as a fan. Most strikingly she adopts the position as the vampire Lestat's best and most devoted fan. She refers to him in *Commotion Strange* as him 'my demon lover', and at the 1995 book-signing she dressed in gothic wedding gear as Lestat's bride. Furthermore, in *Commotion Strange* she also adopts the tone of a 'fan'. In the edition after the film was released in the US in 1994, she discusses the film *Interview With the Vampire* as a fan would (preserving her status as top of the fan hierarchy by referring to her insider knowledge of Lestat). She starts, 'So here goes, point by point'. This is followed by discussion of the 'sets' and 'atmosphere'. She then goes on to discuss the actors with statements like:

Favorite Brad Pitt moments for me: Brad's soft voice saying the single syllable 'No' when Lestat prepares to give the Dark Gift to Claudia; Brad's last real scene with Claudia, their discussion on the balcony outside the hotel room – another contribution from Jordan which was never in my original script.

The informality of tone and address suggests that Rice is a fan like anyone else. But Rice is both fan and author in this traversing of two positions within the field, and she reminds us of her authorship. This movement is continuous in *Commotion Strange*; Rice clearly will not 'play the game' of 'position taking', and while at one level she is thumbing her nose at the media establishment, which is quite good fun, at another level she is making it impossible for the fans to find an 'available position' for themselves without playing her own micro-game of hierarchies which exist in the sub-field of fandom more generally.

Rice is also a millionaire businesswoman with her own company Kith and Kin whose personnel is literally populated by 'kith and kin'. Rice seems to have established a kind of kingdom-cum-theme-park in New Orleans by buying up a variety of properties in the Garden District which are all settings for her novels.[3] The only people who are allowed access to these properties are people who hold official positions in the Rice kingdom, whether they be family, employees, fan club personnel or friends.

Rice has also taken up an (unofficial) position in the political domain, taking out ads encouraging votes for the Democratic Party and an 'open' letter to the Clintons. She has taken an (unofficial) position in the city's cultural politics again by taking out adverts in the *Times Picayune* condemning the architectural design of a new restaurant in the Garden District,[4] and taking up a position within the field of culture, this time as critic. While Rice is very vocal in the public domain, she also positions herself contradictorily as a 'recluse', by making it known through her newsletter and the ARVLFC fanzine that she refuses to 'do' interviews for fear of misquotation.

Rice's simultaneous adoption of a variety of 'available positions' has an important impact on vampire fandom in New Orleans. It has produced a distinction between 'official' fandom which is intimately associated with Anne Rice and unofficial fandom, which is not. The official fans have adopted 'available positions' as functionaries and ground keepers within the Kith and Kin hierarchy, and the rules which govern this position in the hierarchy are 'usefulness' to Rice in 'official' fan capacities. Unlike the 'inclusive' fan culture described by Jenkins, the unofficial fans I talked to found the culture exclusive, in other words, there was no available position for them to occupy as fans in terms of fandom as they understood it through their own more autonomous dispositions. Although I conducted the original research about this fan club in 1998, it has continued to be beset with tensions. Indeed, it appears as though the 2003 'Coven Ball' may have been the last for this fan club. One member has recently claimed on her own web page, 'they really aren't officially together or accepting members anymore'. If this is true, it may partly be due to the prominence of

Buffy fandom in vampire fan culture (but other Anne Rice fans sites still seem to be operating), but it is also possible that the tensions in the fan club hierarchy have imploded. In a review of Jenkins' study, Martin Barker comments that Jenkins' approach gives a sense of 'a world of democratic collectivism, busily creating cultures, freely and against the grain of oppressive cultures' and he asks, 'yet how does fan culture police its own boundaries?' (1993: 673). The border controls operating in this fandom are not the exception that proves the rule,⁵ but is part of a wider struggle in fan culture to establish, through the taking of positions, the legitimate interests and concerns of the fan. Bourdieu argues that the 'opposition between the "commercial" and the "non-commercial" reappears everywhere' (1993: 82), and as we have seen, it takes place in vampire fan culture in the US as seen in the antagonisms between official fans and unofficial fans in vampire fan culture in New Orleans.

DIFFERENT FAN CLUBS, DIFFERENT TENSIONS, SAME STRUGGLE FOR POSITIONS

The opposition between commercial values and the values of cultural distinction can be found across vampire fandom, not only in the ARVLFC. In Britain for example, tensions between members of the British Vampyre Society resulted in a number of members' expulsion from the group and the setting up of a rival group, the London Vampire Group. Accounts from fans seem to indicate that the conflict centred on who had the right to legitimately determine the practices of this fandom. One fan, Dee, commented that during the time of the 'troubles' in the British Vampyre Society, the president of the Society contacted the membership:

> She wrote everybody a really nice letter to tell everybody what was going on *without* telling us what was going on. So I think she's feeling persecuted and there's been – some people broke off from her group and tried to form their own group, the London Vampire Group, and I think she thinks it's these people. I don't know who they are anyway, I'm not able to go to meetings ... She sends out lists of things that are going on, then supposedly they've taken computer files or an address book or something and they've been sending out these things, copies of them, but not exact, they've got all the wrong dates on and stuff like that and people weren't turning up for her meetings, you know. Things like that ... I mean, this is (the president's) side. And then she's never accused them right out, she insinuated that it may possibly have been them who burgled her house one night when they all knew she was out. And somebody else stole her motorbike, and maybe they could have put somebody up to it. But she keeps saying 'it's not fair, I live on my own, why are people doing this to me', oh you know.

Another fan, Karen, explains the 'troubles' from a different perspective:

Milly: So the two groups, do they not get on then?

Karen: No! There was a big court case and everything. Apparently – oh yes, one of the founder members of the Vampire Society writes slander-ous information and sent it out to all members without forewarning the people she was talking about, which would have led to a civil court case which I think has now been dropped. Everything got totally out of hand. All she had to do was write an apology to each of the persons involved and a written retraction in the magazine and that would have got her out of the wrong which, she was totally in the wrong because you don't slander someone. That's defamation of character.

Milly: What was she saying?

Karen: Oh, that they had used funds for their own personal purposes and stuff like that which is totally inaccurate. It is basically that she founded the group and it was her baby. She was in total control and she snapped her fingers and they did as she wanted them to do. But they organised all the events, they collected all the money, they got all the air tickets and the boarding passes and everything sorted out and then she turned on them and you don't do that to people you're working with.

Whether one is inclined to accept Dee's account or Karen's, the crux of the matter is this: who occupies dominant positions in this strata of the field of culture?; who organises events, decides what kinds of events and activities run?; who is legitimate or not? Bourdieu suggests that the autonomous end of the field is where confrontations are 'more continuous' because the terrain is more uncertain. He writes: 'Offering positions that are relatively uninstitutionalised, never legally guaranteed, therefore open to symbolic challenge ... it is the arena *par excellence* of struggles over job definition' (1993: 62). We can see from these accounts from vampire fans that this struggle in fandom often includes tumul-tuous relations between different fractions, split-offs and groups.

The existence of opposing commercial and non-commercial values in fandom can also bee seen recently in the struggles to keep the *Buffy* spin-off show, *Angel*, on the air. For example, SupportAngel.org urges its supports to

> contact the WB network; show love to the people who make *Angel* happen; demonstrate your support to Twentieth Century Fox – pur-chase DVD sets; contact the show's sponsors.

This strategy is based on the commercial notion of consumer power, which sees itself in support of commercial media organisations such as Fox, and com-mercial sponsors. Leave aside for the moment that it is a woefully misplaced strategy due to the fact that Fox will make considerable sums of money from merchandising (including DVDs) whether or not *Angel* is aired; the strategy is in marked contrast to SavingAngel.org, who urged it supporters to join a rally in March 2004 and send postcards to weekly targets, usually to sympathetic television critics. The message the organisations suggested for the postcards read 'Fight for Quality TV: Save Angel'. Here, the campaign to save Angel is run in line with autonomous cultural values, both in terms of its assumed allies (the critical establishment) and in terms of its deployment of the idea of 'quality television'.

Many scholarly accounts of fandom ignore the conflicts and struggles in fandom that this chapter has addressed in relation to vampire fandom; Andrea Macdonald's 1998 analysis of *Quantum Leap* fans is a notable exception, as is Lyn Thomas's complex analysis of the 'functioning of social hierarchies of distinction in actual social interactions' (2002: 20) amongst fans of *Inspector Morse* and *The Archers*. Vampire fans are not unusually quarrelsome people and the conflicts outlined in this chapter are a prevalent feature of all media fandoms. I have attempted to make sense of strife on the terrain of fandom by turning to Bourdieu's model of the cultural field in which the conflict between the opposing principles of cultural worth that dominate the field provide the dynamic of the field. I have suggested that the values of the dominant principles of heteronomy (bourgeois commercialism) and less influential but still dominant autonomous values ('pure taste') influence the sub-field of fandom and those take positions there, and I have contested the view that fandom is automatically a resistant and oppositional cultural formation.

However, although this chapter has demonstrated that fandom as a cultural formation does not necessarily subvert dominant cultural values of legitimacy, I will also argue in the following chapters that fans are not simply the functionaries of the commercial cultural industries, as the widespread influence of the autonomous disposition demonstrates. Further, the following chapter will demonstrate that fan opposition to dominant values is not *only* a process of position-taking and distinction. Although such activity often falls into this structure, what motivates one to take an oppositional pose stems often from the experience of other social constraints and incidences. A number of critics have questioned the rigidity of Bourdieu's schema in this respect. For instance, Mandy Mander, in defence of the intellectual, argues that 'Bourdieu's metaphorical preferences deny the moral dimension of human pursuits and refuse to recognise the ludic and expressive quality of human experience' (1987: 445). While I do not share her defence of academia, her broader point about human motivation offers a useful critique of Bourdieu's insistence that all human activity can, as Lyn Thomas puts it, 'be reduced to struggles for ascendancy (2002: 17). Indeed, the following chapter will argue that the sartorial practices of female vampire fans are understood by the fans themselves as a form of rebellion and that this cannot simply be put down to subcultural rhetoric or elitist practices of distinction, but a part of a rejection of conventional femininity. Thomas also argues that the 'class-based taste cultures identified by Bourdieu exist, but that they are fissured rather than monolithic systems' (2002: 175). This is a point I support, for it is problematic to adopt an entirely uncritical stance in relation to Bourdieu's analysis of the cultural field. Terry Lovell also comments that there is in Bourdieu's analysis 'a strong sense of political paralysis' (2000: 17). As the previous chapter argued, it seems that Bourdieu's focus on the elitist aspects of avant-garde movements is made at the expense of underplaying the significant destabilisation which results from the struggle in the field of cultural production that Bourdieu himself identified, and that he ignores the way that some movements have posed challenges to conventional ways of seeing. The following chapters will demonstrate that women vampire fans are not paralysed by the cultural designations that surround them, and while they cannot step outside of the cultural field, neither are they fixed into place by it. While vampire fans are implicated in the system of position-taking, they are also involved in expressions of the self bound up with imagining future possibilities.

CHAPTER 7

DONNING FANGS: GENDER, THE VAMPIRE AND
DRESSING THE SELF

This chapter will examine female vampire fans' accounts of the self in terms
of their *sartorial practices* and the inspiration they draw from the realm of the
vampire in their sartorial schemes. Dressing the part or 'costuming' is a widespread practice in vampire fandom in Britain and the US, particularly among
women, just as 'costuming' in fandom more generally is. Yet this is an aspect
of fandom that is associated with the frivolous and the feminine. It is also an
area of fandom that receives little scholarly attention. One exception is Jackie
Stacey's (1994) analysis of female fans of Hollywood stars. Stacey examines the
sartorial inspiration that women take from their favourite stars and the way
this impacts on their sense of self. This chapter will be drawing on Stacey's
analysis of the paradox and experiences of femininity in the production of the
dressed female self. However, many academic accounts of fandom concentrate
on fan fiction and slash fiction, and I suggest that this may be to do with the
way that such activities share ground with academic practices and dispositions.
But also, Camille Bacon-Smith has given an account of science fiction fandom
which demonstrates that this fandom too does not consider 'costuming' to be
one if its legitimate activities (2000: 18). She comments that one particularly
chaotic convention in 1987 resulted in the organisers 'dramatically cutting back
on the activities it would support at the conventions' (2000: 19); mostly those
activities which were attractive to young undisciplined members. The organisers see the convention as one 'for readers' and at future conventions 'costuming
was discouraged, and the convention no longer supported activities like gaming
and electronic media' (ibid.). It is interesting that costuming is associated with
the new media and that both are seen as providing the grounds for the trouble,
and again this points to the different dispositions among fans and the struggles
that erupt as a result. In vampire fandom, costuming is generally (although not
exclusively) an activity engaged in by women,[1] and often by women who have
been excluded from the educational capital necessary to engage in the more
'acceptable' pursuit of writing.

However, I will suggest that costuming or dressing the part is not an
activity that can be fully understood through Bourdieu's schema of position-taking that structures the cultural field, particularly because of the fixed
manner in which he discusses the gendered aspect of position-taking, in which
he suggests that the impositions of gender are insurmountable and embod-

ied. In *Masculine Domination* (2001) Bourdieu argues that women are objects of exchange between men with women operating either as carriers of male systems of family honour or (among the Western middle-class and bourgeoisie) as carriers of symbolic capital through their domestic role. Bourdieu's analysis seems unable to account for the partial gains made by the women's movement and the changes this has brought about in a woman's sense of her self and her role. As Terry Lovell argues: 'Even if it is conceded that "women universally have the social status of objects" it must remain questionable whether women universally or exclusively *position* themselves as objects, and indeed whether it is possible to do so unequivocally' (2000: 21). Women do not necessarily accept their role nor do they inevitably assume a feminine identity, and female fan accounts below will demonstrate this. However, Lyn Thomas points out that it is not only Bourdieu who struggles 'between the sense of the power of social structures which their analysis must inevitably convey and a political commitment to the importance of collective and individual political agency' (2000: 22) and suggests that feminism displays similar theoretical tensions. Indeed, it seems that grappling with the question of agency versus structure has been a central concern of politically engaged scholars for many years and is still unresolved. But Bourdieu's account of gender ignores the way that 'femininity is always deeply problematic, a status that is never fully and wholeheartedly embraced' (Lovell 2000: 17). For this reason I will be drawing on a number of feminist scholars of dress and fashion (Wilson 1985; Hollander 1993; Stacey 1994; Macdonald 1995; Tseëlon 1995; Entwistle 2000) who have pointed out the contradictory role of dress in gender and class relations, and by drawing on their work, I hope to add a small contribution to this discussion through an examination of contradictions in female fans' sartorial practices.

I will argue that women vampire fans' engagement with the vampire is connected to their experiences in 'culture', and that a sartorial engagement with this figure provides fans with means of handling paradoxes of the 'self'. I will specifically address the gendered dimension of the experience of 'self' to argue that the sartorial choices of the women vampire fans are not only to do with their experience in 'culture', but that these are specific responses to the ambivalent category of 'femininity'. Part of the pleasure of appropriating vampiric symbols is in producing a sense of self (as outsider) not tied to a feminine ideal which the fans find impossible to achieve. The women fans' self-presentation as vampiric, it will be argued, is a specific response to the broader context of gender that all women face, but experience and deal with differently.

This chapter will begin with a discussion of the category of femininity and the potential experiences that may be generated by its paradoxical status. It will then examine how the women vampire fans articulate their experience of femininity and their motivations for adopting vampiric sartorial schemes. The relationship between these will be examined through three interrelated themes: the first is the women's experience of 'not fitting in' to ideas about feminine norms. Connected to this is the appropriation of vampiric imagery in their dress as a way of producing identities that 'stand out' as different; a connection which suggests that the process of 'standing out' exceeds the system of position-taking as outlined by Bourdieu because of the way that it is motivated initially, not by the quest for distinction, but by the impossible contradictions faced by the female self. Thirdly the role of a particular gothic use of black apparel (drawing on the colour's anti-fashion or oppositional symbolism) in the construction of these identities will be examined. Subcultural analyses of sartorial behaviour have often theorised it as a mode of rebellion (Hebdidge 1979). However as Angela McRobbie (1976) and Bill Osgerby (1998) have pointed out, subcultural theory has tended to present sartorial revolt as a masculine phenomenon. In this chapter I will examine its feminine manifestation among vampire fans.

FEMININITY AS AMBIVALENCE: EXPERIENCING A PARADOX

Feminist critics from such diverse fields as the sociology of the body (Tseëlon 1995) and film theory and spectatorship (Stacey 1994) argue that women's experiences of themselves in the West are framed by the paradoxical category of femininity. For both Tseëlon and Stacey, the paradox of femininity is focused on the female body, producing impossible and contradictory 'norms' which women face as cultural expectations. As Jackie Stacey puts it, feminine ideals are 'by definition, never realisable, since they fundamentally contradict each other (such as the constructions of motherhood and sexual desirability)' (1994: 65). The image of 'woman' is at once equivocal and unattainable. Stacey argues that 'femininity is conventionally reproduced within dominant culture through the circulation of idealised images, constructed as desirable and yet unattainable' (1994: 116). She comments that 'the female body, in particular, can always be guaranteed to be at fault' (1994: 208).

For Efrat Tseëlon, woman is an 'impossible creature who is given a space and no space at all, who is offered a position while being denied that position, who embodies a thing and its opposite at the same time' (1995: 2). Furthermore, Tseëlon argues that this ambivalence is centred on the notion that femininity is constructed as artifice and then derided for lacking authenticity. This leads to a further paradox that woman signifies beauty, but that women do not embody beauty. As Tseëlon argues, 'woman is placed in a no-win situation. She is expected to embody a "timeless" cultural phantasy [sic], but is not naturally more attractive than a man. Her special beauty is at best a temporary state, and it takes hard work and concerted effort to maintain' (1995: 79).

Stacey, Tseëlon and Joanne Entwistle analyse the different ways that women handle this contradiction. Tseëlon argues that as a result of this ambivalence, 'personal appearance' comes to frame women's social positions and influences 'the way she comes to think of herself' (1995: 3). She suggests that women are highly conscious of their 'visible self' (1995: 54) when dressing. Women, argues Tseëlon, make subtle distinctions not only about the situation, but also about the audience and their own state of mind. They distinguish between 'significant' audiences, whose opinions 'matter' and those that do not; between 'comfortable' and 'uncomfortable' situations taking greater effort, care and conscious-ness of what they wear in the latter. In other words, women worry about being dressed inappropriately because they are made conscious of their appearance. Tseëlon argues therefore, that feeling 'visible, exposed, observed or on show appear to be internalised into the self-conception' (ibid.)

Entwistle also argues that dressing ones' body is a social activity that can never be divorced from both micro 'individual experiences of dress' and macro social processes (2000: 4). She suggests that the 'consciousness of bodily appearance is gendered' and that 'women more than men view their bodies as objects "to be looked at"' (2000: 31). Entwistle suggests that 'women may have to think more carefully about how they appear in public than men' and she offers an example of professional women who will take off their jacket at work only in the privacy of their own office in order to 'avoid sexual glances from men' (2000: 34). Drawing on Goffman's work, Entwistle emphasises the relationship between situation, dress and moral order. She argues, like Tseëlon, that when we are dressed 'inappropriately, we feel vulnerable and embarrassed' (2000: 35). However, this is not simply a 'personal *faux pas*, but the shame of failing to meet the standards required of one by the moral order of the social space (ibid.). For Entwistle too, then, women 'internalise particular rules or norms of dress' (2000: 34).

Stacey's study focuses on women and their female Hollywood idols to analyse how women negotiate a match and mismatch between self and ideal self through a favourite star image. She argues that 'since desirable ideals are always changing with new fashion trends, and feminine ideals are actually never fully realisable, the one is always contradicted by the other' (1994: 208). Stacey also suggests that feminine insecurities about 'the attainment of bodily per-fection are a reasonably sure bet for the endless reproduction of commodities for feminine self-improvement' (ibid.). She argues that female fans of female Hollywood stars 'attempt to close the gap between self and desired femi-nine other through the consumption of commodities for the improvement of the female body' (ibid.) which are associated with particular Hollywood stars.

Each of these theorists has emphasised the relationship between dressing the female body, acting on the female body to improve it and the culture dis-courses of femininity which structure experience and a woman's sense of self. Tseëlon and Stacey in particular emphasise the paradoxical nature of cultural discourses on femininity. By drawing on these analyses, it will be suggested that the identities produced by the women vampire fans might also be understood as responses to the paradox of femininity, but that they are specific responses and, as Entwistle puts it, are 'situated' (2000: 29).

I have suggested that women fans sympathise with the vampire's predica-ment; the pathos of being locked in circumstances beyond one's control, forced to be an outsider. The following section will examine how the women relate the vampire's predicament of 'outsiderdom' to their own feelings of 'not fitting into' the norms of femininity as expressed through appearance and dress.

THE EXPERIENCE OF 'NOT FITTING IN'

The context of 'femininity' which Tseëlon and Stacey suggest is the realm of impossible contradictions also frames the experiences of women vampire fans in Britain and the US, for they face the same ambivalent category of 'femininity' that other women face. But their experience of femininity, and the sartorial identities they construct as a result, are *specific* responses to these more general conditions. Women vampire fans, rather than struggling to internalise the impossible, instead experience themselves as 'not fitting in'. They have a notion of 'normal' femininity which is symbolised in the colour pink and is to do with competently following fashion trends, which many of the fans have never felt able to manage. Many of the fans comment that 'pink frilly dresses' and 'little pumps' were not for them. The notion of 'not fitting in', of 'being different' is evidenced in the following comments from different fans in Britain:

> Cheryl: At school I found it difficult to make friends and wear trendy clothes. I didn't fit in, I didn't like the way I looked – or the way I was supposed to look and I started getting into the Goth look.
>
> Dee: I went Goth at the age of 16 when I was training as a hair dresser ... [because] I just didn't fit in and I didn't like the way I looked ... I guess I have always been a little bit different.

Pam and Janet have a similar sense of not fitting in:

> Pam: We went through a stage of trying to be normal. I think that is why we got married so young, and had kids so young and was trying to fit in somewhere...
>
> Janet: ...and then realising that actually you were just different and that's it...
>
> Pam: We've done some strange things together...
>
> Janet: You stand out.
>
> Pam: You stick out like a sore thumb
>
> Janet: Yeah, well, I never did fit in and besides I look terrible in pink.

The fans are experiencing the paradoxical demands of contemporary femininity as ones that they are unable to meet and thus their sympathy with the vampire's 'outsiderdom' echoes their own diffident relationship with notions of femininity. Like the British fans, many of the American fans make comments about 'not fitting in', about their inability to follow fashion and their dissatisfaction with themselves in 'normal' women's clothes.[2] Shirin who comments that she wears 'basic black' says:

> Well, it started out more because I didn't want to go around in the normal thing for girls back then. It was interesting. It was intriguing.

It was mysterious ... Then, when it used to really annoy a lot of people back in the 1960s and 1970s if people wore black in this town, they were all odd to say the least. So I got a lot of flak. So the more annoyed they were, the more bent out of shape they became, the more I would definitely show up in black.

For Andrea, pink is 'a little bit happy, cheerful and bright'. She comments:

Well it's, I think because the rest of, um, the time, like my work, I would not normally dress in a hot pink suit, you know with little pumps. That is not what I'm comfortable with. Um, or you know a navy blue you know suit ... Or whatever, you know, that I wear to work ... I don't like, um, having to wear glasses, wear my hair plain and boring and have to be you know that ... I guess, I feel like I'm boxed in. I prefer to be able to go out and do what I want, say what I want and that's the way I am the rest of my life. I mean, even if all I'm wearing is a black outfit and fangs, you know?

This sense of 'not fitting in' could be interpreted along psychoanalytic lines that the fans are experiencing themselves through the distorting mirrors that patriarchy holds up to women (Williams 1984). Feminist psychoanalysis has suggested that the woman is fixed by the 'male gaze' which objectifies and/or distorts her image through the processes of fetishism and voyeurism. This in turn robs her of the power of self-definition. This view was inaugurated by Laura Mulvey's (1975) ground-breaking article on the cinema and visual pleasure. However, many feminists have criticised this perspective as monolithic not only in terms of the processes of spectatorship (Gledhill 1988; Pribram 1988; Byars 1991) but also in terms of women's experiences of 'self' through appearance. Stacey, for instance, takes issue with psychoanalytic models in which subjectivity is 'only conceptualised as an effect of textual polarities' (1994: 25) and criticises the way this theorises identification and object choice 'within a framework of binary oppositions (masculinity/femininity: activity/ passivity) that necessarily masculinises active female desire' (1994: 27). Tseëlon similarly argues that such models ignore the 'plurality, contradiction or resistance that exists' (1995: 68) in the realm of feminine identification. She suggests that the effect of the general framework of femininity on women's sense of self is also influenced by local environment, on the people and situations and whether one feels secure or insecure. Entwistle is also critical of approaches that 'impose upon the world reified structures and rules which are seen to be independent from agency and practice' (2000: 36). The comments from the women vampire fans demonstrates that they do not feel secure with trends and 'normal' femininity and they experience this as 'not fitting in'. But this in turn has led to a more potent self-definition as 'different'. Once more, this is not to argue that the women's sense of self is cut off from, or resides outside of, the framework of 'femininity'; the women's comments illustrate an unhappiness not simply with the 'norm', but also with themselves (as misfits) in that context. However, the fans are not immobilised by the context of femininity, as the following section will demonstrate. The sense of not fitting into the norms of femininity has led to the construction of vampire identities that enable women fans to transcend their ambivalent attitude to their mismatch with femininity and develop a stronger sense of self by taking pride in standing out.

STANDING OUT

Women vampire fans have through sartorial means transformed a sense of not fitting into femininity into a defiant sense of standing out as different. Lea comments that her reason for wearing antique black gowns and fangs is to show that 'you're not just following everybody else'. Pam comments with a certain amount of pride 'you do stand out 'cause you dress like this':

Janet: It's modern clothes, I hate modern clothes. We are like in a time warp aren't we?
Pam: Yeah.
Janet: Like we belong somewhere else, it's like we just don't belong in this century because its like - that's why I love the way Louis and Lestat dress. I would love to dress like it all the time, I would, I'd walk around our town dressed like it ... I wear my black cape around. I get a few odd looks, people think you're strange but I don't care, I wear it...
Pam: We do stand out if we are in a supermarket and everyone else is dressed in tweeds and brogues which does look sort of...
Janet: Perhaps we're just trying to make a point. I don't know, perhaps it is part of me that wants to make a point.
Pam: You are different and you are saying you're not just following everybody else.

Similarly in New Orleans, Shirin takes pride in being 'one of the first' and comments of the new vampire scene:

...and all these young gothic types come along and act like they discovered the idea. All by themselves, you know ... I was wearing black before they were born.

This sense of pride also takes on a defiant edge as Shirin states:

I went to a shopping centre and there was some young teenager who was walking with someone else, a girl, and he said something about 'sure is a dark day around here'. So I yelled out, 'There sure are a lot of assholes around here'.

It is perhaps not surprising that the women fans' identity construction has focused on dressing and modifying their bodies in particular ways, given, as Stacey puts it, 'the centrality of physical appearance to femininity in this culture' (1994: 167). Myra Macdonald, in an analysis of femininity in the popular media, also suggests that 'the body has historically been much more integral to the formation of identity for women than for men' and that this is problematic for women because of the way women have been denied the right to self-definition in 'the history of cultural representation' (1995: 193). Macdonald argues that from the 1970s on, this has led to practices of reshaping the body and dressing in unusual ways in order to transfer claims of power from the public arena onto one's body, allowing groups 'threatened by cultural invisibility to assert their presence in striking and innovative ways' (ibid.). These vampire fans, while continuing to define themselves in relation to their appearance (thus demonstrating that they have not overthrown the structuring context of femininity), have nevertheless made active decisions to reject certain trappings by taking pride in standing out as different and being seen (by others) as different. The positive side of the dual sense of considering oneself as 'different' and expecting to be seen by others this way is summed up by Pam and Janet's comments about 'making a point' of not following normal dress trends.

Tseëlon maintains that the sense of self is always produced in relation to others and this is the case for women fans whose sense both of 'not fitting in' and 'standing out' comes from how they feel they are perceived by others as is demonstrated by the comments above. The vampire women dress the way they do, despite negative reactions in public. Tseëlon argues that the self is a 'social process', residing not in the individual but as an 'outcome of human interaction' (1995: 40). This is paradoxical for women because women are expected to be authentically feminine and yet femininity is a construct, not a given. Tseëlon draws on Sartre to pull out this 'twofold paradox' (1995: 38). The very attempt to be authentic (i.e. feminine) for Sartre suggests that originally 'one is being what one is not' in that women can only become 'authentically feminine' with considerable effort (quoted in ibid.). Furthermore, Tseëlon suggests that being authentic for woman is not 'being' for herself. Because 'authentic' femininity is constructed, it 'implies objectifying oneself, of seeing oneself through the eyes of the Other' (ibid.). Women experience a relationship between appearance – how they are seen by others – and a sense of self and so come to experience the self through appearance in the eyes of others. Furthermore, a woman's essence and appearance are intertwined and therefore her essence is ultimately conceived of as inessence; artifice, vanity, insincerity and display. Tseëlon argues that women manage these cultural expectations and the fragile sense of self that can result by having many sartorial faces and wearing their clothes like armour. Tseëlon emphasises that women are not being insincere or deceptive about self but that confidence is bound up with feeling good about one's appearance.

The women vampire fans too experience themselves through the eyes of others and are adopting sartorial identities which make them feel good about

Women with alter egos

'I am a part-time vampire'

By day this woman works in telemarketing; at night she transforms herself with elaborate costumes and ornate Gothic jewellery. Throughout Britain there are women who undergo a metamorphosis after hours. By Sarah Wise. Photographs by Fergus Greer

Tina Rath
51, telemarketing trainer and adviser/vampire fan

Tina is self-employed and has been involved in The Vampyre Society for several years. With over 450 members throughout Europe and the US, the society meets regularly to share an interest in vampires and associated Gothic themes.

'To meet clients at work, I wear a respectable black dress and pin my hair up. For meetings of The Vampyre Society, I wear lots of velvet and lace – it's amazing what you can find at Marks & Spencer. I also have clothes made for me, from my own detailed descriptions, including a custom-made corset.

'Vampire fans are seizing an opportunity to play games that is rarely offered to adults today. When I dress up, I am liberating the child in me who wants to show off and be the centre of attention. As a vampire, I am larger than life, I am worth looking at. In my everyday clothes I am competent, trustworthy, capable and pretty much invisible in a crowd. I am diminished.

'The Vampyre Society is dedicated to fun. ▷

Fig. 14 'I am a part-time vampire', as featured in *Marie Claire*, October 1998

themselves. But for the vampire women feeling good does not translate into looking 'good' for others. Instead looking 'good' means looking different to others by rejecting 'pink', 'frilly' femininity. Indeed Andrea calls the way she is required to dress for her work in hospital administration her 'frump gear'. She describes herself as having two faces, the one for work which she calls her 'stage' face and the 'real' Andrea, her vampire face:

Well, that's more like my true person ... when I get dressed and I'm fully dressed with my make-up done and my teeth and everything else – that's when I feel most comfortable and I would, like I said, I would live that way 24 hours a day if I could because that's basically how I am.

Pam and Janet make similar comments:

> Janet: We go to work conventional but come home and whip it
> off and put something different on straight away.
> Pam: Yeah I can't stand it and that's not me.
> Janet: Er, take it all off and I hate it...
> Pam: And I used to wear a *lovely* blue uniform and a navy blue skirt and
> a blouse, a firm white blouse and think 'that's it', come home and
> 'that's it', all off.

The claims these fans make about the authenticity of their vampire identities, the sense that this is the 'real' me, may be partly a response to the dominant notions of femininity as artifice that Tseëlon has argued shapes women's self-perception. Andrea transformed from one of her faces to the other in the course of our interview. The interview began with Andrea in her 'frump gear' and it took the course of our two-hour taped interview for her to dress and apply make-up before we were taken to a club by Andrea, her younger brother and her boyfriend. Andrea had utterly transformed herself from a female office worker into a glamorous vampire. White foundation make-up was sponged to her face followed by cheeks and chin shaded with purple to create a translucent and bruise-like effect. Blonde hair extensions were applied to her peroxide hair to create a thick, wavy blonde mantle and realistic home made fangs were attached to her teeth. Andrea then put on a tight-bodiced gown of black velvet trimmed with satin lace, a hooded black satin cape and black pumps pointed at the toes. Andrea's rejection of 'cheerful' and 'pink' femininity has found positive expression in a striking vampiric identity which she feels expresses who she has come to be. It is clear that the fans' empathy with the vampire's outsiderdom, combined with their appropriation of the elegance and drama cut by the figure of the vampire, has provided a means of converting the experience of 'not fitting in' into a pride in difference and often this is expressed in claims of authenticity: 'this is my true person'.

The women vampire fans' sartorial identities are actually no more nor less artificial or authentic than other 'outfits' that other women armour themselves in. That the women 'stand out' as a result of their sartorial choices and feel themselves to be different in the eyes of others is a reminder of how taken-for-granted are the standards of dress for women in each epoch, but also how women have challenged norms to create innovative styles through which to express the self. For the women vampire fans, then, the experience of not 'fitting in' to the perceived expectations of others has not led to an increased attempt to internalise 'ideal femininity'. Instead it has led to a rejection of those norms and the construction of an alternative sartorial identity. The women fans dress the part of the vampire with long capes in velvets and satins, silky dresses with flared sleeves and lace gloves, converting 'not fitting in' to 'standing out' as different. The following section will discuss the women's use of black to 'stand out' in the context of Western ideas about this colour in sartorial schemes. It will then examine what the women are telling others about themselves through their vampiric sartorial identities.

DRESSING IN BLACK AND STANDING OUT

Combined with a rejection of 'pink' femininity, the fans' alternative dress is intended to ensure that they 'stand out' as different. Their sense of 'not fitting in' has not led to a self-effacing sartorial identity, but one that calls attention to their 'difference'. Like Andrea in New Orleans and Pam and Janet in Britain, Cheryl and Lea also feel most themselves when they dress in black and stand out. The following exchange, when asked why they dress in black, demonstrate this impulse:

> Lea: It's difficult to explain it really. Part of it is that you don't want to feel like normal people...
> Cheryl: Yeah, not conforming...
> Lea: It's a lot of things ... the style of dress, it's different. People look at you if you dress like this.

Again the sentiments are echoed by Andrea in New Orleans who comments:

> The whole appearance of being a vampire gives you a lot of attention to feed off of. Either people are afraid of you, or they just adore you.

The women fold together their dislike for fashion trends, wanting to feel different and wanting to be seen to be different by cladding themselves in vampiric black. Black is the central colour in these women's wardrobes and is central to their sartorial identities. That the women choose black as the symbolic polar opposite of pink is not only to do with their perceptions of the norms of femininity. Black has long provided its wearers with the mark of difference. Anne Hollander argues that there is a tradition of wearing black 'which seeks to isolate and distinguish the wearer' (1993: 377). For Hollander black can offer power and distinction drawing on its 'ancient flavour of anti-fashion' (1993: 365). Furthermore, leading up to and following the Romantic era, black accrued connotations of the sinister and satanic. As Hollander argues, 'black appears as the colour suitable to delicious forbidden practice and belief – the courting of death, not the mourning of it – in a great deal of Romantic literature' (1993: 376).

   The powerful symbolism invoked by black attire, its ability to isolate and draw attention to its wearer as well as its ability to conjure 'fear of the blind darkness of night and the eternal darkness of death' (Hollander 1993: 365) makes it a particularly appealing colour to the women fans who are drawing on this symbolism. Here we can see that the choice of black might be considered to be part of Bourdieu's system of distinction, except that it is also more than this because it is bound up with handling the paradox of the female self in a sexist society, and thus is a way of attempting control for the self which wider society attempts to deny. As Karen puts it:

Fashion trends, fine, you can keep them. Because that is not me. I am always in black. It's a strong colour, people look at it as a very negative colour, but it isn't, black will stop negativity. Anything light or bright will attract negativity 'cause it is bright. It is a welcoming colour ... [but] black keeps people at a distance, it gives people the image of, you know, 'don't approach me, back off, leave me alone'. I'm not the sort of quiet little mouse that sits in a corner. I will not tolerate any one trying to invade or to put me down.

This fan is drawing positively on black's ominous symbolism and it is clear that a link is being made between self-perception (black 'is me'), the perception of others ('black keeps people at a distance from me') and sartorial behaviour. This woman is using black to say to *others* 'I am different', 'I am unapproachable' and 'I am strong'.

While the women's self-presentation is intended to 'stand out' as different, it is a particular kind of 'standing out'. By appropriating vampiric images they are presenting themselves specifically as 'outsiders' and expect others to recognise the symbolism. As Hollander notes, there are different ways of wearing black. Black has expressed bourgeois respectability, a professional demeanour and mourning. It can also mock these connotations through exaggerated display. In the latter half of the nineteenth century it was considered the suitable colour for those of 'straightened means' (Hollander 1993: 379); the shop girl, clerk and domestic servant. But simultaneously, Hollander argues, 'rich and idle men were considered properly dressed in black in the evening, and rich and idle women properly dressed in black for ostentatious mourning or, suitably décolleté, for occasional dramatic evenings' (ibid.). In the twentieth century, black has taken on a variety of symbolic connotations; indeed Hollander argues that in the late twentieth century black has lost its symbolic significance, 'through the fragmentation and multiplicity of styles in dress' and 'chiefly through the self-consciousness of fashion' (1993: 388). For Hollander, to wear black today is to 'refer to a variety of earlier manifestations of black clothes – earlier styles, former meanings, obsolete conventions' (ibid.).

Women vampire fans adorn themselves in a black that harks back to the 'former meanings' of the Romantic era. They emphasise the sinister drama of black through the use of 'antique' and out-of-fashion clothing styles, worn in silks and velvets which many combine with dyed black or blonde hair and sometimes the donning of dental caps fashioned as vampire fangs and yellow contact lenses. The intention is to 'stand out', to adopt an aloof stance. But the vampiric symbolism is also intended to startle and shock in its difference. As Karen comments about wearing fangs:

> So, you walk into a pub, you sit down, you order a drink and you sort of look around and you smile at someone, and it's just a look of shock, of disbelief as if to say 'I know what I'm seeing doesn't exist', but it still doesn't stop them from backing away ... so I feel better with them in, well I'm quite a confident person anyway, but again it gives me the upper hand because it keeps people at a very safe distance.

This sense of being remote and startlingly different echoes the connotations of black attire worn by the Romantic man. As Hollander argues, the Romantic man wore black to establish his remoteness. It was a style with strong literary connections which marked him out as a 'fatal man'. For Hollander, the fatal man was 'specifically connected with spiritual unrest and personal solitude', in league with 'a dark power that exempted him from the responsibilities of common feeling and experience' (1993: 375). Vampire fans too want to display their 'outsiderdom' and draw sartorial inspiration from the vampire as Romantic outsider. Yet, as already argued in previous chapters, the women fans do not view the vampire as the wicked villain depicted in numerous adaptations of *Dracula*. Instead they look to the vampires in Anne Rice's *Vampire Chronicles* or to the sympathetic vampires in *Buffy the Vampire Slayer* who offer a contemporary reinterpretation of the vampire as a sympathetic eighteenth- and nineteenth-century Romantic hero; one who suffers his isolation from humanity with the pathos more appropriate to the heroine of the gothic novel than its black-clad villain. Black keeps its demonic edge in the women's sartorial schemes, but it signifies the pathos of outsiderdom as well as its force, evidenced in the women's comments about 'not fitting in' and feeling a 'misfit'.

BLACK AS REVOLT

Added to the Romantic implications of black-as-difference are those of black-as-revolt. Elizabeth Wilson, in her analysis of fashion, has suggested that black has long been the appropriate colour of 'revolt'. This is because it is the 'colour of bourgeois sobriety, but subverted, perverted, gone kinky' (1985: 189). For Wilson, 'black is dramatic and plays to the gallery, as the costuming of revolt must always do' (ibid.). But more specifically, Wilson proposes that it was the Romantics and dandies, influenced by the revolutionary upheavals in the latter half of the eighteenth century that actually inaugurated the notion of dress as revolt. She argues that it was the 'combined influence of the dandies and the Romantics that made of black a resonant statement of dissent' (1985: 186). While Hollander suggests that black has long signified 'anti-fashion', Wilson argues that it was actually the style invented by the dandies that led to conventional menswear and thus to 'anti-fashion' (1985: 183). Furthermore, Wilson argues that style of the dandy led in another direction; it 'contained the germs of something utterly different, of oppositional style' (1985: 184).

This notion of black-as-revolt chimes with the women's accounts of their sartorial identities as non-conformist. Black not only affords the women fans the means to stand out as 'different', they are also drawing on its oppositional connotations of sartorial revolt. Karen sums up the views expressed by many of the fans:

> It just makes people think. They see me in black, they see the fangs, they see the contact lenses ... They say you can't fight the system or buck the system, well yeah you can, but in your own way, and you do it in such a way that people don't realise that you're actually being a little revolutionary in your own way.

The attitudes expressed by the women in their choice of black as declaring their difference could be interpreted as a sign of the women producing elitist distinctions between themselves and 'normal' people (Thornton 1995) and indeed Wilson suggests that oppositional style aims to express 'views hostile to the conformist majority' (1985: 184). Alternatively, we could interpret their accounts as the proto-political act of subverting mainstream society (Jenkins 1992). However, Wilson offers an alternative explanation which sits on neither side of this binary. She argues that while black has been a sign of 'anti-bourgeois revolt' (1985: 186) it has also been a deeply contradictory sign, 'as contradictory as the society that gave it birth' (1985: 183). Just as this 'transitory epoch of capitalism' (ibid.) was an era poised between the extension of democracy and the politics of reaction, so too did the style of revolt appeal equally to the 'republican radical' and 'the reactionary, the disaffected aristocrat' (1985: 182). Thus it was of both past and future. Baudelaire, for example, wore black in protest against the 'sartorial vulgarity of French bohemian circles' (1985: 183). In fact, Baudelaire seems to express the contradictory impulses of the dandy. For Baudelaire the dandy was a disenchanted 'rebel' who celebrated 'decadence', but he was also one who 'attempts to create a new aristocracy of genius, or at least of talent' (ibid.). Nevertheless for Wilson, this oppositional dress, whether looking to past or future was always 'anti-bourgeois' and she reminds us that capitalism is *permanently* transitory', and condemned to perpetual change, it repeatedly throws up 'ambiguous rebels whose rebellion is never a revolution, but instead a reaffirmation of Self' (ibid.). In other words, sartorial opposition is contradictory; its anti-conformity tends towards elitism and its anti-bourgeois stance moves the other way and these processes are simultaneous, which render any revolt ambiguous.

Women vampire fans can be seen as latter day versions of Wilson's 'ambiguous rebels'. For the women, the appropriation of black attire is to do with a non-conformity which is centrally about the construction and affirmation of 'self'. It is also significant that the women look to the past for sartorial inspiration and look precisely to the (Romantic) period in history that Wilson defines as producing the contradictory germs of oppositional style. Women vampire fans are drawing on the idea of black as a rebellious colour but conceive of the styles of the past contradictorily as both 'more feminine' than today as well as offering them nonconformity with femininity. So Pam, who comments that 'pink' (as the standard colour of femininity) is 'not for her' and wants her sartorial identity to say 'look, I'm different' also comments:

> I don't think women look feminine now-a-days. I think the velvets and the satins and the laces of the past look so feminine. It emphasises you as a woman, I think, more.

Here there is a simultaneous sense of not fitting in to the norms of femininity (expressed in a rejection of pink and preference for black) which nevertheless continues to embrace notions of femininity by looking to the past for sartorial inspiration. This seems explicable in terms of Wilson's formulation of the contradictory character of oppositional dress. Wilson emphasises the way that the conditions that give rise to oppositional style are ambiguous, and that, as a response to those conditions, oppositional style is itself filled with contradictions. The experience of the paradox of femininity that frames the women's choice of black can lead to ambiguities in their sense of what being 'different' means. Wilson has highlighted how sartorial revolt is simultaneously a mode of past and future; that the impulses for nonconformity in dress can appeal to those looking to the past while also drawing those who desire the potential of the future. The following section will propose that for the women vampire fans, the past/future impulses of oppositional dress are simultaneous. Rather than looking to past or future, the women vampire fans are looking in both directions at once.

THE DIALECTICS OF PAST AND FUTURE

The implication of a preferable and 'emphasised' femininity in historical dress may be conceived of as a form of regressive nostalgia for the past. But this is complicated by the ambiguity of the vampire figure with whom the women travel. The Romantic connotations of the vampiric that the women draw on are those of 'otherness' in past as well as present, which problematises any simple notion of their looking to the past for a better way of life. The vampire simultaneously symbolises the pathos and power of outsiderdom. It is a figure which expresses, as Richard Dyer comments, 'the despicable as well as the defiant, the shameful as well as the unashamed, the loathing of oddness as well as pride in it' (1988: 11). It is through vampiric modes of the past that the women express ambivalence about femininity and self. The vampire offers a way for the women to conceive of their identities as both 'not' feminine and 'more' feminine, and it also leads to the women questioning the very boundaries of gender and the associated sexualities. The homo-eroticism which infuses the image of contemporary male vampires is widely recognised (Dyer 1988; Hodges and

Doane 1991; Gelder 1994; Auerbach 1995) and does not go unnoticed by these women fans. For instance Janet comments about Louis and Lestat:

> I don't think they're so male- or female-looking. I think they sort of cross both lines don't they ... aren't vampires bisexual anyway? So it doesn't matter that I'd be a skinny little vampire with no bosoms.

This comment articulates the many issues of 'self', gender and sexuality raised by the vampire, for the women. The idea that having 'no bosoms' as her vampire self 'doesn't matter' echoes the notion of not 'fitting in' to femininity and expresses the duality raised by Dyer above, an uneasy recognition of difference which converts to pride. But this conversion is at least partly possible through engagement with the vampire's bisexuality – it is crossing both lines. The women comment positively on the love between the (same sex) vampires and approve of their androgynous looks. Pam says:

> Armand loves Louis if you read the books through, he really loved him but they also had women. He was quite happy to go chomping around but he loved Louis maybe in another sense but, well, he loved him more than anything in one way. So I think they are quite happy in whichever.

Later Janet comments:

> I've watched that film [Interview With the Vampire] with men ... They don't like the part with Armand and Louis, it puts men off, and I think so many men are like that, whereas women ... It doesn't bother us does it? That love women have for each other. Why should it bother men you know, why should it, if men love men, why should it bother men that much? It's not affecting men but they just can't hack it can they?

These fans relate the close bond between two gay male vampires to the close bonds which exist between women. Indeed Richard Dyer has suggested that 'you could argue for there being something "lesbian" about the vampire by pointing to the fact not only of lesbian gothic but also the tradition of female gothic in general' because lesbian vampires and lesbian gothic are an 'extension of female literary and cultural traditions' (1988: 50); they are 'a continuation of aspects of female culture' whereas gay gothic is a deviation from male culture' (ibid.). It is also the case that some female fans of the vampire have drawn on their fan practices around vampire texts as part of their coming out as lesbians and I will discuss this in more detail in the next chapter.

Some post-Freudian theorists have suggested that the vampire signals an end to gender distinctions. For Christopher Craft (1990) and Sue-Ellen Case (1991) the vampire is a subversive borderline figure which problematises representation and destabilises the boundaries of gender. For Case, the vampire 'disrupts' because it exists between the boundaries through which we conceive of 'being'; the 'bi-polarities that enclose the heterosexist notion of being' are punctured and 'new forms of being, or beings, are imagined through desire' (1991: 4). For Craft, it is the vampire's mouth that poses the vampire as a multi-gendered being by displacing sexuality onto this ungendered space. Craft's vampire exposes the insubstantiality of gender barriers; it 'exists to dissolve opposites' (1990: 109). Both Case and Craft then, pose the vampire as symbolic of ways of 'being' beyond what they consider to be unstable gender distinctions. From this perspective the women's self-presentation as vampiric combined with their articulation of the vampire's bisexuality would suggest that through sartorial means, the women are producing subversive identities beyond the constructs of gender. However, this position cannot take into account that these women look to the past as a time when clothes for women were more feminine. This suggests that they accept gender differences despite their own difficult experiences of contemporary feminine dress.

Other theorists warn against analyses of the vampire that prematurely pose the end of stable gender categories. Devon Hodges and Janice L. Doane (1991), as discussed previously, for example, argue that the fictional blurring of gender categories found in the texts of Anne Rice actually mask a deeper acceptance of difference with its oppressive construction of woman. Analysing the women's comments from this perspective would suggest that the fans' identification with the 'line-crossing' of the vampire is a deeply conservative fantasy to mask their deeper acceptance of the precarious place of the feminine in the symbolic order. However, neither the celebrations of the vampire as subversive of gender representations nor the claims to the contrary capture its duality and equivocal status in culture, nor the ambivalence in women fans' articulation of their appropriation of this symbol in their construction of self.

The women read the vampire as crossing the lines of gender and blurring the boundaries of heterosexuality and they draw sartorial inspiration from what is (at least nominally) a male figure of the past to express their own desire for the future acceptability of androgyny. Yet the past to which they are looking and drawing sartorial inspiration is one in which women are conceived of as more feminine in dress. However, alongside these attitudes, the women's repeated emphasis on not fitting into present feminine norms and *wanting* not to, suggests that they consider the unwanted boundaries of gender to be in place. This complex blend of attitudes, expressed in dress, cannot be accounted for by the either/or explanations discussed above. Walter Benjamin offers an alternative way of understanding these contradictions, ambivalence and ambiguities.

THE VAMPIRE AS 'WISH IMAGE'

Benjamin contributes the concept of 'wish image' to the discussion of the modern consciousness, noting the tendency to 'thirst for the past' (quoted in Buck-Morss 1989: 110) to symbolise a reality that has not yet come into being. According to Benjamin, the 'not-yet' of the new is expressed in archaic symbols rather than in the new forms 'commensurate with it' (1989: 114). Wish images then, express the desire for the not-yet by 'intermingling the old with the new in fantastic ways' (1989: 115). The imagination looks to the past to express the new because of the fetters of the present; the potential of the new is constrained by still-existing social relations and so wish images 'reach back to a more distant past in order to *break from* conventional forms' (1989: 116). For Benjamin 'every epoch dreams the one that follows it' (quoted in Buck-Morss 1991: 114), but because a dream is not yet knowledge of a new reality, dream wishes take on the symbols of the past. Susan Buck-Morss comments that Benjamin's evocation of the wish image is not utopian. She comments that 'Benjamin was reluctant to rest revolutionary hope directly on imagination's capacity to anticipate the not-yet-existing' (ibid.) because a wish image is interpreted through the 'material objects in which it found expression' (1989: 115). The material through which the women fans' identity construction finds expression are the garments of self-presentation and their wish image of a strangely gloomy undead figure from the past. The wish image cannot dream the future, rather it dreams desire for the not-yet. The women fans' 'not-yet' is one of personal emancipation from the paradoxical parameters of femininity and the potential for a more androgynous, less rigidly gendered way of being. This finds expression in past modes of dress inspired by their interpretation of both the (male) Romantic vampire and the feminine cuts of the past. But it has been argued throughout this chapter that women experience themselves in the context of femininity, and while they are not immobilised by this context, neither can they step outside it. Thus their desire for the potential of a new way of being is contained in the inescapable present; they desire something different but (like any member of society) cannot anticipate it, for as Benjamin argues, we 'stand in the darkness of the lived moment' (quoted in Buck-Morss 1991: 114).

If it is the case, as Benjamin proposes, that the wish image must look to the past to dream the future because the imagination is limited by the present, this may explain why the women look to the Romantic past for their modes of sartorial rebellion and why they simultaneously continue to hold to a feminine self-definition while raising the desire for a potential beyond this. If none can transcend the horizons of the present in imagining things not-as-they-are, then as Buck-Morss asks 'where else *but* to the dead past can imagination turn in order to conceptualise a world that is not-yet?' (1991: 124). The vampire women are aware, despite their construction of self as 'vampiric', that the vampire raises desires and potentials rather than realities. None of these women believe that they 'are' vampires and this recognition is evidenced in comments which illustrate their rueful distance from the vampire rather than identity with it. The women have not achieved the desired state:

> Dee: it would be just the perfect life style, it really would ... you could live a life that you had always wanted to.

> Karen: I'd love it [to be a vampire] yeah, I'd love it. You could do what you wanted to do, nobody could oppose you, you'd be very dextrous ...

you'd work under the shadow of darkness, you know. Who'd miss the sunlight, who'd miss the day?

Janet: We could have lived that life quite happily ... And back in where they live, that would suit us to a tee. We could live there.

Pam: They don't have to bother with the rigmarole and the palaver that us humans have to go through sometimes. I'd love to dispense with it all and just have none of it. It would be ideal wouldn't it?

The vampire offers a way of imagining the past for the women which poses potential, not realisation; a desire for a different way of being, not its fulfilment. The women clearly feel that the vampire offers an alternative possibility to 'the way things are' which casts a particular light on their passion for the past. The past is a mode of engaging with present desires about self and trying out alternative possibilities of self by the creation of vampiric sartorial identities through which they can stand out as different to current normative definitions of self for women. The vampire is an appropriate symbol for these women who want to 'be' different both because of the experience of not 'fitting in' and the desire for alternative ways of being in the world. The vampire's duality captures these impulses; the pathos of 'not fitting in', of being an outsider, a desire for alternatives tinged with a recognition of non-fulfilment.

WOMEN AND THE VAMPIRE: THE POSSIBILITY OF SELF

Jackie Stacey suggests that the relationship between female spectators and stars is an intense attachment actually to do with possibilities for the self. She argues that Hollywood stars may have significance for women 'in terms of their representation of a fantasy self never realised' (1994: 65). The following comment from Janet demonstrates that she recognises aspects of herself in the vampire Lestat and that this is the basis of thinking about a self that is not realisable:

I'm not conventional, I obviously don't go to the extremes as what Lestat goes to, but I'd love to. I'd love to do what he does – we've decided that there's nothing that he wouldn't sort of challenge.

Stacey argues that 'forms of recognition of the self in the idealised other, or indeed recognition of the desired self in the idealised other, inform the choices and selection of favourite stars made by spectators' (1994: 209). This is clearly in operation in Janet's choice of Lestat. Stacey's notion that stars offer 'the possible fantasy of something better' (1994: 126) is applicable to these fans' relationships to their favoured vampires. There is a 'negotiation between spectators and their star ideals [that] is the recognition of similarities and differences' (1994: 128). However, it must be recognised that testing out a potential self as a vampire is not entirely the same as testing out possibilities of self in a female Hollywood star such as Betty Grable (although both are rather glamorous). There are common themes to do with recognising the self in an other and recognising the difference between self and other, but there are significant differences. Vampires, unlike Hollywood stars, are not social ideals but social renegades. The vampire, outcast and undead, can never be simply an optimistic ideal self. In this cultural choice, the fans are openly revealing their pain (at their sense of outsiderdom and pathos). But they are also demonstrating defiance at their sense of difference. This is discernible in Cheryl's comment, 'it's appealing, being a vampire and living forever and being a tortured soul really'. Karen expresses a stronger version of this sentiment, 'they say ... you have got to conform to society, I have never conformed to society and I never will, you know?'

Stacey suggests that trying out possible selves through an ideal other is a complex mix of recognising similarities and differences and this explanation is one which accords with the women vampire fans accounts of their engagement with vampires. The fans who wanted to be interviewed in pairs or in small groups make use of vampires to discuss with each other what kind of people they are. For example, throughout their interview Pam and Janet define themselves in relation to each other. They discuss their favourite vampire characters to describe, criticise and value the self and each other. This takes place in an atmosphere of intense mutual affection and decades of friendship:

Janet: I'm more like Lestat. We've always said that even when we first started reading the books. She's a Louis and I'm a Lestat from the books, I suppose I am really ... Pam is more of a...

Pam: I think it all out.

Janet: 'Oh, I don't know, we didn't ought to do that, oh dear.'

Pam: I'm methodical. I think about it and I think of any outcomes, you just dive in. I'll think about a situation. We get presented with a situation, I'll think about it...

Janet: She's a Louis...

Pam: Yeah, what'll happen...

Janet: 'Ah, but what if?'

Pam: And the consequences and so we know how to deal with the consequences *when* they happen...

Janet: [laughs] I mean when we were going to join this group and I went head long in and said 'yeah, I'll do it'...

Pam: She said, 'I'm just going out for a walk, I'll be a while, I'll just borrow a wine glass' and I never saw her again.

Janet: I never came back.

Pam: Some chap goes riding by in his tight trousers on his charger and you're off [they both laugh a lot].

Janet: But Louis was always there for Lestat even the trouble he got into, Louis was always there...

Pam: Yeah, I know.

Janet: I want to be him, I want to be Lestat.

Pam: Well I'm not going to rescue you if you take on Beelzebub [both laugh]. .

This exchange epitomises the interviews with pairs of fans in that they use the vampire characters' types to talk not just about themselves but also about their relationships. Janet may want 'to be Lestat', but she demonstrates enough self-awareness to recognise both that she is *not* Lestat and that his character is trouble. She also relies on Pam's more cautious approach to life to help her out of her own trouble. The fans' cultural choices, then, are not totally directed at the self, but are part of their wider sets of relations, friendship networks and club memberships. These fans are as interested in how the vampire can be applied to a friend as to themselves. The importance of relationships seems particularly relevant to the fans because despite the emphasis on personal and individual meaning, the relationship between the vampires is also central to the structure of many modern vampire tales. This is a melodramatic form of the gothic in which, as Peter Brooks puts it, 'interpersonal relations are not merely contacts of the flesh but encounters that must be carefully nurtured, judged, handled as if they mattered' (1995: 22). Thus the fans' cultural interests are not simply about the self. The exchange quoted above also demonstrates a clear awareness that the vampires embody 'types' (she's *a* Louis) with distinct values (Louis/caution – Lestat/rebellion). The fans relate these values to themselves and each other, but not as simple idealised projections of self. They also articulate the hazards of those values as well as recognition that they are not the vampire they would like to be. There is recognition of difference between self and the vampire 'other'.

The fans are matching themselves and each other to favoured versions of the sympathetic vampire, but while they may see themselves as similar to a particular vampire, they also recognise the difference, and it is in the gap between self and imagined self that resides the desire to test out a potential self. Also, rather than compulsive identification with the vampire, there is a recognition that one cannot lead the (vampiric) life one desires. It may be that the fans' simultaneous construction of vampire selves and recognition of their difference to their vampire 'ideals' is part of the appeal of the gothic and melodramatic structuring of the fans' vampire favourites. As Christine Gledhill argues, melodrama typically produces an 'over-investment in the symbol, combined with the impossibility with actually living it' (1987: 35). The fans' attachment to the melodramatic vampire, then, is not only to do with its pathos, but also its strength; a strength one recognises that one does not fully possess, but nevertheless aspires to. This structuring enables the fans to recognise themselves in the vampire and its predicament, but also to try out potential selves, imaging themselves through the strength of the vampire. Rather than being 'dupes' of the melodramatic structuring, the fans clearly acknowledge the 'impossibility of living it'. But this does not stop them wishing that things could be different for the self and that the vampire offers images of new potential selves. As Karen puts it:

the vampire is a free spirit ... things can still damage them, but it's just pure freedom, really. It really is freedom.

This chapter has attempted to demonstrate that dressing the part of the vampire for the women fans is a complex means of self-expression. By drawing on the dualistic connotations of the vampire as Romantic rebel and pathos-steeped outsider, the women are 'rebelling' and they are testing out possibilities of self in a manner which recognises non-fulfilment. The women's desire for alternative ways of being takes expression in their appropriation of black and vampiric attire as a means of producing nonconformist identities though oppositional dress. I have argued that this manner of rebellion is as contradictory as the context that produced its impulse; both rejecting and retaining ideas of femininity, producing distinctions and producing a more democratic sense of self, looking to the past to imagine the future, expressing the pain of outsiderdom and the strength of non-conformity. These contradictions stem from the inability of the self to transcend the constraints of the present while still being able to imagine things not-as-they-are. The women vampire fans are not fixed by the framework of femininity but neither can they simply step outside of social context and thus their desire for potential identities outside of this context are akin to the vampire with whom they engage; they are desires that do not die but neither do they live. Throughout this chapter there has been an emphasis on the women's sartorial practices as a response to cultural dilemmas, rather than seeing the women as outside of the cultural set up. An examination of the women's writing practices in the next chapter will demonstrate that this aspect of fandom too is affected by cultural discourses, but that more than in the arena of dress, it is affected by the unequal distribution of cultural capital.

CHAPTER 8

RE-WRITING THE VAMPIRE: GENDER, SEXUALITY AND FAN FICTION

Fan fiction in vampire fandom (and other fandoms I would suggest) is an activity which both eludes categorisation through Bourdieu's schema of position-taking in the hierarchy of the cultural field, *and* most fully expresses it. It simultaneously exists in a place that is stratified by the possession (or not) of appropriate cultural capital and it is a space of genuine creativity whose originating impulse does not begin with a quest for ascendancy – even if the structure of fandom transmits it in that direction. In this chapter I will begin by exploring the creativity of vampire fan fiction. I will examine the focus of much fan fiction on the moment of vampiric attack on the human protagonist and her or his painful physical transformation. While these stories are not part of the slash (erotic and often homoerotic) genre, I will suggest that they share certain characteristics. However, I will also examine issues to do with the experience of female embodiment that women fans have regularly referred to when explaining their writing to me, which exceeds the arena of the sexual, but often focuses on the experience of the body in pain and the fantasy of transcendence.

I will then move on to discuss slash fiction specifically in relation to *Buffy* fandom and will consider the way that this 'cult' text has expanded the ground of slash because of its own flirtation with this genre in the series – overtly through the character pairing of Buffy and Spike, but also implied in the depiction of the loving lesbian relationship of Willow and Tara and the kinky heterosexual one of Xander and Anya. We shall see how slash fiction writers' disruption of these pairings adds new dimensions of polymorphous sexuality which seemed to be missing from some accounts of slash fiction where the emphasis is on male/male pairings.

This chapter will then move on to analyse the cultural politics of vampire fan fiction. I will argue that this form of creativity seems to be strongly marked by differences in class and education. The evidence from women vampire fans in Britain and New Orleans, it will be argued, contradicts accounts from fan theorists that writing in fandom takes place in an egalitarian and 'nurturing atmosphere' for women (Jenkins 1992: 159; see also Bacon-Smith 1992). Instead, I will argue that while small support networks exist, there is a hierarchy of value at work in the field of fan writing which mirrors traditional autonomous cultural capital. The 'level' of writing engaged in is very much a matter of an individual fan's level of personal confidence which seems to correlate directly to class and educational background. Thus the modes of creativity open to women vampire fans in terms of their writing practises are not equal. I will examine both the lack of self-confidence that stops some fans from writing fan fiction in favour of forms of writing they deem more appropriate to their skills (or else who feel unable to write at all), as well as the impositions from some Internet groups, fanzines, newsletters and journals which stipulate who can write and about what.

WRITING THE VAMPIRE: PHYSICAL PAIN AND PHYSICAL TRANSFORMATION

Fan writing about the vampire takes a myriad of forms: it takes place on-line and on paper; it takes the form of narrative; is a response to fan 'challenges'; participation in role-playing games; it can be poetry, reviews, word games, criticism, and other forms of experimental writing. Also, unlike other fandoms, writing the vampire is not exclusively tied to the characters of an already existing imaginative universe. Many fans do write about the characters from the *Vampire Chronicles* or *Buffy* and *Angel*, but fans also write about the 'virtual vampire star' (as discussed in chapter three), who is disconnected from any individual actor or textual instance, but who embodies a specific set of sympathetic characteristics. I am characterising this work as fan fiction because, like other fan fiction, it is distributed through fan-club networks, is talked through and reworked in small fan-based support networks. This fiction has a tendency to examine the process of physical transformation that a fledgling vampire undergoes. One fan, Karen, explained why her writing dwelt on the moment of vampiric transfomation and it is clear that the emphasis is on the experience of physical pain:

> It is everything that I would imagine that I would go through because you have got to put yourself in either one of the roles, I mean it would be excruciating pain. I can draw on the feeling of what it would be like to have the flesh severed and penetrated ... because I have experienced that, so I know the pain factor that is involved in that when I had [my daughter] ... Very, very hard how you are gasping for breath and how your heart is beating so fast that you can't breathe. I have experienced that, I have been under quite a few major operations so going under anaesthetic, that kind of in-between here and there, I know how that feels.

Karen is using her experience of pain to help her to create a believable account of vampiric transformation, but there is also the reverse sense that she is addressing her own experience of pain by repeatedly writing about the moment of human-to-vampire transformation and by discussing this plot with other fans. Camille Bacon-Smith (1992) points out that fan fiction contains a genre known as 'hurt/comfort' that focuses on the paring of two males; one half of a male pairing being injured and comforted by the other half. Although the vampire transformation stories that vampire fans write do not always follow this pattern (although sometimes the vampire who attacks the human does comfort the vampire the person has become) they do share with this genre an emphasis on pain. Bacon-Smith suggests that physical pain represents a psychic pain in hurt/comfort stories that the author is struggling with. Like Bacon-Smith's science fiction fans, vampire fans often 'talk story'; they discuss plots, structure and characterisation and they are simultaneously talking about their pain. The vampire transformation story, however, emphasises physical pain and the mental anguish it generates, rather than psychic pain. Becoming a vampire is both the source of the pain and is the solution to the pain; it symbolises a variety of womanly pains and then symbolically transcends them. In this sense it addresses the particularly female (and paradoxical) experience of embodiment and yet it is a more individualistic genre than 'hurt/comfort' because it relies, not on a caring partner, but on the self. Karen describes the final part of the vampire transformation sequence – the fledgling vampire's first moments in its new body:

> As soon as it [blood] enters her stomach that is when the metamorphosis takes hold. It is changing her blood structure and is changing her body so what she has always had inside – that has now been vomited out ... It is the most intense fear she is ever gonna feel. After the fear there comes a calm – a peace – no more pain, ever. Everything is vital, eyesight, hearing, everything takes on a totally different vision and then ... this new life she has been given – immortality ... how she can see differently through vampire eyes with a vampire eyesight, how everything is louder, how she takes her first breathe as a living corpse, bewilderment at her newly-born vampire body, basically that is the essence of a new born ... Fear, bewilderment, excitement, it really is a cocktail. She knows she is dying, she is trying so desperately to hold onto life and she knows that she can't because she knows she is dying. She is torn between – will she live or won't she? She knows that the only way she can live is to accept blood, but to drink blood is immoral and horribly wrong.

This description of her story concentrates on the physical aspects of transformation, so while she demonstrates a fascination with moving beyond the limits of the body ('vomiting out' the old and 'no more pain, ever') there is a continued emphasis on physical sensation. Also, the description of the transformation into a vampiric body is abject ('what she always had inside – that has now been vomited out'). Like many transformation stories, it lingers on the visceral detail of painful physical death which precedes the entry into vampirism. This is a fictional body which, in its transformations, breaches the body's boundaries. The human body has been penetrated and then it vomits out *all* of what is human inside. In turn, it penetrates in its own 'feeding' (blood-drinking), thus destabilising the notion of inside and outside the body, it blurs that boundary. Theories of abjection propose that societies mobilise the body in their classification systems and through ritual set up demarcation lines between the human and the non-human (Kristeva 1982; Douglas 1984; Creed 1993). Barbara Creed, for example, applies Kristeva's theory of abjection to a variety of horror texts and characters to suggest that the 'concept of a border is central to the construction of the monstrous in the horror film' (1993: 11). For Creed, the vampire is abject because 'the act of vampirism mixes the idea of blood/semen/milk and ... the vampire's union is brought about by the opening up of a wound' (1993: 70). Creed argues that 'with its repeated emphasis on marking the skin, opening up a wound, the vampire narrative points continually to the imperfection of the body and the particularly abject nature of the maternal body' (1993: 71). The maternal body has specifically been considered to be abject, leaky, transgressive and confusing the border between outside and in. It is interesting therefore how the descriptions this fan produces of her vampire's moment of transformation parallels her descriptions of the pain of childbirth and how she sees the vampiric transformation as a form of birth. It is also interesting that her descriptions take abjection to its logical conclusion; it is not just opening a wound that destabilises her vampire, it is the ejection of *everything* from the body. Her descriptions, though, do not demonstrate repulsion with these border transgressions since they are necessary integral parts of becoming anew, although there is ambivalence at becoming anew because it involves appetites that are 'horribly wrong' (and this signals that this vampire has not had all human sensibility burned out, for as we saw in chapter two, the rejection of blood is a key symbol of vampiric innocence). The abjection of the vampire for the fans is not a source of disgust, but it is a source of ambivalence; it is both anxiety inducing, and it is the means of transcending the human body and its pain.

Some post-structuralist feminisms might consider this desire to disconnect from biological imperatives to be 'somatophobic' because of the way they pose female bodies as 'troublesome bodies' (Price and Shildrick 1999: 4). Indeed Janet Price and Magrit Shildrick criticise second-wave feminism for its separation of gender and biology and describe Shulamith Firestone, a symbol of second-wave feminism, as 'somatopobic'. They write: 'Firestone ... looked forward with optimism to a time when the then incipient advanced reproductive technologies might free a woman from the "oppressive 'natural' conditions" of procreation' (ibid.). Yet the women vampire fans share with this strand of second-wave feminism an equivocal relation to the body and a desire to transcend the limits of the body, which at least for some is connected to reproduction. The critiques of the 'transcendence paradigm' do not seem to address the question of pain which is at the forefront of these fan accounts of their own body. The women fans' experience of different forms of pain, their articulation of that pain and their appropriation of the figure of the vampire to imagine a 'beyond', takes place in and through a history of discourses about feminine pain and I would like to suggest that second-wave feminism has added to this discourse two 'norms' popularly available for women to make sense of 'womanly' pain such as childbirth. The first is to celebrate these physical experiences as a natural part of womanhood (which seem to differ little from traditional ideas about women). The second is to insist that women should not be defined through their biology and thus it celebrates the transcendent possibilities of science, the ability to control fertility, and to control pain. The transformation stories sit somewhere in-between because pain has not been erased from them (in fact it has been dwelt upon) but it is ultimately surpassed in a new (undead) ontology. Some contemporary feminists also celebrate the transcendent possibilities of science and technology. Donna Haraway, for instance, advocates cyborg feminism because the 'cyborg is a kind of disassembled and reassembled, postmodern collective and personal self ... No objects, spaces, or bodies are sacred in themselves; any component can be interfaced with any other if the proper ... code can be constructed' (2000: 55). The rewritten vampire, however, is not Haraway's optimistic cyborg metaphor, where leaky bodies are the basis of a new ontology and feminist politics, but is perhaps her underbelly. For, while Haraway's cyborg points to future potentials, the vampire points to alternatives and their non-fulfilment simultaneously, the vampire after all will never be alive. Nevertheless, fan fiction is grappling with the same issues of 'being' and embodiment that has long concerned feminism. The vampire figure of the fans' writing is an imaginative and creative examination of different ways that a body might be inhabited and felt and the transcendence paradigm perhaps loses somatophobic edge in the context of the physicality of the vampire stories the fans write. Although it is not 'slash' fiction, it explores similar issues to 'hurt/comfort' stories around the issues of pain and risk. It is through addressing their own struggles with pain that fans explore alternative ways of being in this fiction.

FAN FICTION: BUFFY AS SLASH

Slash fiction is an important feature of the fan fiction surrounding *Buffy* and *Angel*, but it is important to remember that although there are dozens of websites dedicated to *Buffy* slash, it is not the only fan fiction engagement with the series. There are many stories which extend existing non-sexual friendships and introduce new story lines which are not sexual in character. For instance, there are stories which further explore the relationship between Buffy's younger sister, Dawn, and Spike. Often these stories focus on Spike's brotherly or fatherly role in protecting Dawn, and what he must sacrifice in terms of his 'cool' image. One very appealing story is entitled 'Be Sober, Be Vigilant' by 'Lady Cat'. We are introduced to Spike attempting to get a depressed Dawn out of bed: 'Get up you silly bint. You look like a frog.' To shake Dawn out of her depression Spike persuades her to escape with him out of her bedroom window and he takes her to 'Frank's' seedy demonic bar. The reader is invited to question Spike's judgement as he offers, 'You want to start with beer, or the hard stuff?' Even Dawn, who thinks its 'cool', hesitates when the beer arrives because she is worried about its contents. 'Bloody hell', Spike responds and takes a gulp. His plan, 'so bad that even *he* was hesitant about implementing it' has worked; as Dawn takes a gulp of beer she chokes on the taste: 'It looks like urine. And it tastes *so* worse.' She spends the remainder of the visit to the bar happily 'blathering on about silly teenager things'; her depression lifted, Spike content. Spike has to stake a Vorshal demon to get Dawn out of the bar safely, which underlines the danger of the place he has taken her, but the reader knows that he is capable of protecting her and even Frank tells her, 'Don't come back here without Spike'. This story not only explores Spike's ambivalent attitude to the 'sodding warm fuzzies he got when Dawn depended on him', it also acts as a symbolic *full* acceptance from the other Scoobies that Spike is denied in the television series. Spike recognises that 'Red didn't come storming into the bar, demanding that they leave right this instant, Mister, and you are in so much trouble', and the story closes with Spike sharing a beer with Xander, the one Scooby who consistently loathes Spike on TV. This is one of numerous examples of non-slash fiction surrounding the series that are concerned with the issue of the 'outcast'. In this story Spike, the ultimate outcast, is accepted. But *Buffy* has also generated enormous amounts of slash fiction.

The cult television text and the rise of the Internet have both had an important impact on the development of slash fiction. Camille Bacon-Smith, writing about the science fiction slash community in the early 1990s, characterised this form of creative activity as one of 'risk' (1992: 208); risk from personal exposure, risk from facing full-on the question of why life 'hurts so much' (1992: 207). Women in the caring professions or who worked in publishing felt exposure of their membership to this kind of fan community could put their jobs at risk. As a result, new members to fandom were only introduced to slash after trust was established with a distribution network. However, slash fiction is no longer an underground or hidden aspect of fandom. Slash fiction websites, webrings and newsgroups abound and many sites openly mix slash and non-slash fiction, as well as fictional and non-fictional material. As a result, slash fiction has increased and undergone transformation. The cult television text has contributed greatly to this transformation. For instance, the slash community that Bacon-Smith was involved with wrote predominantly about male/male parings which led her to question why women would write about male homosexual encounters. Bacon-Smith suggested that this was part of the process of the conservation of risk. It removes the woman from the direct experience about which she writes and allows her to engage in fantasy sexual situations that she would not want to experience in reality. Furthermore, writing about gay sex 'means writing about the risk inherent in pursuing an oppressed sexuality' (1992: 147). Like other scholars who have written about slash fiction (Russ 1985; Lamb and Veith 1986; Penley 1992), Bacon-Smith suggests that slash writers are female writers articulating their desires about relationships with men. Women are writing about men because men are for them, 'the alien, the other'. However, ten to fifteen years has changed slash fiction considerably. Significantly, shows such as *Xena: Warrior Princess* have provided a model for depictions of female/female pairings of the strong women protagonists and has generated considerable amounts of lesbian slash.

Furthermore, cult television texts such as *Xena* have openly encouraged audiences to play with its homoerotic subtext in order to attract large and intense fan audiences (cf. Gwenllian Jones 2000).[1] The slash subtext is even more overtly encouraged in the case of *Buffy the Vampire Slayer*. Joss Whedon, the series creator, posted a message on the *Buffy* fan discussion board, The Bronze, suggesting that the attraction of the Buffyverse is that:

> It lends itself to polymorphous perverse subtext. It encourages it. I personally find romance in every relationship [with exceptions], I love all the characters, so I say B. Y. O. Subtext!

I suggested in chapter four that *Buffy*'s extended plotlines, intertextual and metatextual references, its serial nature and lack of closure, is deliberately intended to produce active fan involvement, and this is equally true for slash fiction involvement, as Whedon's comments indicate, and as we shall see in the sexual encounters depicted on the show. Esther Saxey, who also argues that *Buffy* is 'slashable', suggests that it is because it is 'dedicated to dwelling on those interesting "expectations" aroused in the middle of texts' (2002: 192). So while slash has traditionally dwelt on 'emotions and sexual attraction that are "off-limits"' (2002: 199), Buffy is already infused with these elements, but it is nevertheless 'frequently slashed' anyway:

> What *Buffy* slashers are most drawn to is not only that which is absent ... but particularly that which has been thrown out of Buffy: themes dwelt on in the middle of episodes or plotlines which are abandoned or overcome. (Ibid.)

For Saxey it is the psychological torture that the characters endure (which is both raised and disavowed in *Buffy*) that provides the ejected content that slash fiction focuses on. This is why *Buffy* slash tends to focus on 'mismatched misery', where sex is the only point of contact for 'a pair of lovers whose own problems are too vast for them to find anything but transitory comfort' (2002: 202). The idea that the act of sex is the only possible comfort seems to be a new theme in slash fiction which is overtly depicted in the show. This focus on sex without tenderness exists alongside the more familiar slash sub-genres; 'hurt/comfort', 'first-time', and 'of-necessity' (the science fiction slash community call this 'Pon Farr'). Saxey seems to have predicted the *overt* direction of the television series in the latter half of season five and season six, while continuing to insist that there is no 'direct relationship between the series and slash' (2002: 209). She argues that it is 'stretching the point' to suggest that *Buffy* encourages speculation to the degree that it 'produces or condones slash' (ibid.). However, *Buffy* not only condones slash, to some extent it *is* slash in these seasons, overtly through the sado-masochistic sexual relationship of

Buffy and Spike, but heavily alluded to in the case of other characters. Buffy assumes the dominant role in this relationship with Spike, and the Spike/Buffy pairing might be seen as an extended 'hurt/comfort' story which looks like a 'hurt Spike' story for a good part of two seasons. Although Spike has long been in love with Buffy, in season six she uses him as her sexual toy. She regularly abuses him – physically, mentally and sexually. She beats him, calls him an 'evil, disgusting thing' and insists on sex even when he says 'no'. In 'Smashed' the pair's first sexual encounter occurs when Buffy throws Spike against a wall, unzips his trousers and has sex with him, and again in 'Gone' she breaks into his room throws him against the wall and initiates sex. To liken this to slash may be uncomfortable to some, particularly as slash is normally considered to depict 'hurt/comfort' between a pair of lovers with violence stemming from outside. The injury of one partner and the (sometimes sexual) comforting of the other partner is seen as an eroticisation of female nurturance. Bacon-Smith suggests that women fans write 'hurt/comfort' slash because of the experience of pain, which is 'so pervasive in the lives of women that it [lies] like a wash beneath all of the creative efforts of a community' (1992: 270). She comments that in a typical 'hurt/comfort' story,

> One hero will be injured ... while his companion worries about him, empathises with his pain, and finally gives comfort. Throughout the victim remains powerless, but the story of domination undergoes a transformation: beginning as the product of force – bad, masculine, power – it becomes the reflection for his need for caring – good, feminine power. While the victim remains powerless, the move from masculine power to feminine power transforms the victim as well. When the woman begins the story, she may identify the victim as female in spite of the male character that represents her, but as the story progresses, the woman as comforter holds power, even when represented by a man ... In this fictional transformation we see the transmutation of the sadistic urge into the maternal role of self-sacrifice, while the masochistic position of victim remains ever problematic, both attractive and repellent. (1992: 272)

A number of critics have commented on the gender slidings that operate in horror (Clover 1992; Creed 1993), and the idea that females can identify with male characters has been demonstrated in women fan accounts of their engagement with the vampire in chapter two, supporting Bacon-Smith's contention about cross-gender identification. Yet *Buffy* complicates these gender identifications by overtly slashing Buffy and Spike, and in doing so the show extends the repertoire of slash because slash writers attempt to move on from the series. In the TV pairing of Buffy/Spike, the sympathy resides with the abused male monster, not the female abuser. However, this is not a simple gender inversion – Buffy as masculine and Spike as feminine. As Dee Amy-Chinn argues, Spike is 'queer' in that he is 'both male *and* female, masculine *and* feminine, vanilla *and* erotically varied' (2005: 316). For Amy-Chinn Spike complicates his biological maleness 'with a performance of gender that switches between testosterone-fuelled masculinity and an extreme form of femininity' (ibid.). Indeed, both characters traverse gender boundaries; Buffy adopts the traditional masculine role of initiating sex and she uses Spike for sex yet does not show him love, whereas Spike is the loving partner whose emotional needs are not met. But as the series moves forward, Buffy comes to occupy the feminised dependent position. In the penultimate episode Buffy falls into a depression when the Scooby Gang have deposed her in favour of Faith and relies on Spike for emotional comfort and support. The final season of *Buffy* finds both characters occupying feminised dependent positions in relation to each other and in the end Buffy comforts Spike too. Their attraction, however, is not primarily an erotic form of nurturing; it is sexual desire. As Amy-Chinn puts it, this is 'sex born out of violence', fuelled by a 'desire for domination and control' (2005: 321), particularly on Buffy's part, although Spike willingly participates out of love and because he can, his 'queerness' gives him 'access to a broader repertoire of behaviours' (Amy-Chinn 2005: 326) than any of Buffy's previous men.

The large female fandom surrounding Spike adopts a position of identification with Spike. This considerably alters the gender dynamics of traditional slash because Spike occupies a female position and is in love with a female character – an expression of lesbian desire. Spike is also being abused by Buffy which undermines any systematically progressive reading of this pairing. Furthermore, Buffy's self-loathing at her attraction to Spike can be read as self-directed homophobia. After Buffy's first aggressive initiation of sexual intercourse she comments 'last night was the most perverse, degrading experience of my life'. Perhaps, but it did not stop her. Saxey argues that 'Buffy-as-Slayer' often stands in for 'Buffy-as-queer', such that when she 'comes out' to her mother, her mother asks: 'Have you tried not being a vampire Slayer?' ('Becoming Part 2'). Amy-Chinn also argues that while 'Buffy may, as Spike asserts, need a little monster in her man ... she also needs quite a lot of woman' (2003: 9). Despite the show's hesitancy regarding the queering of Buffy's sexuality, we can see how the gender relations of traditional slash are disrupted. Where Bacon-Smith's women occupied a male role in a homosexual relationship in order to explore heterosexual desire, female Spike fans occupy a male position in a heterosexual relationship to explore polymorphous sexual desire – the moving back and forth between lesbian desire and heterosexual desire. One might wonder where slash fiction could go from a series that has so thoroughly slashed itself. But the male/male pairing boundaries of slash have been extended considerably around *Buffy*. For instance, Spike (as nominally male but symbolically female), is regularly paired with other female characters. When Spike is paired with Tara, who is Willow's lesbian lover, the encounter is still 'queer', but the forbidden and elicit edge to the pairing is intensified by the depiction of shifting desire as Tara is confused at desiring his masculine body.

Saxey has suggested that there is a sense in *Buffy* that sexual encounters do not only allude to emotional conditions, they are a temporary defence against them – the sex itself is the comfort. There is much *Buffy* slash that similarly focuses on the sexual act itself, but not necessarily for comfort. It is not only the case that emotional suffering is turned into sexual encounters, it is also the case that sex is depicted primarily to sexually arouse. Alongside the usual 'hurt/comfort' stories, 'first-time' stories and 'of-necessity' stories for instance, *Buffy* slash fiction includes numerous depictions of sado-masochistic sex. One example is a Spike/Xander pairing which begins with Xander on his own playing with Spike's highly symbolic belt and erotically imagining Spike beating him with it. Spike enters and the two engage in graphic S/M sex which involves Spike strangling Xander with the belt to consummate the sexual act. There are also S/M encounters between Buffy, Spike and Riley which focus on rough anal sex, which causes Buffy pain (that she enjoys) and other acts which humiliate Riley and Spike, and so on. Whether or not slash is pornographic has been much debated by fan scholarship. Like Bacon-Smith, Patricia F. Lamb and Diana L. Veith (1986) focus on emotional intimacy of the sexual encounters in slash and Mirna Cicioni argues that slash is not pornographic on the basis that pornography endorses sexual behaviour that is depicted as degrading or abusive to at least one of the participants 'even if the person has chosen or consented to it' (Helen Longino quoted in Cicioni 1998: 168). For Cicioni, slash scenes, 'far from representing degrading behaviour, are usually set in contexts of deep emotional closeness, which ... are as much a part of the fantasy as the sexual activities themselves' (ibid.). However, this is clearly not the case in much *Buffy* slash, including the slashed relationship between Buffy and Spike in the show itself. As Amy-Chinn argues, the sex between Buffy and Spike is not a tender, loving encounter between two people who have made a mutual commitment, but a hard, fast, frenzied, encounter between two people whose desire is excessive and out of control' (2005: 321).

In at least one version of the threesome described above, the characters are not depicted as emotionally close, but rather, are alienated from each other. Spike degrades Buffy, and Buffy degrades Riley and Spike by insisting that Spike bite him against his will. So acute are Riley's feelings of humiliation at the encounter that he tells Buffy, 'I have no dignity when it comes to you'. Constance Penley, in contrast to Bacon-Smith, Cicioni and Lamb and Veith, has argued that the academic emphasis on romance 'slights the pornographic force' (1992: 491) of much slash. She points to a range of sado-masochistic slash stories in science fiction fandom, but she does not condemn them entirely because she sees them as sexual fantasies rather than actions that women would want to happen in reality.

It seems that many of the slash stories based on *Buffy* characters are primarily intended to sexually arouse the reader through the graphic depiction of forbidden and polymorphous sexual encounters. Much of the writing in *Buffy* slash fiction is pornographic, whether it is nice to admit it or not. I am not suggesting that this makes slash unacceptable politically, for I concur with Penley that slash exists as imaginary sexual encounters and not real ones. But neither is slash to be simply celebrated; it is hard to celebrate erotically depicted rape and torture sequences even if they are only fantasy. Slash also is clearly no longer a matter of the politically progressive endeavour of women building a culture outside of 'masculinist' norms, to nurture and comfort each other, as Bacon-Smith suggests; much *Buffy* slash instead is a matter of sexual arousal. But this does not mean that romance is dead in vampire fandom, as the following section will demonstrate.

VAMPIRES IN CYBERSPACE

Two of my contacts in New Orleans, Hannah and Melinda, met through a non-moderated vampire newsgroup on the Internet. They described themselves as 'previously heterosexual' women who met each other in cyberspace, fell in love, came out as lesbians, moved to New Orleans together, got married, and lived happily every after. It is a heart-warming story that seems to support those who make claims about the possibilities offered by on-line fandom. For instance, Sherry Turkle, in discussing on-line, text-based computer games such as the *Star Trek* game 'Trekmuse', argues that in cyberspace 'we can talk, exchange ideas, and assume personae of our own creation'; this is taking place in the context of 'eroding boundaries between the real and the virtual, the animate and the inanimate, the unitary and the multiple self' (1998: 6). This sense of the Internet providing new spaces in which to explore identity is echoed in Melinda and Hannah's own accounts of finding love in cyberspace. They met during a role-playing game where the male homoerotic possibilities that they wrote for the characters opened up possibilities for them and their relationship:

> Melinda: As I say, I still trace it back to the game personally. Well the way we were playing the game ... before we started actually talking to each other. We would be up most nights just passing email posts back and forth on the game, and the characters we were playing were engaged and romantically inclined and going to get married and – you know, it started getting kind of hot and heavy on the scenes, and we decided we clicked really well, and who proposed to whom?
>
> Hannah: I proposed to her...
>
> Melinda: You see, what happened ... this was Hollywood Vampires, about right in the middle of it, I had taken on Armand ... She was playing Marius, who I hated ... Well, she played him so beautifully, so sympathetically that I started seeing a tremendous amount of her in the character. So finally – when you play these games, don't misunderstand, it's not – I post one post in the vacuum and they all respond to it, and then somebody else posts a post through a vacuum and everybody else responds. We plan out each one of these steps, so for every post that you see in these games, you've got at least ten or twenty emails behind the scenes saying 'okay, now what are you going to do and how are we going to react and how are we going to write this, and how are we gonna deal

with this' ... so there's a tremendous amount of work behind the scene planning ... and the preplanning that took to create this story, to make it a beautiful piece of work, that's how we got to know each other.

Hannah: I remember one night in particular. She quoted one poem and I recognised it, because it was on a tape that I have. So I'm like, 'oh I recognise that', so without telling her I recognised it, I ran and got the tape and wrote out another one of the poems from it and sent it to her. And she's like 'oh this can't be quite happening', so she wrote out another one to me, and I'm just like, I don't know what that's from ... That was when we actually started talking to each other about, you know, what we like, what we didn't like, and all this sort of stuff and actually getting to know each other. We found out we had a lot of similarities ... and it was always going simultaneously because we had just written this amazingly hot and heavy scene between Armand ... I remember when I woke up the next morning, I was feeling a case of the nerves. But I remember how I felt and I felt so astounded about it all and I wrote back to her immediately, going 'what did we do, and how did you feel'? And she wrote back immediately saying to me 'this is the first morning that I could face going to work with a smile on my face and joy in my heart, and this is what you've done to me. Regardless of what happened, this is what comes of it' ... that's how it all came about.

I wanted to quote extensively from this discussion because it demonstrates the complexity of communal writing of vampires on the Internet, and also shows how playing with homoerotic desire between fictional characters has allowed them to develop a romantic cyber-relationship that carries into the rest of their lives. There is very little written about 'finding love' in cyberspace. However, in a study of couples who met on the Internet, Andrea Baker (1999) suggests that couples meet 'through particularised, rather than general places on-line'. Furthermore, she suggests that physical attraction takes second place to 'intellectual and emotional compatibility' adding that, 'with these couples, the knowing of the "inner person" occurs before the revelation of the outer shell' (ibid.). These observations seem to ring true in the account of the relationship between Hannah and Melinda. The emphasis in the exchange above is on sharing intellectual pursuits (poetry) and practices (writing) as well as emotional compatibility, followed by the 'hot and heavy' desire. Thus the practices of vampire fandom in that space that is called 'cyberspace' enabled the connections and explorations of identity which opened up possibilities about sexual identity and self and enabled these women, through a fan community, to come out as lesbians and fall in love.

These two women and the others in their writing circle refer to each other as 'cybersisters' and 'cyberfamily' and have found on the Internet an alternative community to traditional family ties. Another female couple from the group were married prior to Hannah and Melinda and joined them in New Orleans, where the four live together as two couples. Their fandom allowed the women to express and act upon, as Bacon-Smith puts it in relation to female science fiction fans, 'feelings that are unacceptable' (1992: 270). But such alternative living arrangements existed long before the Internet and those who argue that it is the changes wrought by the Internet *per se* that have permitted these alternatives are quite one-sided in their view of technology. Sadie Plant, for instance, proposes that virtual worlds 'undermine both the worldview and the material reality of two thousand years of patriarchal control' (2000: 265) and that in spite of itself 'patriarchy is subsumed by the processes that served it so well' (2000: 269). She maintains that 'it takes an irresponsible feminism – which may not be feminism at all – to trace the inhuman paths on which woman begins to assemble herself [in] the cracks and crazes now emerging across the once smooth face of the patriarchal order' (2000: 274). However, Plant's claim that such power has never before revealed cracks or that logging on to one's computer is the mode of overturning such power, is highly dubious. Saxey has argued in relation to *Buffy* slash that the Internet is not the 'playground of mobile identity it has been proclaimed to be – its middle-class Western slant is evident' (2002: 189). This echoes the damning critique of Internet euphoria by Kevin Robins and Frank Webster (1999) which was followed by numerous other critics (Balsamo 2000; Gonzales 2000; Lykke 2000; Morley 2000). For Robins and Webster, the community on the Internet is part of modernity's desire to hide alterity and banish difference. Commenting upon the predominantly male, white, middle-class American inhabitant of cyberspace, they argue that 'cyberspace, with its myriad of little consensual communities, is a place where you will go in order to find confirmation and endorsement of your identity' (2000: 249). The idea of 'connectivity – being in touch through interest and affinity rather than the accident of geographical location' (2000: 240) is not a new form of interaction, but relates to an old desire to deny difference. For Robins and Webster the 'new virtual space is a pacified space [because] virtual culture is driven by the desire to suppress the complexities, difficulties and divisions that characterise real geographies' (2000: 239). Furthermore they argue that 'technoculture' seeks to revalidate Rousseau's ideal of social transparency in which 'persons cease to be other, opaque, not understood, and instead become mutually sympathetic, understanding one another as they understand themselves' (2000: 244).

It is true that Melinda and the other members of their Internet group have found a small 'consensual community' based on mutual interest and affinity. Melinda explains:

> We met from all over the world ... But we all met on the Internet, we all got together, we all found a common interest, we all found a common talent, and we said 'cool, let's go'. So we all have our own web pages, we all are very deeply into this as far the characters ... these characters speak to us ... You know, there's a concept and there's a core in there that is very romantic and very appealing, and these concepts are alive ... the nerves that they touch within the human heart gives them a certain life ... So that's what captured us and drove us forward.

However, Robins and Webster's critique of both the theories of cyberspace and cyberspace itself, while providing a much needed unpacking of the 'e-topia' claims about cyberspace, seems to be unable to fully account for these women's experiences on-line. When they write that 'encounters with others should not be about confirmation but about transformation', they are ignoring crucial questions of subordination linked to (among other issues) gender and sexuality, and perhaps such a statement is only easily made by those whose identities are confirmed rather than hidden by wider culture. In the case of these women, finding 'confirmation' of their identity in their on-line community is less about hiding differences, and more about finding support and friendship circles that allow their (socially unacceptable) identities as lesbian women to emerge. What is interesting, though (and at odds with much of the literature about on-line communities), is that, for these women, finding a family and a home in cyberspace did not curtail their desire for close physical proximity to their new family. The space/time compression, so lauded by theorists of cyberspace as recreating new geographies, was not enough for these women who wanted to be together physically as well. Melinda explains:

> We all travelled to New Orleans independently, thinking we'd all hate each other, because whenever you meet somebody off the Internet, you always hate them, even though you really, really like them on the net, you hate them in person, and when we all left, it was one of the most traumatic things in our lives. [When] we all went back to the four corners of America ... it was one of the worst days of our entire lives. And we decided right there and then we had to be together. We all shared a vision.

David Morley suggests that while new communication technologies are producing new definitions of community, they are not erasing, but rather 'overlaying' older understandings. It is not, he argues, the case that physical space no longer matters; 'it is rather a question of how physical and symbolic networks become entwined around each other' (2000: 176). These fans' symbolic networks on-line have indeed become inextricably bound up with their sense of home and place.

This examination of the lesbian community set up by these fans via the Internet does not indicate that cyberspace has inaugurated a new era of identity subversion. Indeed, Morley concurs with Robins and Webster's view that 'the space of the Internet is in fact more socially homogenous than that of the physical world, because those who have access to it have already been selected by ethnicity, nationality, class and gender' (2000: 187). However, my point is that it is not entirely homogenous and is populated by many people who are privileged in some ways and subordinated in others and our understanding of the on-line world has to accommodate such complexity. Melinda and Hannah share some, but not all, of the privileges by which access to the Internet is selected. Both are university-educated Americans and Hannah, who has formal computer training to degree level, works as a network engineer at one of the university hospitals in New Orleans. However, their gender and sexual orientation works against that privilege in a society in which heterosexuality continues to be judged the norm. Also, Hannah struggles in particular in a very male-oriented work environment. Therefore it is both the experiences of subordination and access to privileges that shape these women's lives and their desire for community.

WRITING BOUNDARIES

Fan fiction is understood predominantly as an interpretive community, an inclusive, encouraging and inclusive space (Bacon-Smith 1992: Jenkins 1992). For Henry Jenkins, 'writing becomes a social activity for these fans, functioning simultaneously as a form of personal expression and as a source of collective identity (part of what it means to be a fan)' (1992: 155). Fans stretch the boundaries of texts 'to incorporate their concerns, remoulding its characters to better suit their desires' (1992: 156). At one level, Jenkins' description is accurate. The examination of Melinda and Hannah's on-line writing supports this point. They also take great pride in infringing copyright when they re-write Anne Rice's vampires. Melinda says:

> The specs are something that Anne hates. I'll tell you right now, she hates them, because she's very possessive about her characters, and would prefer that others not write about them. But it's done anyway, so give it up, and there's no way you can control this. The only author I know that ever tried to stop it was [inaudible] and not only did she get a singularly negative reputation amongst the Internet fans, but as far as I know, the stories within her world are going as strong as ever, in fact redoubled, simply as a backlash, and now they're just underground. You know, all you have to do is ask, 'oh where do I get this'? They say 'here's my private little archive that nobody knows about, and there's all the stories', so you can't stop it.

In this sense, these fans are 'poaching' Rice's characters and re-writing them to suit themselves. But that is not all there is to speculative stories. There is a very firm etiquette about writing which Bacon-Smith describes in relation to science fiction fandom and which Melinda explained to me. For instance, one fan is not allowed to take up the threads of another writer's story without permission. Also, killing off of favourite characters is forbidden, and taking over a character that another fan has already claimed is not acceptable. Hannah described some 'flamewars' that have erupted on their newsgroup as a result of just such breaches of protocols (one particularly galling incident came from a PhD candidate who killed off favourite characters in order to assess the group reaction for her thesis). But often, new or inexperienced participants are bounced off, ignored, or else taken under someone's wing in order to 'learn the ropes'. Bacon-Smith discusses these issues in her analysis of science fiction fandom. She argues that

> experienced fans work consciously to *preserve the standards* [my italics] of fan fiction developed over time in *Star Trek* and other fan literature; at the same time, the very depth of their experience gives them the freedom to explore new ways of expressing the messages most important to them. (1992: 215)

Although Bacon-Smith does not acknowledge it, it is clear from her description that fans are taking positions to sanction themselves as experienced fan fiction writers, who can legitimately designate who is and who is not experienced enough to be considered, and to endorse others like themselves, thus securing their position within the fandom. This becomes even clearer in her description of the writing of fan fiction. Newcomers are labelled 'neophytes', and are told to occupy positions of newcomers. Bacon-Smith writes:

> Roberta frequently suggests that newcomers amend well-worn plots with a humourous twist. She recognises that the beginning writer may not have mastered the codes and conventions she needs to write a story that the group, her readers, will take seriously. In humour, however, the neophyte inhabits a liminal area where she may practice the manipulation of the community's codes. (1992: 153)

Like other areas of cultural life, fans are expected to accumulate the appropriate cultural capital (or internalise the appropriate habitus) deemed to merit inclusion by those who police the boundaries of legitimacy. Bacon-Smith addresses this issue when she proposes that editors of fanzines act as 'arbiters of taste' by suggesting changes to stories that have not met the aesthetic criteria of the group. But she skirts over the issue by emphasising the editor's role is to maintain the 'integrity' of the circuit (1992: 215). These attitudes are repeated among vampire fans, where appropriate behaviour is utterly expected. For example, Melinda had written a series of letters between two of the vampires which she posted on the site. I asked her about the surrounding etiquette:

Milly: *But how would you feel if somebody else from wherever,*
    London or something, wrote extra letters?
Melinda: Yeah, you see, I'd go crazy!
Milly: *Would you really?*
Melinda: Yes. Exactly, I'm such a hypocrite. I don't deny it in the
    slightest. But what we try and do, we try to be very polite.
    The characters are not exclusive, but once you begin a story,
    unless you ask the author to jump in on that particular story,
    you can't do it. Write your own story with the same charac-

ters, the same set, the same concept, do whatever you like. Just don't jump in on this story.

Rather than fan writing on the Internet being a space where 'anything goes', it seems that computing norms have emerged which do not constitute a 'radically new discursive space' (MacDonald 1998: 133) in terms of the game of position-taking and the struggles for legitimacy based on cultural capital, even while it has clearly opened up a space to explore questions of sexuality.

In Britain, Dee and Karen comment on the way that fanzine editors act as 'arbiters of taste' and systematically reject material that they deem unsuitable or not up to standard. When I asked Dee if she sent fictional stories to a particular fanzine, she replied in the negative and explained:

> Well, simply because they reject, I mean, I thought about writing something for them, and then they reject all such things like comedy horoscopes ... I have a friend who sent them some stories but they rejected her stuff and also when the Dracula Society, they were gonna do a book for the Centenary, but they didn't get enough interest, and they wanted people to send in stories. And she sent some of her stories, but she'd noticed it in the Vampyre Society booklet. It said you could send them to them, and because she'd had more dealings with them, she sent her stories to them, who didn't pass them on to the Dracula Society.

This account paints an entirely different picture to Jenkins' picture of a 'nurturing atmosphere', with editors who 'take pride in their receptiveness to new contributors' and his claim that 'anyone who wants to can probably get published within fandom' (1992: 159). Indeed, Constance Penley (1991) discusses the tension of competing impulses that *Star Trek* editors face. Editors are 'torn' between 'professionalism' and 'acceptance'. Such an observation seems to support the suggestion that fandoms are influenced by the discourses of legitimisation circulating around the two antagonistic dominant poles in the field of cultural production.

But it is not only the constraints of fan publishing which present a barrier to publishing fan fiction. Writing is also bound up with one's self-confidence as a writer, which again seems to be related to class background and educational level. Dee, who left school at 16 with very few qualifications, worked in a hairdresser before she had her children and she is now a full-time single parent. Her level of confidence in her abilities and her general level of humility contrasts sharply with the confidence which university-educated fan writers exude. When I asked her if she now writes vampire fiction she replied, 'No, I don't write stories because I'm bad at it'. She explains that:

> Book reviews, I used to be able to do them, I just used to pick up a book and review it, but then when they started sending them me ... some

books are hard to do it with. And then I'm thinking 'at the end of the day, it's only my opinion. I think it's crap, but what if I get caught out', because I can't actually write reviews. So what if somebody realises ... I couldn't bear them to say 'we can't use this, it's crap'. I'm sure they wouldn't say that, they'd just say it's not suitable for this month's issue or something.

Here is a fan being encouraged by the fanzine to do more reviews, but her confidence in her own abilities stops her from writing. She does not possess, in educational terms, official cultural capital and fandom does not provide her with the means of acquiring alternative cultural capital. When Jenkins characterises fan fiction for women as 'an alternative source of status' and writes, 'women who have low-prestige jobs or who are homemakers can gain national and even international recognition as fan writers and artists' (1992: 159) he ignores the very stark ways that the unequal distribution of cultural capital can effect self-esteem. It may be the case that some women gain confidence through writing fan fiction, but it is not axiomatic of fandom as this fan's comments demonstrate. Furthermore, Jenkins' weekend utopia ignores the way that one's life outside fandom can impact on fan activity. Dee made these comments in the context of discussing a number of difficulties, mainly financial (as a single mum she had limited income) and emotional (one of her sons was very ill). She told me:

> Now, it takes me sometimes three hours to write a letter ... but I used to do two an hour, now I couldn't do half in that time, because my mind's on other things. Because my house is falling down, the roof needs mending, my kitchen needs doing, and there's something wrong with my son ... I just – I am a great worrier.

Also, it is important to recognise that fan fiction is not only an 'alternative' source of status. Would-be professional writers use fan fiction as a training ground. Even if this does not entirely motivate some to write fan fiction, it is certainly clear that the national and international recognition as a fan writer is seen by some as a very useful strategy for breaking into professional writing. Melinda who wants her work to be published, sees fan fiction thus:

> I'm writing my first serious novel. And you see, fan fiction isn't exclusive to Anne Rice by any means. When I first ran into fan fiction it was to another fandom entirely ... And one of the authors that I particularly admired was just brilliant, and she wrote her own fan fiction, and you see when you do this, you can sell it, but only for cost, and so you print it up and you sell it for the cost of the printing. You can't make a profit off of it, no problem. But it gets your name out there and it establishes you as you, but I have the talent, I have the conviction to complete a novel. I have what it takes.

The author mentioned by Melinda did 'break in' to publishing and had her novel published, providing Melinda with the inspiration that she could do the same. There is nothing wrong with using fan fiction as a way to practice professional writing, for getting feedback and for establishing a reputation. The point is not to castigate Melinda. Instead the point is that fans do participate in the official world of authorial meaning, stratified as it is by class, reputation and the possession of appropriate cultural capital. This fan is (at least partly) participating in fan fiction as a way of entering the 'official' world of publishing as a professional author. It seems to me to be a rather positive side to fan culture, that aspiring authors have a resource to help them 'break into' what is often an exclusive world. But it does not subvert mainstream culture.

Writing the vampire for these women fans is a complex cultural practice involving processes that are often at odds with each other. Fan fiction is a creative means of exploring issues to do with body boundaries, transformation and selfhood. Yet while fans are blurring boundaries in their fiction, other boundaries are erected. The validity to designate who can write what and for whom, invested in fanzine and webring editors, is not part of a fan cultural project of subverting mainstream conventions of cultural production, but rather seems to be influenced by the ideas of cultural production in a quest for 'distinction'. Furthermore, fan culture does not necessarily offer alternative forms of cultural capital denied to subordinate groups, but rather the lack of cultural capital experienced by some fans is carried into the arena of fandom and limits their participation.

THE VAMPIRE AND THE SELF: THE DILEMMAS
OF THE DEAD AND THE REALM OF THE POSSIBLE

The Western vampire is a creature of capitalism; it enters the Western imagination concurrently with the emergence of the culture of the bourgeoisie, giving expression to its fears, denials and contradictions. Marx famously likened the workings of capitalism to the vampire,[1] and drawing on Marx, David Punter suggests that the literature of the Gothic (the vampire's early Western landscape) cannot be disconnected from the 'economic life of the age' that gave birth to it (1996: 196). It was the tumultuous eighteenth century that shaped Gothic literature and Punter comments that this was a time wracked by contradictions in the economic and cultural spheres, particularly in relation to official explanations of the world. The vampire enters the permanently transient culture of capitalism, adapting and evolving in order to keep pace with the cultural moment. It is for this reason that the Western vampire is an ambiguous figure; it is a rebel and aristocrat, bohemian and nobility, it looks to the past and to the future. But the vampire is a creature of capitalism in another sense, for as a borderline figure, one that is marginal to the culture to the point of undeath, the vampire expresses the pathos of the condition of the many in the West – the condition of alienation. Indeed, Punter describes the Gothic as the 'literature of alienation' (1996: 197), demonstrating how Marx's four main categories of alienation are persistent themes in the Gothic. Ever ambivalent, the vampire expresses our alienation from our very human-ness and it offers an imaginary transcendence to culturally-imposed limitations on the body and the self. Its duality therefore explains the vampire's longevity and its popularity today, as Anglophone culture increasingly celebrates a sense of self that most cannot or will not conform to. Our own time too, then, is marked by the contradictions and limits of its official discourses, widening the gap between these discourses and our experiences of ourselves in the world. Thus the vampire is no longer an expression of terror, it is the expression of the outcast and this helps to explain its enormous popularity and the existence of a large vampire fan culture.

However, rather than consider this fan culture as *per se* subversive of the dominant system I have suggested that the cultural politics of vampire fandom (and fandom in general) is contradictory and often focused on the self. Vampire fandom sits within the field of cultural production; it cannot step outside of this field into a utopian space and it is thus subject to the struggles and dynamics, the position-taking and the hierarchies, that structure modern cultural engagement. But it is not adequate to suggest that vampire fandom rubs along easily with the dominant values of culture – not least because they do not rub along easily with each other. But more than this, the vampire's undead existence raises the unspoken pain of not fitting into societal norms and the misery of insignificance, and this in turn gives rise to creative works. This creativity takes numerous shapes; sartorial self-expression, fan fiction, role- playing, the creation of clubs, journals, websites and more. There is something to be appreciated in this creative endeavour, despite the fact that its source is often pain, and despite the way that is exists (and must exist) in the hierarchical cultural field.

I have suggested that due to the structure of relations in culture, vampire fandom's activities are necessarily influenced by one or other set of values that dominate the field of cultural production. Some fans accept the 'heteronomous' values of culture and link cultural production and engagement to the profit motive. Others eschew these economic values and seek fandom-for-fandom's sake, sharing the cultural values with the 'autonomous pole' of dominant culture, including the often concomitant elitist distinctions. However, I have also suggested that, despite the potential for elitism, fandom-for-fandom's sake has, if nothing else, rejected the notion of culture for profit, and I suggest that this is a precondition for radicalising culture, even if it is not a revolution itself. Stephen Duncombe makes a similar point about underground 'zine' culture in the US and he too draws on Marx's theories of alienation to explain this. Duncombe reminds us of Marx's insight that most work under capitalism is not organised for the satisfaction of those who engage in it, it is organised for profit. Under these conditions, we are alienated from our work. Duncombe comments that 'the idea of non-alienated labour may not be ready for the ash heap of history just yet' (1997: 94). This is because, while creative production has been largely harnessed for profit, the idea of doing something for its own sake rather than for money is 'a type of work that runs counter to the norm within capitalist society' (ibid.). The writers of underground 'zines', like the 'not-for-profit' vampire fans are engaging in cultural production and consumption at odds with bourgeois values, even though it is often the case that such work is accompanied by elitist distinctions and contradictory ideas. One of the strengths of Duncombe's analysis is that he investigates these contradictions in zine culture systematically. Duncombe notes that the fragmented bohemia (of which both zine culture and vampire fandom are apart), divides the world into two polar opposites 'our world and theirs, integrity and selling out, purity and danger'. He examines the inwardness of this 'bohemian elitism' (1997: 168) and considers how it 'pits "us" against "them", its identity being contingent upon this distinction' (1997: 185). Nevertheless, he argues that zines 'reject the dominant justification for production and creation in our society' and by their very existence critique the 'pecuniary and narrowly instrumental nature of nearly all work' (1997: 95). While I have suggested that some vampire fans accept the economic rational for creativity, those who do not, who strive for fandom-for-

fandom's-sake, are rejecting the values of the dominating pole of cultural production – values which inhibit the possibilities for the self. As Terry Eagleton
puts it, 'to live a really fulfilling life, we have to be allowed to do what we do
just for the sake of it' (2003: 115), and he argues that this self-actualisation runs
counter to the ethos of capitalism.

The subset of fandom that rejects economic imperatives can and does
engage in its activities as its own reward, but it has also been unable to detach
the idea of 'for its own sake' from the drive towards hierarchy and elitism of the
autonomous values of culture. However, this does not alter the fact that these
ideas exist and really are opposed to the dominant idea of culture for profit.
As Duncombe argues, 'the politics of underground culture, like all "counter-
hegemonic cultures" and "pre-political" formations, offer a *necessary* but not
sufficient condition for social change. I don't see this as a pessimistic conclusion, just an honest one' (1997: 193) [my italics]. To reject the idea of culture for
profit is a necessary starting point for a more democratic culture, but in itself,
it is not enough to realise it.

Yet I have suggested that it is the cultural insistence on success, on visibility,
on significance and on the impossibility of 'living it' that has shaped the modern
Western vampire and has shaped our sympathetic responses to it, that is, to the
pain of our experience of this paradox. Engaging with the vampire is connected
to recognising our pain; a recognition that the promises that our culture holds
out to us are both contradictory and impossible to achieve. This throws up
different experiences, and for many this begins with a sense of not fitting in.
The most convincing accounts of fandom are not the euphoric ones, but the
ones that emphasis pain. For instance, Camille Bacon-Smith examines the risk
and the pain that surrounds female science fiction fandom, where members
share the experience of suffering with each other and through their fiction.
Like vampire fandom, it is dualistic: 'pain is present, recognised, shared, but
art is also present, and art is joyful' (1992: 269). Duncombe's zine writers experience themselves as 'losers'. But Duncombe comments that, 'while there isn't
much they can do about being losers in a society that rewards interests they
don't share and strengths they don't have, they can define the value of being a
loser, and turn a deficit into an asset' (1997: 20). Vampire fans do not consider
themselves losers – rather they are outcasts – but there persists a sense of the
pain of being rejected by the 'success'-orientated and patriarchal culture that
many want to stand out from.

The vampire's own curtailed experience and its outsiderdom resonate with
this experience for many vampire fans because of its plight – wrongly damned
and misunderstood. Fans sympathise with this predicament, relate to the
vampire, and relate it to themselves. Vampires are forgivable (and glamorous)
outcasts and the fans engage with the pain of the vampires' sense of outsiderdom. Cheryl, for instance comments on her adolescence:

> I was having problems with friends at school and stuff so I started
> getting into it a bit. Perhaps that's it. I don't know, perhaps that's why

you identify with vampires – because you feel a bit of a misfit. And let's face it, there's more of a better image associated with vampires than like werewolves and witches (laughs).

This quotation sums up both the duality of the vampire and the appeal of this duality – a misfit with a good image. Dee also says that 'she has always been a little bit different' as does Karen who 'never fit in'. Pam and Janet comment that although they have always been different, they 'went through the stage of trying to be normal', they got married and had children but realised that they could keep up the 'pretence' no longer. Pam says:

I think what we both did was because we felt so different, didn't we, even when we were young. We were sort of at odds with the little communities we were in. We were just totally different even though we had brothers and sisters and that.

Andrea comments that at work she puts on an act – 'a little too happy, cheerful and bright, but that's not my true person' – and Melinda recognises the loneliness of the vampire and states that 'it made enough of an impression on me and I decided this was something I identified with and deeply'. These feelings of outsiderdom, and feelings of 'not fitting in' jar against the official discourses of an inclusive society. There is a sense that it is a personal failing rather than a social failing to feel oneself an outsider and it is to such unacknowledged anxieties that the sympathetic vampire today speaks.

Vampire fans are experiencing and articulating what numerous critics have pointed out – that contemporary society promises personal fulfilment and significance as well as creating the conditions which ensures its achievement is unattainable. Lucien Goldmann observed that bourgeois society produces an 'internal contradiction between individualism as a universal value ... and the important and painful limitations that this society itself brought to the possibilities of the development of the individual' (1975: 12). This comment points to the contradictions of bourgeois culture that are hidden by its promises and the dilemmas for the self that can result. Chris Rojek asks how recognition and belonging are to be attained under such paradoxical conditions and suggests that the majority suffer from 'achievement famine' (2001: 49). Peter Brooks reminds us that universal values have struggled to assert themselves in a modern post-sacred society and points out that cultural forms have tried to stand-in for the missing totality of meaning by offering *individual* characters who – through melodramatic structuring – take on the transcendental values. The vampire is a creature of capitalism in a final sense, then, which is that it is imbued with the ideas of individualism and a focus on the self so central to modern society, even as it poses the problem of the lack of individual significance.

The following comment from Janet expresses a common attitude amongst the fans that one's everyday life is rather meaningless and lacking in significance, and that the image of the vampire poses an alternative to this:

I just can't believe that this is all there is to it – we're born and then we live and then we die ... I mean Lestat made such a big impact on everyone he met.

Later on in the interview Pam comments:

He's never satisfied, he always has to look for more things, to challenge one more thing. It's what you and me keep doing.

Also Andrea, who remarks a number of times about the boredom of work, and on how she hides her real self and would 'like to live that way [like a vampire] all the time' comments, 'I can feel boxed in'. Andrea claims, however, that she has 'an affinity' with the vampires who always 'go one step further'. Melinda concurs that

immortals can take it to a deeper level and they can explore things in much more depth – they have the luxury of time. And you toss in the vampiric beauty and perfect pitch [laughs].

These comments express both the frustration at the quest for fulfilment and significance ('one more challenge') *and* the pleasure in the fictional representation of the vampire who can make 'such a big impact' and take things to a 'deeper level'.

The lure of the gothic and melodramatic vampire is to do with its ability to represent what is disavowed, to speak to anxieties and desires that are difficult to name. As David Punter has argued, the gothic form has persisted beyond the life of the gothic novel into contemporary horror fiction both on the screen and on the page because, like its ancestor, it is concerned with the contradictions of contemporary society that have no name. However, while the classic Gothic novel has been considered a way for middle-class audiences of the eighteenth and nineteenth centuries to cope with anxieties about modernity, and in particular that the Enlightenment did not fully bring about the civilised Augustan age of reason; the late twentieth-century transformations of the gothic can be said to reflect the popular anxieties of our cultural moment: 'contemporary manifestations of the Gothic open up deeply wounded and wounding questions about how fulfilment is to be achieved' (Punter 1996: 189). The vampire's undead existence is a symbol of unfulfilled selfhood and its outsiderdom chimes with experiences of not belonging.

This sense of the pain of not belonging is expressed by many twentieth-century vampires, but none so clearly as Rice's vampires. When the vampire Armand tells Louis that he is the 'spirit of the age', Louis responds, 'I'm not the spirit of any age. I'm at odds with everything and always have been! I have never belonged anywhere with anyone at anytime!' Armand replies, 'But Louis ... This is the very spirit of your age. Don't you see that? Everyone feels as you feel. Your fall from grace and faith has been the fall of a century' (Rice 1976: 288).

This passage is open to interpretation and at least one academic critic, Ken Gelder, considers Louis' character to embody the current crisis of knowing, but perhaps it is more to do with a current crisis of the 'self', of how the self is to have meaning, to signify. For, just as the monsters who stalked the eighteenth and nineteenth centuries reminded those times of the limits to the promises of 'reason', our vampires remind us of the limits of the promises of our own time; the promises for the individual to *be* fulfilled, significant and content. As I have suggested, our times do not just promise these things, they *demand them of us* and when we do not achieve the success we are promised is open to all, we too are outsiders to the Anglo-American dream. The melodramatically constructed sympathetic vampire addresses the bourgeois myth about the unfettered pos- sibilities for the self, and its corollary – the individualisation of notions of the successful self. It is not an accident, then, that the impulse towards transcen- dental significance should take the sign of the individual in bourgeois culture.

Yet today's vampires (as Jules Zanger has complained) are not only express- ing the pain of individualism, they also pull against it in that they are communal rather than solitary. The pre-Dracula nineteenth-century vampire was intimate with humans, as were a number of early twentieth-century screen adaptations. Rice's late twentieth-century vampires lived together and also occasionally related to humans. Buffy's vampires are searching for acceptance and redemp- tion from humans and she comes to love them for this. Indeed, Gelder points out the use of certain conventions in the *Vampire Chronicles* that is common to many contemporary vampire tales; they 'share a number of characteris- tics usually associated with women's fiction – notably, the tracing out of the vampire's search for fulfilment, for a "complete" love relationship' (1994: 109). Many women fans counterpose outsiderdom and the impossible paradoxes of the self with 'love', which persistently works against the cultural demands of individualism. For women fans in particular, the notion of 'ideal' love is a central element in the attraction of their favourite vampire tales. Pam makes this comment about the love between the vampires:

> It's a brilliant love to love like that unconditionally and just it doesn't matter – it doesn't matter whether you love a male or you love a female, I mean, why should you be ashamed because you love a female.

The view of ideal love as something that disrupts conventional male/female relations is one that many female fans share and many talk of a special female connection. (This relates to the possibilities identified by many critics in the image of the lesbian vampire.) These themes connect to the search for ful- filment and remain salient in the fans' engagement with the vampire and in relating these themes to themselves. This is demonstrated in the following exchange between Pam and Janet:

> Janet: I think everyone would love not to grow old, to be immortal and to have those strengths and the knowledge that they've had to

go off through the centuries and just gain all that knowledge...

Pam: Instead of cramming it into a few short years...

Janet: And never forget it and the love they feel for each other, that sort of binding love that they never lose for each other, no matter where they are or how separate they are, they always feel it...

Pam: And that's what you and me always feel. It's always been there [Janet nods agreement] – no matter what.

This exchange articulates a dissatisfaction with life's 'few short years', but also the importance for fulfilment which is discussed in ways 'usually associated with women's fiction' – fulfilment in personal relationships and the importance of 'binding love'. Vampire fans empathise both with the vampires' outsiderdom *and* the love between the vampires that makes living their existence bearable. These fans have found in the vampire a figure that expresses painful outsiderdom and love in a way that echoes own their experiences in the world.

I have argued that the vampire is dualistic in a number of ways; it presents an image of glamorous (and often infamous) individualism and that it represents the pain of insignificance – an invisible and shadowy existence. The vampire lives outside the rules of ordinary society (underlining its bohemian distinction and potential for elitism) and lives communally. It thus gives expression to many of the dilemmas of the Western modern self that are generated from the persistent discourses of individualism and 'achievement' culture. That the vampire comes to personally represent the dilemma of insignificance and the imaginary means of overcoming this can be seen to be an example of the gothic/melodramatic sensibility. For, as Brooks argues, melodrama and the gothic are 'peculiarly modern' forms (1995: 16) precisely because they insist on viewing the social in *personal* terms.

The vampire addresses the question of personal fulfilment in a society that continues to ensure that the potential for self is curtailed. Melodrama and the gothic form 'are modes which insist that reality can be exciting, can be equal to the demands of the imagination' (Brooks 1995: 6), and this structuring of vampire narratives appeals to fans by offering the means of achieving excitement and significance. Melinda recognises this clearly when she comments that

These extraordinary characters ... are the best and the worst, but always the ultimate of what a human can become.

The vampire offers an imaginative means of managing the experience of a central cultural paradox; the promise of personal fulfilment and significance in a social set up which curbs the potential of the majority. The vampire, however, is not an ideal, but a member of the undead; it not an idealised figure, but a borderline figure. This seems to emphasise the difficulty in attaining the potential residing in the image of the vampire, as it holds in tandem both possibility and its negation. Vampire fans read the vampire not as death but as possibility

– yet this is laced with recognition that it is an outsider and a pathos-steeped creature so that the vision of the possibilities residing in the vampire may not be dead, but they are 'undead'.

The images that vampire fans are drawing on, then, are not the optimistic vision of a potential utopia that critics have suggested other popular art forms offer their audiences (Dyer 1985; Jenkins 1992). In fact, Brooks argues that the gothic and melodramatic diverge in their presentation of imaginative universes; melodrama offering optimistic 'angelic spheres' (1995: 20) and the gothic that of pessimistic 'demonic depths' (ibid.). Punter agrees that the gothic,

> unlike utopian fiction ... actually demonstrates within itself the mechanisms which enforce non-fulfilment. Rather than jumping straight from an existent situation to a projection of its opposite, the gothic takes us on a tour through labyrinthine corridors of repression, gives us glimpses of the skeletons of undead desires and makes them move again. (1996: 188)

This is culturally valuable because it dares to 'speak the unspeakable' (1996: 197), but as Punter suggests, 'the very act of speaking it is an ambiguous gesture' (ibid.). The gothic melodrama that vampire fans favour is inscribed by the contradictions that it speaks to: the potentials raised and the desires articulated are of the self rather than society; there is an offer of defiance, but also a strong sense of individualism; of personal transformation rather than social transformation. They are also transformations that cannot be realised, for one cannot really become a vampire. However, as Duncombe points out, 'impossible dreams are essential today because a key aspect of bourgeois society is to deny any alternatives to it' (1997: 196). Vampire fandom (or any fandom) cannot bring about these alternatives, but can only imagine them, and this through a figure of the undead, an outcast who both rebels against the society it haunts and is marginal to it. The vampire is probably the most potent symbol of the outcast today, speaking to our culture's unacknowledged pain, dramatising a desire to transcend the socially imposed definitions of what it means to be human, and demonstrating that such transformations are just beyond our reach.

CHAPTER ONE

1   See Auerbach 1995 and Moretti 1988.
2   See D. J. Skal (1990) *Hollywood Gothic: The Tangled Web of Dracula From Novel to Stage to Screen*, London: Andre Duetsch, for a history of the cinematic *Dracula*.
3   Moretti himself argues that *Dracula*, like all horror fantasy, forces its readers to consent to normality through fear. The social function of the novel is to frighten readers into compromising with an unacceptable social system (1988: 40). This interpretation might be seen to share the very problem of the '*Zeitgeist* fallacy' that Moretti so cogently identifies.
4   There is, however, at least one account of the vampire that draws on Freud's notion of the return of the repressed to suggest that the vampire is symbolically female; see F. Moretti (1988) 'The Dialectic of Fear', in *Signs Taken for Wonders: Essays in the Sociology of Literary Form*. London: Verso, 83–108.
5   Others agree. Judith Weissman argues that Lucy and Mina 'occasionally say things which reveal – without Stoker's conscious knowledge, I am sure – his anxieties about women's sexuality'; see J. Weissman (1988) '*Dracula* as Victorian Novel', in M. L. Carter (ed.) *Dracula: The Vampire and the Critics*. Ann Arbor: UMI Press, 74.
6   J. Twitchell (1985) *Dreadful Pleasures: An Anatomy of Modern Horror*. New York and Oxford: Oxford University Press. She is also referring to D. J. Skal (1990) *Hollywood Gothic: The Tangled Web of Dracula From Novel to Stage to Screen*, London: Andre Duetsch, and W. Kendrick (1991) *The Thrill of Fear: 250 Years of Scary Entertainment*, New York: Grove Weidenfeld.
7   For a reading that agrees with this interpretation, see G. B. Griffin (1988) '"Your Girls That You All Love Are Mine"; Dracula and the Victorian Male Sexual Imagination', in M. L. Carter (ed.) *Dracula: The Vampire and the Critics*. Ann Arbor: UMI Press, 138–9.
8   According to Harry M. Benshoff, the author of this tale was a well-known sexologist who considered homosexuality to be a biologically determined 'Third Sex'. Benshoff suggests that Ulrich perhaps unwittingly 'contributed to the monster-homosexual equation' (1997: 18) during the course of his career and only wrote 'Manor' very late in his career where the male lovers embrace, 'but only in death' (1997: 19).
9   Sue Ellen Case suggests that if the vampire is coded as feminine, then to suggest sympathy rather than sexual desire between the vampire and the female is heterosexist; see S. E. Case (1991) 'Tracking the Vampire', *Differences*, 3, 1-20. But there is no reason why the vampire cannot evoke both sympathy and sexual desire, even in the same female reader.
10 In 1832 the Anatomy Act was passed in Britain permitting the unclaimed bodies of paupers to be used for medical purposes, such as the teaching of anatomy to medical

students.

11 According to Elizabeth Miller, the line 'stripped off her clothing in her sleep whilst living' was removed for the 1901 popularised edition of Dracula that was aimed at a larger and less affluent reader. Nevertheless, the erotic implications remain clear; see E. Miller (2002) 'Shapeshifting Dracula: The Abridged Edition of 1901', in J. C. Holte (ed.) *The Fantastic Vampire: Studies in the Children of the Night*. Westport, CT and London: Greenwood Press, 3–10.

12 For example, the anatomist William Hunter, when conducting dissections on pregnant corpses, 'also sectioned the clitoris' (1989: 61) although this organ was not the object of enquiry.

13 See P. Brantinger (1986) 'Victorians and Africans: The Genealogy and Myth of the Dark Continent', in H. L. Gates, Jr. (ed.) *"Race", Writing and the Difference It Makes*. Chicago and London: University of Chicago Press, 62–88. See also S. Gilman, 'Black Bodies, White Bodies: Towards an Iconography of Female Sexuality in Late Nineteenth-Century Art, Medicine and Literature', in the same volume, 89–101.

14 The quotation in Doerksen 1997 comes from J. J. Virey (1819) 'Negre', *Dictionnaire des sciences medicales*, 41 vols., 35, 398–403.

15 This theme can be found in the work of Stoker's literary contemporaries also. For instance, Arthur Conan Doyle's 'The Case of the Lady Sannox' (1894), tells the story of a surgeon, Douglas Stone, who has an affair with the married Lady Sannox. One night a rich Turk offers him £200 to treat his wife who has been cut by a poisoned Smyrna dagger and who will die if the lip is not cut off. The Turkish woman is completely veiled and all Stone can see are her eyes and exposed 'under lip'. As Showalter explains, he proceeds with the operation 'not so much because he is greedy as because he has stopped seeing the person in the veil as a human being: "This was no longer a woman to him. It was a case". She has become the Other...' (1990: 136). Stone cuts a 'V-shaped piece' from her lip, the veil is taken from her face revealing a screaming Lady Sannox, while the Turk is revealed to be her vengeful husband. Showalter suggests that the operation is punishment for her sexuality and as such, 'is a displaced clitoridectomy' and that Stone is 'forced to confront both the horrible operation that he has performed ... on his mistress and the fact of female sexual difference itself: the "bloody gap" that paralyses him with terror' (ibid.). It additionally seems that his terror is based on the realisation that he performed this operation on a *white* woman, his lover, rather than on an Other, the Turkish woman behind the veil who to him was just a 'case'. Unlike Lady Sannox, the idea of a Turkish mutilation did not produce terror in Stone, for he had agreed to carry out the operation.

16 Richardson notes that opponents of the Bill suggested that this include people at the other end of the social scale, 'the numerous government nominees in receipt of state pensions and sinecures'. But to the Select Committee and their parliamentary colleagues 'this phrase could only have one meaning: paupers' (1987: 125).

17 Indeed, Richardson argues that the Act 'profoundly influenced working-class death culture, a culture so potent as to survive into our own century, and even into our own time' (1987: 262).

18 Frederick Donaghey, review of Deane and Balderston's *Dracula*; *Chicago Daily Tribune*, 3 April 1929, 37, quoted in D. J. Skal (1997) 'Theatrical Adaptations of *Dracula*', in Nina Auerbach and David J. Skal (eds) *Bram Stoker's Dracula: Authoritative Text, Context, Reviews and Reactions, Dramatic and Film Variations, Criticism*, New York and London: W. W. Norton, 372.

19 Sigmond (1849) 'Impulsive Insanity – The French Vampire', *Journal of Psychological Medicine and Mental Pathology*, 2, 577–89.

CHAPTER TWO

1   Indeed, as Peter Brooks (1995) has demonstrated, melodrama arises out of the same impulses as the Romantic movement and comes to be a mode of artistic expression found across the aesthetic divide of modernity.

2   Fred Saberhaagen went on to write the screenplay for Francis Ford Coppola's *Bram Stokers Dracula* (1992), noted for its sympathetic romantic take on Dracula despite selling itself as the 'real thing'.

3   *Dark Shadows* ran to 1,225 episodes until it was finally cancelled in 1971. Dan Curtis was approached for a new tele-film and miniseries which aired in 1991 and according to the Nielsen ratings had a viewership of 24 million making it the show with the highest viewership of the year.

4   However, she was indeed not 'the first writer to narrate her stories in the first person from the vampire's point of view' (Gelder 1994: 109).

CHAPTER THREE

1   Yet Gwenllian Jones reverts to similar language when she suggests that fans are 'seduced ... into intense engagements with the fictional worlds and fantastic logics of the cult television series' diegesis' (2003: 166).

2   'Scooby Gang' is the name given to Buffy's group of friends who help her combat evil; clearly an intertextual reference to the American television cartoon, *Scooby-Doo*.

CHAPTER FOUR

1   Although, not always. Buffy's mother, Joyce, dies, not at the hands of a demon, but as a result of cancer.

2   This merger was approved by the Federal Communications Commission (FCC) despite the new conglomerate exceeding the 35 per cent audience share regulation. Viacom-CBS has a 41 per cent audience reach (see Holt 2003: 22; http:mediasharx. com/index.php.news/119).

3   <http:///www.usatoday.com/life/telelvision/2001-04-05-buffy.htm>

4   <www.pazsaz.com/toptv.html>

5   Jennifer Holt suggests that network television had a combined audience share of 90 per cent in the 1970s which shrank to 57 per cent in the 1990s (2003: 16).

6   Occasionally these accounts produce very interesting results. In different ways, Lyn Thomas and Mark Jancovich offer first-hand accounts of their fandom in order to complicate the fan/academic binary and to raise the issue of cultural distinctions that are manifest on both sides.

7   Indeed, part of the reason for my embarking on this study was to challenge the (masochistic) theoretical assumptions that were made about a feminine engagement with the figure of the vampire.

8   This is not to suggest that there are no working-class vampire fans; I will discuss the implications of class differences between vampire fans in chapters seven and eight.

CHAPTER FIVE

1   As we have seen, for Bourdieu, there is no popular culture, only a popular aesthetic which exists in relation to the autonomous and heteronomous poles of cultural production from a position of subordination: 'There is no *neutral*, impartial, "pure" description of either of these opposing visions (which does not mean

that one has to subscribe to aesthetic relativism, when it is so obvious that the "popular aesthetic" is defined in relation to "high" aesthetics and that reference to legitimate art and its negative judgement on "popular" taste never ceases to haunt popular experience of beauty). *Refusal or privation?* It is as dangerous to attribute the coherence of a systematic aesthetic to the objectively aesthetic commitments of ordinary people as it is to adopt, albeit unconsciously, the strictly negative conception of ordinary vision which is the basis of every "high" aesthetic (1993: 237) [my italics].

2   This is the translator's insert.

3   Bourdieu exemplifies this in his analysis of 'Flaubert's Point of View' in *The Field of Cultural Production* from 1993. He demonstrates that in writing Madame Bovary, Flaubert situated himself actively within the space of possibilities and possible choices. Flaubert chose to write a novel and thus risk association with what was considered to be an inferior form as well as a form in which a variety of different writers and sub-genres were lumped together – where no 'great' author stood out. But Flaubert positioned himself against genre writing on the one hand and the (successful) sentimental writing of Feuillet on the other. However, he also positioned himself against the 'realist' school. Thus, Flaubert was putting himself in an impossible position in relation to the positions available in the field at the time. He manages, according to Bourdieu, to create a new range of possible positions. Bourdieu states, 'taking the point of view of a Flaubert who had not become Flaubert, we try to discover what he had to do and wanted to do in a world that was not yet transformed by what he in fact did, which is to say, the world to which we refer to him by treating him as a "precursor"' (1993: 205).

4   Bourdieu argues that the autonomisation of the cultural sphere began in Quattro Centro Florence, but accelerated in the Industrial Revolution and the Romantic reaction. This was a period of growth in the culture industry which coincides with the growth of the reading public 'which turned new classes (including women) into consumers of culture' (1993: 113). These conditions began the process of differentiation between the various fields of production and created conditions that were favourable to the construction of 'pure theories' (ibid.). Art-for-art's-sake was born in this period of differentiation because of the combined impact of the artists' liberation from the 'patron' and the simultaneous submission to the laws of the impersonal market. The ideologies of disinterestedness and the insistence of the separation of art from the commodity 'appear to be just so many reactions to the pressures of an anonymous market' (1993: 114). These conditions extended into the logic of cultural distinction and the development of taste, which excludes the taste of others. In particular was the development of the 'pure gaze', or the 'aesthetic gaze': 'It did so by dissociating art-as-commodity from art-as-pure-signification, produced according to a purely symbolic intent for purely symbolic appropriation, that is, for disinterested delectation, irreducible to simple material possession' (ibid.).

5   Lyn Thomas has complicated the 'pure gaze' of the intellectual in her own work on fan culture. She argues that while her analysis showed that intellectuals who focused on form rather than content produces 'an empirical illustration of Bourdieu's theory', she also comments, 'it is also clear that the picture is more complicated than his structures would suggest, and the purest of gazes is interesting in content and narrative, as well as the niceties of form' (2002: 175).

CHAPTER SIX

1   Advertised in *The Savage Garden* (1997) without prices listed and also in *The Time*

Picayune (Sunday 9 February 1997).

2 Newletters after early 1997 are entitled *The Savage Garden*.

3 In the Garden District alone (where the properties are large) Rice owned the following properties in 1998: her own home, another house, St Elizabeth Orphanage and a local chapel. I was also told repeatedly of the controversy between Rice and Al Copeland over the building of his restaurant 'Straya's' in the Garden District. Melinda told me during one of our conversations that 'she is having a fit because Al Copeland built his place on the spot where she last saw Lestat'.

4 See 'The Rice Versus Copeland fracas' by James Gill in the *Times Picayune*, 9 February 1997.

5 The ARVLFC is not the only fan club that has direct endorsements from the object of fandom who is also the producer of the texts which fans engage in, nor it is the only one to receive financial support from the object of fandom. See Abercrombie and Longhurst (1998) for a discussion of modes of fandom.

CHAPTER SEVEN

1 This is complicated where vampire fandom overlaps with the Goth scene which is a sartorial and music scene primarily, populated by male and female participants.

2 While all of the female fans interviewed in Britain considered dressing the part of the vampire the central activity of their fandom, in the US the same unanimity is not found. For instance, Diane seldom dressed as a vampire and Lisa did so only on special occasions, such as the Memnoch Ball.

CHAPTER EIGHT

1 Sara Gwenllian Jones considers this to be a phenomenon of the 1990s cult television text, but Bacon-Smith demonstrates that it has been developing since the 1970s. She suggests that shows such as *Starsky and Hutch* also encouraged their own slash – 'hurt/comfort'. Bacon-Smith notes that in 33 per cent of the episodes of the show, 'the press releases mentioned as central to the plot injury or direct threat of death to one of the two heroes, while the other worried or saved him' (1992: 158) and concludes that 'fans drew basic concepts from the screen' (1992: 258).

CONCLUSION

1 'Capital is dead labour, which, vampire like, lives only by sucking living labour, and lives the more, the more labour it sucks' (Marx 1978: 274).

Abercrombie, N. and B. Longhurst (1998) *Audiences: A Sociological Theory of Performance and Imagination*. London: Sage.

Abbott, S. (2001) 'A Little Less Ritual and a Little More Fun' *Slayage*, 3, June <www.slayage.tv/essays/slayage3/Abbott.htm>

Abel, K. (1999) 'Buffy Slays Parental Sensibilities, FamilyEducation.com <familyeudcation.com/article/0,1120,1-7884, 00.html>

Acker, J., Barry, K and Esseveld, J. (1983) 'Objectivity and truth: problems in doing feminist research', *Women's Studies International Forum*, 6, 4, 423-35.

Alasuutari, P. (1995) *Researching Culture: Qualitative Method and Cultural Studies*. London and New Delhi: Sage.

Amsley, C. (1989) 'How to Watch *Star Trek*', *Cultural Studies*, 3, 3, 312-20.

Amy-Chinn, D. (2002) 'Queering the Bitch: Spike, Transgression and Erotic Empowerment', in D. Amy-Chinn and M. Williamson (eds) 'The Vampire Spike in Text and Fandom: Unsettling Oppositions in *Buffy the Vampire Slayer*', special issue, *European Journal of Cultural Studies*, 8, 3, 313-28.

Ang, I. (1982) *Watching Dallas: Soap Opera and the Melodramatic Imagination*. London: Methuen.

_____ (1991) *Desperately Seeking the Audience*. London: Routledge.

Ang, I. and J. Hermes (1991) 'Gender and/in Media Consumption', in J. Curran and M. Gurevitch (eds) *Mass Media and Society*, second edition. London: Arnold, 127-43.

Anglo, M. (1977) *Penny Dreadfuls and other Victorian Horrors*. London: Juniper Books.

Astle, R. (1980) 'Dracula as Totemic Monster: Lacan, Freud, Oedipus and History', *Substance*, 25, 98-105.

Auerbach, N. (1995) *Our Vampires Ourselves*. Chicago and London: University of Chicago Press.

Auerbach, N and D. J. Skal (eds) *Bram Stoker's Dracula: Authoritative Text, Context, Reviews and Reactions, Dramatic and Film Variations, Criticism*. New York and London: W. W. Norton.

Bacon-Smith, C. (1992) *Enterprising Women: Television, Fandom and the Creation of Popular Myth*. Philadelphia: University of Pennsylvania Press.

_____ (2000) *Science Fiction Culture*. Philadelphia: University of Pennsylvania Press.

Baker, A. (1999) 'Relationships in Everyday Life Online: Finding Love in Cyberspace', in J. Armitage and J. Roberts (eds) *Exploring Cyber Society: Social, Political, Economic and Cultural Issues*. Newcastle upon Tyne: University of Northumbria at Newcastle.

Balsamo, A. (2000) 'Reading Cyborgs, Writing Feminism', in G. Kirkup, L. Janes, K. Woodward and F. Hovenden (eds) *The Gendered Cyborg: A Reader*. London and New York: Routledge, 148-58.

Barbas, S (2001) *Movie Crazy: Fans, Stars, and the Cult of Celebrity*. New York and

Basingstoke: Palgrave.

Barker, M. (1984a) *A Haunt of Fears: The Strange History of the British Horror Comic Campaign*. London: Pluto Press.

—— (ed.) (1984b) *Video Nasties: Freedom and Censorship in the Media*. London: Pluto Press.

—— (1989) *Comics: Ideology, Power and the Critics*. Manchester: Manchester University Press.

—— (1993) 'The Bill Clinton Fan Syndrome', *Media, Culture and Society*, 15, 669–73.

—— (1997) 'Taking the Extreme Case: Understanding a Fascist Fan of *Judge Dredd*', in D. Cartmell, I. Q. Hunter, H. Kaye and I. Whelehan (eds) *Trash Aesthetics: Popular Culture and its Audience*. London: Pluto Press, 14–30.

Barker, M. and K. Brooks (1998) *Knowing Audiences: Judge Dredd, its Friends, Fans and Foes*. Luton: Luton University Press.

Barrett, M. (1992) 'Words and Things: Materialism and Method in Contemporary Feminist Analysis', in M. Barrett and A. Phillips (eds) *Destabilizing Theory*. Cambridge: Polity Press, 201–19.

Barrett, M. and D. Barrett (2001) *Star Trek: The Human Frontier*. Cambridge: Polity Press.

Barrett, M. and A. Phillips (eds) (1992) *Destabilizing Theory*. Cambridge: Polity Press.

Bavidge, J. (2004) 'Chosen Ones: Rereading the Contemporary Teen Heroine', in G. Davis and K. Dickinson (eds) *Teen TV: Genre, Consumption and Identity*. London: British Film Institute, 41–53.

Baym, N. (1998) 'Talking About Soaps: Communicative Practices in a Computer-Mediated Fan Culture', in C. Harris and A. Alexander (eds) *Theorizing Fandom: Fans, Subculture and Identity*. Cresskill, NJ: Hampton Press, 111–30.

Becker, S. (1999) *Gothic Forms of Feminine Fiction*. Manchester: Manchester University Press.

Benjamin, W. (1973a) *Charles Baudelaire: A Lyric Poet in the Era of High Capitalism*. London: NLB.

—— (1973b) *Illuminations*, ed. and trans. H. Arendt. London: Fontana.

Bennett, T. and J Woollacott (1987) *Bond and Beyond: The Political Career of a Popular Hero*. London: Macmillan.

Benshoff, H. M. (1997) *Monsters in the Closet: Homosexuality and the Horror Film*. Manchester and New York: Manchester University Press.

—— (1998) 'Secrets, Closets, and Corridors Through Time: Negotiating Sexuality and Gender Through *Dark Shadows*', in C. Harris and A. Alexander (eds) *Theorizing Fandom: Fans, Subculture and Identity*. Cresskill, NJ: Hampton Press, 199 218.

Bentley, C. (1988 [1972]) 'The Monster in the Bedroom: Sexual Symbolism in Bram Stoker's Dracula', in M. L. Carter (ed.) *Dracula: The Vampire and the Critics*. Ann Arbor: UMI Press, 25–43.

Beynon, H. and Nicholls, T. (1977) *Living With Capitalism: Class Relations and the Modern Factory*. London: Routledge, Keegan and Paul.

Birke, L. (1999) *Feminism and the Biological Body*. Edinburgh: Edinburgh University Press.

—— (1986) *Women, Feminism and Biology: The Feminist Challenge*. Brighton: Wheatsheaf.

Bishop, F. (1991) *Polidori! A Life of Dr. John Polidori*. Chislehurst: The Gothic Society at The Gargoyle's Head Press.

Bloom, C., B. Docherty, J. Gibb and K. Shand (1988) *Nineteenth-Century Suspense: From Poe to Conan Doyle*. London: Macmillan.

Bobo, J. (1995) *Black Women as Cultural Readers*. New York: Columbia University Press.

Botting, F. (1996) *Gothic*. London: Routledge.

Bourdieu, P. (1984) *Distinction: A Social Critique of the Judgement of Taste*. London:

Routledge.

_____ (1993) *The Field of Cultural Production: Essays on Art and Literature*. Cambridge: Polity Press.

_____ (1998a) *Acts of Resistance*. Cambridge: Polity Press.

_____ (1998b) *Practical Reason: On the Theory of Action*. Cambridge: Polity Press.

_____ (2001) *Masculine Domination*. Cambridge: Polity Press.

Boyette, M. (2001) 'The Comic Anti-hero in *Buffy the Vampire Slayer*, or Silly Villain: Spike is for Kicks', *Slayage*, 4, <Slayage.tv/essays/slayage4/Boyette.htm>

Bradley, L. (1996) *Writing Horror and the Body: The Fiction of Stephen King, Clive Barker and Anne Rice*. Westport, CT, and London: Greenwood Press.

Brantlinger, P. (1986) 'Victorians and Africans: The Genealogy and Myth of the Dark Continent', in H. L. Gates, Jr. (ed.) *"Race", Writing and the Difference It Makes*. Chicago and London: University of Chicago Press, 62–88.

_____ (1988) *The Rule of Darkness: British Literature and Imperialism, 1830–1914*. Ithaca, NY: Cornell University Press.

Braun, B. (2000) '*The X-Files* and *Buffy the Vampire Slayer*: The Ambiguity of Evil in Supernatural Representations', *Journal of Popular Film and Television*, 28, 2, 88–94.

Brooks, P. (1995 [1976]) *The Melodramatic Imagination: Balzac, Henry James, Melodrama and the Mode of Excess*. York: York University Press.

Brower, S. (1992) 'Fans as Tastemakers: Viewers for Quality Television', in L. Lewis (ed.) *The Adoring Audience: Fan Culture and Popular Media*. London and New York: Routledge, 163–84.

Brown, M. E. (ed.) (1990) *Television and Women's Culture*. London: Routledge.

Brunsdon, C. (1989) 'Text and Audience', in E. Seiter, H. Borchers, G. Kreutzner and E-M. Warth (eds) *Remote Control: Television, Audiences and Cultural Power*. London: Routledge, 116–29.

_____ (1997) *Screen Tastes: Soap Opera to Satellite Dishes*. London: Routledge.

_____ (2000) *The Feminist, the Housewife, and the Soap Opera*. Oxford: Clarendon Press.

Buck-Morss, S. (1989) *The Dialectics of Seeing: Walter Benjamin and the Arcades Project*. Cambridge, MA and London: MIT Press.

Budd, M., R. M. Entman and C. Steinman (1990) 'The Affirmative Character of U.S. Cultural Studies', *Critical Studies in Mass Communication*, 7, 2, 169–84.

Burke, V. and J. Dunadee (1990) A *Collection of Memories: The Beauty and The Beast Phenomena*. Grand Rapids: Whispering Gallery Press.

Butler, K. (2003) 'James Marsters on Life after Buffy', *United Press International*, 6 November.

Butler, J. (1993) *Bodies That Matter: On the Discursive Limits of 'Sex'*. New York: Routledge.

Byars, J. (1991) *All that Hollywood Allows: Re-reading Gender in 1950s Melodrama*. London: Routledge.

Byron, Lord George Gordon (1988 [1816]) 'Fragment of a Novel' in A. Ryan (ed.) *The Penguin Book of Vampire Stories*. Harmondsworth: London, 1–7.

Calvi, M. (1849) ''Lunier 'd' un Cas de Monomie Instinctive, *Union Medicale*, 17.

Campbell, A. (1993) *Out of Control: Men, Women and Aggression*. London: Pandora.

Carby, H. (1982) 'White Women Listen', in Centre for Contemporary Cultural Studies (eds) *The Empire Strikes Back*. London: Hutchinson, 128–42.

Carroll, N. (1990) *The Philosophy of Horror: Or Paradoxes of the Heart*. London: Routledge.

Carter, M. L. (ed.) (1988) *Dracula: The Vampire and the Critics*. Ann Arbor: UMI Press.

_____ (1997) 'The Vampire as Alien in Contemporary Fiction', in J. Gordon and V. Hollinger (eds) *Blood Read: The Vampire in Contemporary Culture*. Philadelphia: University of Pennsylvania Press, 27–46.

Cartmell, D., I. Q. Hunter, H. Kaye and I. Whelehan (eds) (1997) *Trash Aesthetics: Popular Culture and its Audience*. London: Pluto Press.

_____ (eds) (1998) *Pulping Fictions: Consumer Culture Across the Literature/Media Divide*. London and Chicago: Pluto Press.

Case, S-E. (1991) 'Tracking the Vampire', *Differences*, 3, 1–20.

Cavicchi, D. (1998) *Tramps Like Us: Music and Meaning Among Springsteen Fans*. Oxford: Oxford University Press.

Charnas, S. M. (1980) *The Vampire Tapestry*. New York: Tor Books.

Chibnall, S. (1997) 'Double Exposures: Observations on *The Flesh and Blood Show*', in D. Cartmell, I. Q. Hunter, H, Kaye and I. Whelehan (eds) *Trash Aesthetics: Popular Culture and its Audience*, London: Pluto Press, 84–102.

Cicioni, M. (1998) 'Male Pair-Bondings and Female Desire in Fan Slash Writing', in C. Harris and A. Alexander (eds) *Theorizing Fandom: Fans, Subculture and Identity*. Cresskill, NJ: Hampton Press, 153–78.

Classen, S. (1998) 'Redeeming Values: Retail Coupon and Product Refund Fans', in C. Harris and A. Alexander (eds) *Theorizing Fandom: Fans, Subculture and Identity*. Cresskill, NJ: Hampton Press, 71–86.

Clemens, V. (1999) *The Return of the Repressed: Gothic Horror from the Castle of Otranto to Alien*. State University of New York Press.

Clery, E. J. and R. Miles (2000) *Gothic Documents: A Sourcebook 1700–1820*. Manchester: Manchester University Press.

Clifford, J. and G. E. Marcus (eds) (1986) *Writing Culture: the Poetics and Politics of Ethnography*. Berkeley and London: University of California Press.

Clover, C. J. (1992) *Men, Women and Chainsaws: Gender in the Modern Horror Film*. Princeton, NJ: Princeton University Press.

Clynes, M. E. and N. S. Kline (eds) (1995) 'Cyborgs and Space', in C. H. Gray (ed.) *The Cyborg Handbook*. New York: Routledge, 29–34.

Couldry, N. (2000) *Inside Culture: Re-imagining the Method of Cultural Studies*. London and New Delhi: Sage.

Coyne, R. (1999) *Technoromanticism*. Cambridge, MA and London: MIT Press.

Craft, C. (1990) '"Kiss Me with Those Red Lips": Gender and Inversion in Bram Stoker's *Dracula*', in E. Showalter (ed.) *Speaking of Gender*. London: Routledge, 216–42.

Cramer, S. (1997) 'Cinematic Novels and 'Literacy' Films: *The Shining* in the Context of the Modern Horror Film', in D. Cartmell, I. Q. Hunter, H. Kaye and I. Whelehan (eds) *Trash Aesthetics: Popular Culture and its Audience*. London: Pluto Press, 132–42.

Cranny-Francis, A. (1988) 'Sexual Politics and Political Repression in Bram Stoker's *Dracula*', in C. Bloom, B. Docherty, J. Gibb and K. Shand (eds) *Nineteenth-Century Suspense: From Poe to Conan Doyle*. London: Macmillan, 64–79.

_____ (1998) 'On *The Vampire Tapestry*', in C. Bloom (ed.) *Gothic Horror*. New York: St. Martin's Press, 27–39.

Creed, B. (1993) *The Monstrous-Feminine: Film, Feminism, Psychoanalysis*. London: Routledge.

Curran, J. (1990) 'The New Revisionism in Mass Communication Research', *European Journal of Communication*, 7, 2, 130–64.

D'acci, J. (1987) 'The Case of *Cagney and Lacey*', in H. Baehr and G. Dyer (eds) *Boxed-In: Women and Television*. London: Pandora, 15–30.

_____ (1989) *Defining Women: Television and the Case of Cagney and Lacey*. Chapel Hill: University of North Carolina Press.

Daugherty, A. M. (2002) 'Just a Girl: Buffy as icon', in R. Kaveny (ed.) *Reading the Vampire Slayer: The Unofficial Critical Companion to Buffy and Angel*. London: I. B. Tauris, 148–65.

Davis, G. and K. Dickinson (2004) *Teen TV: Genre, Consumption and Identity*. London:

British Film Institute.

De Certeau, M. (1984) *The Practice of Everyday Life*. Berkeley and London: University of California Press.

Dell, C. (1998) '"Look at that hunk of a man!": Subversive Pleasures, Female Fandom and Professional Wrestling', in C. Harris and A. Alexander (eds) *Theorizing Fandom: Fans, Subculture and Identity*. Cresskill, NJ: Hampton Press, 87–110.

Dickstein, M. (1980) 'The Aesthetics of Fright', *American Film*, 5, 10, 32–7; 56–9.

Dijkstra, B. (1986) *Idols of Perversity: Fantasies of Feminine Evil in Fin-de-Siècle Culture*. Oxford: Oxford University Press.

_____ (1996) *Evil Sisters: The Threat of Female Sexuality and the Cult of Manhood*. New York: Alfred A. Knopf.

Dinsmore, U. (1998) 'Chaos, Order and Plastic Boxes: The Significance of Videotapes for the People Who Collect Them', in C. Geraghty and D. Lusted (eds) *The Television Studies Book*. London and New York: Arnold, 315–76.

Doerksen, T. A. (1997) 'Deadly Kisses: Vampirism, Colonialism and the Gendering of Horror', in J. C. Holte (ed.) *The Fantastic Vampire: Studies in the Children of the Night – Selected Essays from the Eighteenth International Conference on the Fantastic in the Arts*. Westport, CT and London: Greenwood Press, 137–44.

Donald, J. (ed.) (1989) *Fantasy and the Cinema*. London: British Film Institute.

Douglas, M. (1970) *Purity and Danger: An Analysis of Concepts of Pollution and Taboo*. Harmondsworth: Penguin.

Duncombe, S. (1997) *Notes from the Underground: Zines and the Politics of Alternative Culture*. London and New York: Verso.

Dyer, R. (1985) 'Entertainment and Utopia', in B. Nichols (ed.) *Movies and Methods, Volume II*. Berkeley, CA: University of California Press, 39–47.

_____ (1988) 'Children of the Night: Vampirism as Homosexuality, Homosexuality as Vampirism', in S. Radstone (ed.) *Sweet Dreams: Sexuality, Gender and Popular Fiction*. London: Lawrence and Wishart, 47–72.

_____ (1993) 'Dracula and Desire', *Sight and Sound*, January, 8–15.

Eagleton, T. (1976) *Marxism and Literary Criticism*. London: Methuen.

_____ (2003) *After Theory*. London: Allen Lane.

Edwards, L. (2002) 'Slaying in Black and White', in R. Kaveny (ed.) *Reading the Vampire Slayer: The Unofficial Critical Companion to Buffy and Angel*. London: I. B. Tauris, 85–97.

Ehrenreich, B., E. Hess and G. Jacobs (1992) 'Beatlemania: Girls Just Want to Have Fun', in L. Lewis (ed.) *The Adoring Audience: Fan Culture and Popular Media*. London and New York: Routledge, 84–107.

Ehrstine, J. W. (1994) 'Byron and the Metaphysics of Self-Destruction', in G. R. Thompson (ed.) *The Gothic Imagination: Essays in Dark Romanticism*. Pullman, WA: Washington State University Press, 47–57.

Enns, A. (2000) 'The Fans from U.N.C.L.E.: The Marketing and Reception of the Swinging '60s Spy Phenomenon', *Journal of Popular Film and Television*, 28, 3, 124–33.

Entwistle, J. (2000) *The Fashioned Body: Fashion, Dress and Modern Social Theory*. Cambridge: Polity Press.

Evans, W. (1990) 'The Interpretative Turn in Media Research', *Critical Studies in Mass Communication*, 7, 2, 147–68.

Ferrell, M (2004) <mediasharx.com/index.php.news/1191>

Fetterley, J. (1978) *The Resisting Reader: A Feminist Approach to American Fiction*. Bloomington, IN: Indiana University Press.

Finch, (1984) '"Its great to have someone to talk to": The ethics and politics of interviewing women', in C. Bell and H. Roberts (eds) *Social Researching: Politics, Problems and Practices*. London: Routledge, 12–22.

Firestone, S. (1979) *The Dialectics of Sex*. London: The Woman's Press.

Fiske, J. (1989) *Understanding Popular Culture*. Boston and London: Unwin Hyman.

—— (1991) *Reading the Popular*. London: Routledge.

—— (1992) 'The Cultural Economy of Fandom', in L. Lewis (ed.) *The Adoring Audience: Fan Culture and Popular Media*. London: Routledge, 30–49.

—— (1996) *Media Matters: Race and Gender in U.S. Politics*. Minneapolis and London: University of Minnesota Press.

Flynn E. A. and P. P. Schweickart (eds) (1986) *Gender and Reading: Essays on Readers, Texts and Contexts*. Baltimore and London: Johns Hopkins University Press.

Flynn, J. F. (1992) *Cinematic Vampires: The Living Dead on Film and Television, from the Devil's Castle (1896) to Bram Stoker's Dracula (1992)*. Jefferson, NC, and London: McFarlane.

Fonesca, T. (1997) 'Bela Lugosi's Dead, but Vampire Music Stalks the Airwaves' in J. C. Holte (ed.) *The Fantastic Vampire: Studies in the Children of the Night: Selected Essays from the Eighteenth International Conference on the Fantastic in the Arts*, Westport, CT, and London: Greenwood Press, 59–68.

Frayling, C. (1991) *Vampyres: Lord Byron to Count Dracula*. London: Faber and Faber.

—— (1996) *Nightmare: The Birth of Horror*. London: BBC Books.

Freedman, D. (1998) 'Globalisation and local consumption: the Labour Party's attempts to sell British media', *Contemporary Politics*, 4, 4, 413–31.

Freud, S. (1953–66) *The Standard Edition of the Complete Psychological Works of Sigmund Freud*, 24 volumes, trans. J. Strachey. London: Hogarth.

Frost, B. J. (1989) *The Monster with a Thousand Faces: Guises of the Vampire in Myth and Literature*. Bowling Green, OH: Bowling Green State University Press.

Frow J. (1995) *Cultural Studies and Cultural Value*. Oxford: Oxford University Press.

Fry, C. L. (1988) 'Fictional Conventions and Sexuality in *Dracula*', in M. L. Carter (ed.) *Dracula: The Vampire and the Critics*. Ann Arbor: UMI Press, 35–8.

Fuller, K. H. (1996) *At the Picture Show: Small-Town Audience and the Creation of Movie Fan Culture*. Washington and London: Smithsonian Institution Press.

Gamer, M. (2000) *Romanticism and the Gothic: Genre, Reception and Canon Formation*. Cambridge: Cambridge University Press.

Gammon, L. and M. Marshment (1988) *The Female Gaze: Women as Viewers of Popular Culture*. London: The Women's Press.

Garnham, N. (1977) 'Towards a Political Economy of Culture', *New Universities Quarterly*, 31, 3, 341–57.

Garnham, N. and R. Williams (1980) 'Pierre Bourdieu and the Sociology of Culture: an introduction', *Media, Culture and Society*, 2, 3, 209–23.

Gatens, M. (1992) 'Power, Bodies and Difference', in M. Barrett and A. Phillips (eds) *Destabilizing Theory*, Cambridge: Polity Press, 120–37.

Geertz, C. (1973) *The Interpretation of Cultures*. New York: Basic Books.

—— (1988) *Works and Lives: The Anthropologist as Author*. Cambridge: Polity Press.

Gelder, K. (1994) *Reading the Vampire*. London: Routledge.

—— (1996) 'The Vampire Writes Back: Anne Rice and the (Re)Turn of the Author in the Field of Cultural Production', in D. Cartmell, I. Q. Hunter, H. Kaye and I. Whelehan (eds) *Pulping Fictions: Consuming Culture Across the Literature/Media Divide*. London and Chicago: Pluto Press, 29–42.

Geraghty, C. (1991) *Women and Soap Opera: A study of Prime Time Soap*. Cambridge: Polity Press.

—— (1996) 'Feminism and Media Consumption', in J. Curran, D. Morley and V. Walkedine (eds) *Cultural Studies and Communications*. London: Arnold, 306–22.

—— (2000) 'Representation and Popular Culture: Semiotics and the Construction of Meaning', in J. Curran and M. Gurevitch (eds) *Mass Media and Society*, third edition.

London: Arnold, 362–75

Geraghty, C. and D. Lusted (eds) (1998) *The Television Studies Book*. London and New York: Arnold.

Gillespie, M. (1995) *Television, Ethnicity and Cultural Change*. London and New York: Routledge.

Gillilan, C. (1998) 'WAR OF THE WORLDS: Richard Chaves, Paul Ironhorse, and the Female Fan Community', in C. Harris and A. Alexander (eds) *Theorizing Fandom: Fans, Subculture and Identity*. Cresskill, NJ: Hampton Press, 179–98.

Gilman, S. L. (1982) *Seeing the Insane: A Cultural History of Madness in Art in the Western World*. New York: John Wiley.

Gledhill, C. (1985 [1978]) 'Recent Developments in Feminist Criticism', in G. Mast and M. Cohen (eds) *Film Theory and Criticism: Introductory Readings*, (third edition). New York: Oxford University Press, 817–45.

____ (ed.) (1987) *Home is Where the Heart is: Studies in Melodrama and the Woman's Film*. London: British Film Institute.

____ (1988) 'Pleasurable Negotiations', in E. D. Pribram (ed.) *Female Spectators*. London: Verso, 64–89.

Glover, D. (1992) 'Bram Stoker and the Crisis of the Liberal Subject', *New Literary History*, 23, 4, 983–1002.

Goffman, E. (1972) *Relations in Public*. Harmondsworth: Pelican Books.

Goldmann, L. (1975) *Towards a Sociology of the Novel*, trans. A. Sheridan. London: Tavistock Publications.

Gomez, J. (1991) *The Gilda Stories*. New York: Firebrand.

Gonzales, J. (2000) 'Envisioning Cyborg Bodies: Notes from Current Research', in G. Kirkup, L. Janes, K. Woodward and F. Hovenden (eds) *The Gendered Cyborg: A Reader*. London and New York: Routledge, 89–100.

Gordon J. and V. Hollinger (eds) (1997) *Blood Read: The Vampire as Metaphor in Contemporary Culture*. Philadelphia: University of Pennsylvania Press.

Grant, B. K. (ed.) (1984) *Planks of Reason: Essays on the Horror Film*, Metuchen, N.J and London: Scarecrow Press.

Gray, A. (1992) *Video Playtime: The Gendering of a Communications Technology*. London: Routledge.

____ (1995) 'I want to tell you a storey: the narratives of *Video Playtime*', in B. Skeggs (ed.) *Feminist Cultural Theory: Process and Production*. Manchester: Manchester University Press, 153–68.

Griffin, C. (1980) 'Feminist Ethnography', *Stenciled Papers*, Centre for Contemporary Cultural Studies, University of Birmingham, 117–29.

Griffin, G. B. (1988) '"Your Girls That You All Love Are Mine"; Dracula and the Victorian Male Sexual Imagination', in M. L. Carter (ed.) *Dracula: The Vampire and the Critics*. Ann Arbor: UMI Press, 137–48.

Griffiths V. (1995) *Adolescent Girls and Their Friends: A Feminist Ethnography*. Aldershot: Averbury.

Gwenllian Jones, S. (2000) 'Starring Lucy Lawless?', *Continuum: Journal of Media and Cultural Studies*, 14, 1, 9–22.

____ (2003) 'Web Wars: Resistance, Online Fandom and Studio Censorship', in M. Jancovich and J. Lyons (eds) *Quality Popular Television: Cult TV, the Industry and Fans*. London: British Film Institute, 163–80.

Haining, P. (ed.) (1978) *Tales from the Gothic Bluebooks*. Chislehurst: The Gothic Society of the Gargoyle's Head Press.

Hakken, D. (1999) *Cyborgs @ Cyberspace? An Ethnographer Looks Into the Future*. New York and London: Routledge.

Hall, S. and T. Jefferson (1976) *Resistance Through Rituals*. London: Hutchinson.

Hall, S., A. Lowe and P. Willis (eds) (1980) *Culture, Media, Language*. London: Hutchinson.

Hallam, J. and M. Marshment (1995) 'Framing experience: case studies in the reception of *Oranges are not the Only Fruit*', *Screen*, 36, 1, 1–15.

Haraway, D. (1991) *Simians, Cyborgs and Women: The Reinvention of Nature*, London: Free Association Books.

Hardwick, C. (1863) *Insolvent Sick and Burial Clubs: The Causes and the Cure; or, How To Choose or Found a Reliable Friendly Society*. (publisher unknown)

Harris, C. and A. Alexander (eds) (1998) *Theorizing Fandom: Fans, Subculture and Identity*. Cresskill, NJ: Hampton Press.

Harris, C. (1998) 'A Sociology of Television Fandom', in C. Harris and A. Alexander (eds) *Theorizing Fandom: Fans, Subculture and Identity*. Cresskill, NJ: Hampton Press, 41–54.

Harrison, T. (1996) 'Interview with Henry Jenkins', in T. Harrison, S. Projansky, A. O. Kent, A. E. R. Helford (eds) *Enterprising Zones: Critical Positions on Star Trek*. Boulder CO: Westview Press.

Hatlen, B. (1988) 'The Return of the Repressed/Opressed in Bram Stoker's Dracula', in M. L. Carter (ed.) *Dracula: The Vampire and the Critics*. Ann Arbor: UMI Press, 117–36.

Havens, C. (2003) *Joss Whedon: The Genius Behind Buffy*. London: Titan Books.

Hebdidge D. (1979) *Subculture: The Meaning of Style*. London: Methuen.

Helford, E. R. (2002) '"My Emotions Give Me Power": The Containment of Girls' Anger in *Buffy*', in R. Wilcox and D. Lavery (eds) *Fighting the Forces: What's at Stake in Buffy the Vampire Slayer*. Lanham, Boulder, New York, Oxford: Rowman and Littlefield, 18–34.

Hetherington, K. (1998) *Expression of Identity: Space, Performance, Politics*. London and New Delhi: Sage.

Hills, M. (2001) *Fan Cultures*. London and New York. Routledge.

Hobson, D. (1982) *Crossroads: The Drama of a Soap Opera*. London: Methuen.

_____ (1989) 'Soap opera fans at work', in E. Seiter, H. Borchers, G. Kreuntzner and E-M. Warth (eds) *Remote Control: Television, Audiences and Cultural Power*. London: Routledge, 150–67.

_____ (1990) 'Women audiences and the workplace', in M. E. Brown (ed.) *Television and Women's Culture: The Politics of the Popular*. London: Sage.

Hodges, D. and J. L. Doane (1991) 'Undoing Feminism in Anne Rice's *Vampire Chronicles*', in J. Naremore and P. Brantlinger (eds) *Modernity and Mass Culture*. Bloomington, IN: Indiana University Press, 158–75.

Hollander, A. (1993) *Seeing Through Clothes*. Berkeley, LA and London: University of California Press.

Hollows, J. (2003) 'The Masculinity of Cult', in M. Jancovich, A. L. Reboll, J. Stringer and A. Willis (eds) *Defining Cult Movies: The Cultural Politics of Oppositional Taste*. Manchester: Manchester University Press, 35–53.

Holt, J. (2003) 'Verticle Vision: Deregulation, Industrial Economy and Prime-time Design', in M. Jancovich and J. Lyons (eds) *Quality Popular Television*. London: British Film Institute, 11–31.

Holte, J. C. (ed.) (1997) *The Fantastic Vampire: Studies in the Children of the Night – Selected Essays from the Eighteenth International Conference on the Fantastic in the Arts*. Westport, CT and London: Greenwood Press.

hooks, b. (1981) *Ain't I a Woman: Black Women and Feminism*. Boston, MA: South End Press.

Howard, M. (1997) 'Slayer-Speak', *Entertainment Weekly*, 31 October, 84.

Howes, M. (1988) 'The Mediation of the Feminine: Bisexuality, Homosexual Desire, and Self-Expression in Bram Stoker's *Dracula*', *Texas Studies in Literature and Language*, 30, 104–19.

Hughes, W. (2000) 'Fictional Vampires in the Nineteenth and Twentieth Centuries', in D. Punter (ed.) *A Companion to the Gothic*. Oxford: Blackwell, 143–54.

Hughs, W. and A. Smith (1998) *Bram Stoker: History, Psychoanalysis and the Gothic*. London: Macmillan.

Hunter, I. Q. (1996) Capitalism Most Triumphant: Bill and Ted's Excellent History Lesson', in D. Cartmell, I. Q. Hunter, H. Kaye and I. Whelehan (eds) (1997) *Trash Aesthetics: Popular Culture and its Audience*. London: Pluto Press, 111–24.

Hutchings, P. (1993) *Hammer and Beyond: The British Horror Film*. Manchester: Manchester University Press.

Huyssen, A. (1986) *After the Great Divide: Modernism, Mass Culture, Postmodernism*. Bloomington: Indiana University Press.

Iragaray, L. (1985) *This Sex Which is Not One*. Ithaca NY: Cornell University Press.

Jackson, R. (1981) *Fantasy: The Literature of Subversion*. London: Methuen.

Jancovich, M. (1992) *Horror*. London: Batsford.

_____ (2000) '"A Real Shocker": authenticity, genre and the struggle for distinction', *Continuum: Journal of Media and Cultural Studies*, 14, 1, 23–37.

_____ (2002) 'Cult Fictions: Cult Movies, Subcultural Capital and the Production of Cultural Distinctions', *Cultural Studies: Theorizing Politics, Politicizing Theory*, 16, 2, 306–22.

Jancovich, M. and J. Lyons (2003) *Quality Popular Television: Cult TV, the Industry and Fans*. London: British Film Institute.

Jenkins, H. (1992) *Textual Poachers: Television Fans and Participatory Culture*. London: Routledge.

_____ (1998) '"The Poachers and the Stormtroopers", transcript of a talk presented at the University of Michigan, posted on Red Rock Eater Digest <commons.somewhere. com/articles/1998/The.Poachers.and.the.Sto>

_____ (2001) 'Henry Jenkins interviewed by Matt Hills at 'Console-ing Passions' conference, Unversity of Bristol, 7 July 2001', *Intensities: the Journal of Cult Media Studies*, <http://www.cult-media.com/issue2/CHRjenk.htm>

Jenkins, H., T. McPherson and J. Shattuc (2002) *Hop on Pop: The Politics and Pleasures of Popular Culture*. Durham and London: Duke University Press.

Jensen, J. (1992) 'Fandom as Pathology', in L. Lewis (ed.) *The Adoring Audience: Fan Culture and Popular Media*. London Routledge, 11–24.

Jones, E. (1991 [1929]) 'On the Vampire', in C. Frayling (ed.) *Vampyres: Lord Byron to Count Dracula*. London: Faber and Faber, 310–30.

Jordanova, L. (1989) *Sexual Visions: Images of Gender and Science and Medicine Between the Eighteenth and Twentieth Centuries*. New York: Harvester Wheatsheaf.

Katz, J. (1999) 'Bootleggin Buffy: Era of Information Control is Over', 8 June, <freedomforum.org/templates/document.asp?documentID=11579>

Kaveney, R. (ed.) (2002) *Reading the Vampire Slayer: An Unofficial Critical Companion to Buffy and Angel*. London: I. B. Tauris.

Kendrick, W. (1991) *The Thrill of Fear: 250 Years of Scary Entertainment*. New York: Grove Weidenfeld.

Kermode, M. (1997) 'I was a teenage horror fan: or, "How I learned to stop worrying and love Linda Blair"', in M. Barker and J. Petley (eds) *Ill Effects: The Media/Violence Debate*. London Routledge, 126–34.

Kilgour, M. (1995) *The Rise of the Gothic Novel*. London: Routledge.

Kirkup, G., L. Janes, K. Woodward and F. Hovenden (eds) (2000) *The Gendered Cyborg: A Reader*. London and New York: Routledge.

Kitchen, R. (1998) *Cyberspace: The World in the Wires*. Chichester and New York: John Wiley and Sons.

Kosofsky-Sedgwick, E. (1980) *The Coherence of Gothic Conventions*. New York and London: Methuen.

⸺ (1985) *Between Men: English Literature and Male Homosocial Desire*. New York: Columbia University Press.

Kraft-Ebbing, R. von (1893 [1886]) *Psychopathia Sexualis: with special reference to Contrary Sexual Instinct: A Medico-Legal Study*, trans. C. G. Chaddock. Philadelphia: F. A. Davis/London: F. G. Rebman.

Kristeva, J. (1982) *Powers of Horror: An Essay on Abjection*. New York: Columbia University Press.

Kuhn, A. (1984) 'Women's Genres', *Screen*, 25, 1, 18–28.

Lamb P. F. and D. L. Veith (1986) 'Romantic Myth, Transcendence, and *Start Trek* magazines', in D. Palumbo (ed.) *Erotic Universe: Sexuality and Fantastic Literature*. New York: Greenwood Press, 296–312.

Laplanche, J. and J. B. Pontalis (1973) *The Language of Psychoanalysis*. New York: W. W. Norton.

Le Fanu, S. (1988 [1782]) 'Carmilla', in A. Ryan, (ed.) *The Penguin Book of Vampire Stories*. Harmondsworth: Penguin, 71–137.

Leading Licensors (2004) report <licensmag.com/licensemag/data/articlesstandard. ususemag/152003/53354/article.pdf>

Lewis, L. (1992) *The Adoring Audience: Fan Culture and Popular Media*. London: Routledge.

Lipsitz, G. (1990) *Time Passages: Collective Memory and American Popular Culture*. Minneapolis, MN: University of Minnesota Press.

Lovell, T. (2000) 'Thinking feminism with and against Bourdieu', *Feminist Theory*, 1, 1, 11–32.

Lull, J. (1990) *Inside Family Viewing: Ethnographic Research on Television Audiences*. London: Routledge.

⸺ (2001) *Culture in the Communication Age*. London and New York: Routledge.

Lykke, N. (2000) 'Between Monsters, Goddesses and Cyborgs: Feminist Confrontation with Science', in G. Kirkup, L. Janes, K. Woodward and F. Hovenden (eds) *The Gendered Cyborg: A Reader*. London and New York: Routledge, 74–88.

Lyndon J. W. (1999) *Count Dracula Goes to the Movies: Stoker's Novel Adapted, 1922–1995*. Jefferson, NC, and London: McFarland.

MacDonald, A. (1998) 'Uncertain Utopia: Science Fiction Media Fandom and Computer Mediated Communication', in C. Harris and A. Alexander (eds) *Theorizing Fandom: Fans, Subculture and Identity*. Cresskill, NJ: Hampton Press, 131–52.

Macdonald, M. (1995) *Representing Women: Myths of Femininity in the Popular Media*. London: Arnold.

Malchow, H. L. (1996) *Gothic Images of Race in Nineteenth-Century Britain*. Stanford: Stanford University Press.

Manchel, F. (1970) *Terrors of the Screen*. Englewood Cliffs, NJ: Prentice-Hall.

Mander, M. (1987) 'Bourdieu, the sociology of culture and cultural studies; a critique', *European Journal of Communications*, 2, 427–53.

Martin, P. (1988) 'The Vampire in the Looking-Glass: Reflection and Projection in Bram Stoker's *Dracula*', in C. Bloom, B. Docherty, J. Gibb and K. Shand (eds) *Nineteenth-Century Suspense: From Poe to Conan Doyle*. London: Macmillan, 80–92.

Marx, K. (1978 [1867–94]) *Capital: A Critique of Political Economy*, trans. David Fernbach.

London: Penguin.

Massey, D. (1994) *Space, Place and Gender*. Cambridge: Polity Press.

Mast, G. (1971) *A Short History of the Movies*. Indianapolis, IN: Pegasus/Bobbs Merrill.

McDayter, G. (1995) '"Consuming the Sublime": Gothic Pleasure and the construction of identity', *Women's Writing*, 2, 1, 55–75.

McGuigan, J. (1992) *Cultural Populism*. London: Routledge.

McNally, R. T. (1983) *Dracula Was a Woman: In Search of the Blood Countess of Transylvania*. London: Hamlyn.

McRobbie, A. and J. Garber (1976) 'Girls and Subcultures' in S. Hall and T. Jefferson (eds) *Resistance Through Rituals*. London: Hutchinson, 209–22.

_____ (1982) 'The Politics of Feminist Research: Between Talk, Text and Action', *Feminist Review*, 12, 46–57.

Melton, J. G. (1994) *The Vampire Book: The Encyclopaedia of the Undead*. Detroit: Visible Ink.

_____ (2002) 'Words from the Hellmouth: A Bibliography of Books on Buffy the Vampire Slayer', *Slayage*, 4 <Slayage.tv/essays/slayage4/meltonbooks.htm>

Merrick, H. (1997) 'The Readers Feminism Doesn't See: Feminist Fans, Critics and Science Fiction', in D. Cartmell, I. Q. Hunter, H. Kaye and I. Whelehan (eds) *Trash Aesthetics: Popular Culture and its Audience*. London: Pluto Press, 48–65.

Metz, C. (1982) *The Imaginary Signifier: Psychoanalysis and the Cinema*. Bloomington, IN: Indiana University Press.

Michéa (1849) 'Des Déviations Maldives de l' Appétite Vénérier', *Union Medicale*, 17, 338–9.

Mighall, R. (1999) *A Geography of Victorian Gothic Fiction: Mapping History's Nightmares*. Oxford: Oxford University Press.

Miles, R. (1994) 'Introduction', *Women's Writing*, 1, 2, 131–41.

Miller, E. (2002) 'Shapeshifting Dracula: The Abridged Edition of 1901', in J. C. Holte (ed.) *The Fantastic Vampire: Studies in the Children of the Night*. Westport, CT and London: Greenwood Press, 3–10.

Mitchell, W. J. (1999) *e-topia: 'urban life Jim – but not as we know it'*. Cambridge, MA and London: MIT Press.

Modleski, T. (1979) 'The Search for Tomorrow in Today's Soap Operas', *Film Quarterly*, 33, 1, 12–21.

_____ (1982) *Loving With a Vengeance: Mass-Produced Fantasies for Women*. London: Methuen.

_____ (1986) *Studies in Entertainment*. Bloomington, IN: Indiana University Press.

Moore, M. (2003) *Bowling for Columbine*. Metro-Goldwyn-Mayer

Moretti, F. (1988) *Signs Taken for Wonders: Essays in the Sociology of Literary Form*. London: Verso.

Morley, D. (1980) 'Texts, readers and subjects', in S. Hall, A. Lowe and P. Willis (eds) *Culture, Media, Language*. London: Hutchinson, 163–76.

_____ (1986) *Family Television: Cultural Power and Domestic Leisure*. London: Comedia.

_____ (1989) 'Changing Paradigms in Audience Studies', in E. Seiter, H. Borchers, G. Kreutzner and E-M. Warth (eds) *Remote Control: Television, Audiences and Cultural Power*. London: Routledge, 16–43.

_____ (1992) *Television, Audiences and Cultural Studies*. London: Routledge.

_____ (2000) *Home Territories: Media, Mobility and Identity*. London and New York: Routledge.

Morris, R. T. (1892) 'Is Evolution Trying to Do Away With the Clitoris?', *The American Journal of Obstetrics and Diseases of Women and Children*, 26, 847–58.

Mulhern, F. (2000) *Culture/Metaculture*. London and New York: Routledge.

Mulvey, L. (1975) 'Visual Pleasure and Narrative Cinema', *Screen*, 16, 3, 6–18.

Neale, S. (1982) *Genre*. London: British Film Institute.

Newman, K. (1984) *Nightmare Movies: A Critical History of the Horror Movie From 1968*. London: Bloomsbury.

Nixon, N. (1997) 'When Hollywood Sucks, or, Hungry Girls, Lost Boys and Vampirism in the Age of Reagan', in J. Gordon and V. Hollinger (eds) *Blood Read: The Vampire as Metaphor in Contemporary Culture*. Philadelphia: University of Pennsylvania Press, 115–28.

Oakely, A. (1981) 'Interviewing women: a contradiction in terms', in H. Roberts (ed.) *Doing Feminist Research*. London: Routledge and Kegan Paul, 30–61.

Osgerby, B. (1998) *Youth in Britain Since 1945*. Oxford: Blackwell.

_____ (2004) '"So Who's Got Time for Adults!": Femininity, Consumption and the Development of Teen TV – from *Gidget* to *Buffy*', in G. Davis and K. Dickinson (eds) *Teen TV: Genre, Consumption and Identity*. London: British Film Institute, 71–86.

Owen, S. A. (1999) 'Buffy and Vampire Slayer: Vampires, Postmodernity and Postfeminism', *Journal of Popular Film and Television*, 27, 2, 24–31.

Palmer, P. (1999) *Lesbian Gothic: Transgressive Fictions*. Cassell: London and New York.

Parks, L. (2003) 'Brave New Buffy: Rethinking "TV Violence"', in M. Jancovich and J. Lyons (eds) *Quality Popular Television: Cult TV, the Industry and Fans*. London: British Film Institute, 118–136.

Parry, M. (ed.) (1977) *The Rivals of Dracula*. London: Severn House.

Pearson, R. (1997) '"It's always 1895": Sherlock Holmes in Cyberspace', in D. Cartmell, I. Q. Hunter, H. Kaye and I. Whelehan (eds) *Trash Aesthetics: Popular Culture and its Audience*. London: Pluto Press, 143–61.

Penley, C. (1992) 'Feminism, psychoanalysis and the study of popular culture', in L. Grossberg, T. Nelson and P. Treicher (eds) *Cultural Studies*. New York and London: Routledge, 479–500.

Penley, C., E. Lyon, L. Spigal and J. Bergstrom (eds) (1991) *Close Encounters: Film, Feminism and Science Fiction*. Minneapolis, MN: University of Minnesota Press.

Pirie, D. (1973) *A Heritage of Horror: The English Gothic Cinema 1946–1972*. London: Gordon Frasure.

_____ (1977) *The Vampire Cinema*. Leicester: Gallery Press.

Plant, S. (2000) 'On the Matrix: Cyberfeminist Simulations', in G. Kirkup, L. Janes, K. Woodward and F. Hovenden (eds) *The Gendered Cyborg: A Reader*. London and New York: Routledge, 265–75.

Playden, Z-J. (2002) '"What you are, what's to come": Feminism, citizenship and the divine', in R. Kaveny (ed.) *Reading the Vampire Slayer: The Unofficial Critical Companion to Buffy and Angel*. London: I. B. Tauris, 120–47.

Polidori, J. (1994 [1819]) 'Fragment of a Novel', in A. Ryan (ed.) *The Penguin Book of Vampire Stories*. Harmondsworth: Penguin.

Poniewozik, J. (2001) 'How the 'Buffy' Coup Could Change TV', <http://www.time/columnist/poniewozik/article/0,9565,107337,00.html>

Pribram, E. D. (ed.) (1988) *Female Spectators: Looking at Film and Television*. London: Verso.

Price, J. and M. Shildrick (eds) (1999) *Feminist Theory and the Body: A Reader*. Edinburgh: Edinburgh University Press.

Punter, D. (1996) *The Literature of Terror: A History of Gothic Fiction from 1765 to the Present day*, second edition. London: Longman.

_____ (ed.) (2000) *A Companion to the Gothic*. Oxford: Blackwell.

Punter, D. and G. Byron (eds) (1999) *Spectral Readings: Towards a Gothic Geography*. London: Macmillan.

Radway, J. (1984) *Reading the Romance: Women, Patriarchy and Popular Literature*. Chapel Hill: University of North Carolina Press.

Ramsland, K. (1991) *Prisms of the Night: A Biography of Anne Rice*. London and New York: Plume/Penguin.

_____ (1993) *The Vampire Companion: The Official Guide to Anne Rice's Vampire Chronicles*. London: Little, Brown.

Read, J. (2003) 'The Cult of Masculinity: From Fan-Boys to Academic Bad-Boys', *Defining Cult Movies: The Cultural Politics of Oppositional Taste*. Manchester: Manchester University Press, 54–70.

Rice, A. (1976) *Interview With the Vampire*. New York: Ballentine Books.

_____ (1985) *The Vampire Lestat*. New York: Ballentine Books.

_____ (1988) *The Queen of the Damned*. New York: Alfred A. Knopf.

_____ (1992) *The Tale of the Body Thief*. New York: Alfred A. Knopf.

_____ (1995) *Memnoch the Devil*. New York: Alfred A. Knopf.

_____ (1998) *The Vampire Armand*. London: Chatto and Windus.

_____ (2000) *Merrick*. London: Chatto and Windus.

Richardson, M. (1991 [1959]) 'The Psychoanalysis of Count Dracula', in C. Frayling (ed.) *Vampyres: Lord Byron to Count Dracula*. London: Faber and Faber, 418–22.

Richardson, R. (1987) *Death, Dissection and the Destitute*. London: Routledge and Kegan Paul.

Rickels, L. (1999) *The Vampire Lectures*. Minneapolis: University of Minnesota Press.

Robins, K. and F. Webster (1999) *Times of the Technoculture: From the Information Society to the Virtual Life*. London and New York: Routledge.

Rojek, C. (2001) *Celebrity*. London: Reaktion Books.

Ross, A. (1989) *No Respect: Intellectuals and Popular Culture*. New York: Routledge.

Roth, L. (1984) 'Film, Society and Ideas: *Nosferatu* and *Horror of Dracula*', in B. K. Grant (ed.) *Planks of Reason: Essays on the Horror Film*. Metuchen, NJ and London: Scarecrow Press, 87–109.

Roth, P. A. (1988) 'Suddenly Sexual Women in Bram Stoker's *Dracula*', in M. L. Carter (ed.) *Dracula: The Vampire and the Critics*. Ann Arbor: UMI Press, 57–67.

Russ, J. (1985) *Magic Mommas, Trembling Sisters, Puritans and Perverts: Feminist Essays*. New York: Crossing.

Ryder, J. M. (1988 [1845]) 'Varney the Vampyre, or, The Feast of Blood', in A. Ryan (ed.) *The Penguin Book of Vampire Stories*. London: Bloomsbury, 25–35.

Sanders, J. (1997) *Science Fiction Fandom*. Westport, CT and London: Greenwood Press.

Sankek, D. (1990) 'Fans Notes: The Horror Film Fanzine', *Literature and Film Quarterly*, 18, 3, 150–9.

Saxey, E. (2002) 'Staking a claim: The series and its slash fiction', in R. Kaveny (ed.) *Reading the Vampire Slayer: The Unofficial Critical Companion to Buffy and Angel*. London: I. B. Tauris, 187–210.

Seiter, E. (1990) 'Making Distinctions in Television Audience Research', *Cultural Studies*, 4, 1, 61–84.

_____ (1995) 'Mothers Watching Children Watching TV', in B. Skeggs (ed.) *Feminist Cultural Theory: Process and Production*. Manchester: Manchester University Press, 112–32.

Seiter, E., H. Borchers, G. Kreutzner and E-M. Warth (eds) (1989a) *Remote Control: Television, Audiences and Cultural Power*. London: Routledge.

_____ (1989b) 'Don't Treat Us Like We're So Stupid and Naïve', in *Remote Control: Television, Audiences and Cultural Power*. London: Routledge, 223–48.

Senf, C. A. (1988) 'Dracula: the Unseen Face in the Mirror' in M. L. Carter (ed.) *Dracula: The Vampire and the Critics*. Ann Arbor: UMI Press, 93–104.

Senf, C. A. (1987) 'Blood, Eroticism, and the Vampire in Twentieth-Century Popular Literature', in G. Hoppenstand and R. B. Browne (eds.) *The Gothic World of Stephen King Landscape of Nightmares*. Bowling Green, OH: Bowling Green State University Press, 20–30.

____ (ed.) (1993) *The Critical Response to Bram Stoker*. Westport, CT and London: Greenwood Press.

Sholle, D. (1991) 'Reading the Audience, Reading Resistance: Prospects and Problems', *Journal of Film and Video*, 43, 1–2, 80–9.

Showalter, E. (1990) *Sexual Anarchy: Gender and Culture at the Fin-de-Siècle*. New York: Penguin.

Sigmond (1849) 'Impulsive Insanity – The French Vampire', *Journal of Psychological Medicine and Mental Pathology*, 2, 577–89.

Silver, A. and J. Ursini (1975) The *Vampire Film*, London: The Tantivy Press, South Brunswick and New York: A. S. Barnes.

Silverman, D. (1985) *Qualitative Methodology and Sociology: Describing the Social World*. Aldershot: Gower.

____ (1993) *Interpreting Qualitative Data: Methods for Analyzing Talk, Text and Interaction*. London: Sage.

Skal, D. J. (1990) *Hollywood Gothic: The Tangled Web of 'Dracula' from Novel to Stage to Screen*. New York: W. W. Norton.

____ (1993) *The Monster Show: A Cultural History of Horror*. London: Plexus.

____ (1996) *V is for Vampire: The A–Z Guide To Everything Undead*. London: Robinson Books.

Skeggs, B. (ed.) (1995) *Feminist Cultural Theory: Process and Production*. Manchester: Manchester University Press.

Skwire, S. E. (2002) 'Whose Side Are You on, Anyway? Children, Adults, and the Use of Fairy Tales in Buffy', in R. Wilcox and D. Lavery (eds) *Fighting the Forces: What's at Stake in Buffy the Vampire Slayer*. Lanham, Boulder, New York, Oxford: Rowman and Littlefield, 195–206.

Smith, J. (1996) *Anne Rice: A Critical Companion*. Westport, CT and London: Greenwood Press.

Smith, M. A. and P. Kollock (eds) (1999) *Communities in Cyberspace*. London and New York: Routledge.

Spelman, E. V. (1999 [1982]) 'Woman as Body: Ancient and Contemporary Views', in J. Price and M. Shildrick (eds) *Feminist Theory and The Body*. Edinburgh: Edinburgh University Press, 32–41.

Stacey, J. (1994) (1994) *Star Gazing: Hollywood Cinema and Female Spectatorship*. London: Routledge.

____ (1995) 'The Lost Audience: Methodology, Cinema History and Feminist Film Criticism', in B. Skeggs (ed.) *Feminist Cultural Theory: Process and Production*. Manchester: Manchester University Press, 97–118.

____ (1999) 'High School Hell', *Buffy the Vampire Slayer*, 3, December.

Stevens, D. (2000) *The Gothic Tradition*. Cambridge: Cambridge University Press.

Stoker, B. (1962 [1897]) *Dracula*. London: Arrow.

Tankel, D. J. and K. Murphy (1998) 'Collecting comic books: A Study of the Fan and Curatorial Consumption', in C. Harris and A. Alexander (eds) *Theorizing Fandom: Fans, Subculture and Identity*. Cresskill, NJ: Hampton Press, 55–70.

Tannenbaum, L. (1990) 'Policing Eddie Murphy: The Unstable Black Body in Vampire in Brooklyn', in J. C. Holte (ed.) *The Fantastic Vampire: Studies in the Children of the Night – Selected Essays from the Eighteenth International Conference on the Fantastic in the Arts*. Westport, CT and London: Greenwood Press, 69–75.

Taylor, H. (1989) *Scarlett's Women: Gone with the Wind and it's Female Fans*. London: Virago.

Thomas, L. (1997) 'In love with *Inspector Morse*', in C. Brunsdon, J. D'acci and L. Spigal (eds) *Feminist Television Criticism: A Reader*. Oxford: Clarendon Press, 184–204.

——— (2002) *Fans, Feminisms and 'Quality' Media*. London and New York: Routledge.

Thornton, S. (1995) *Club Cultures: Music, Media and Subcultural Capital*. Cambridge: Polity Press.

Tomc, S. (1997) 'Dieting and Damnation: Anne Rice's *Interview With the Vampire*', in J. Gordon and V. Hollinger (eds) *Blood Read: The Vampire as Metaphor in Contemporary Culture*. Philadelphia: University of Pennsylvania Press, 95–114.

Tonkin, B. (2002) 'Entropy as Demon: Buffy in Southern California', in R. Kaveney (ed.) (2002) *Reading the Vampire Slayer: An Unofficial Critical Companion to Buffy and Angel*. London: I. B. Tauris, 37–52.

Topping, K. (2000) *Slayer: The Totally Cool Unofficial Guide to Buffy*. London: Virgin.

Tracy, K. (1998) *The Girl's Got Bite: An Unofficial Guide to Buffy's World*. Los Angeles: Renaissance Books.

Travers, A. (2000) *Writing the Public in Cyberspace: Redefining Inclusion in the Net*. New York and London: Garland.

Trencansky, S. (2001) 'Final Girls and Terrible Youth: Transgressions in 1980s Slasher Horror', *Journal of Film and Popular Television*, 29, 2, 63–73.

Tseëlon, E. (1995) *The Masque of Femininity*. London: Sage.

Tudor, A. (1974) *Theories of Film*. London: Secker and Warburg.

——— (1989) *Monsters and Mad Scientists: A Cultural History of the Horror Movie*. Oxford: Blackwells.

——— (1997) 'Why Horror? The peculiar pleasures of a popular genre', *Cultural Studies*, 2, 3, 443–65.

Tulloch, J. and H. Jenkins (1995) *The Science Fiction Audience: Dr. Who, Star Trek and Their Fans*. London and New York: Routledge.

Turkle, S. (1998) 'Treckmuse', in R. Holetone (ed.) *Composing Cyberspace: Identity, Community and Knowledge in the Electronic Age*. Boston: McGraw-Hill, 52–71.

Twitchell, J. B. (1981) *The Living Dead: A Study of the Vampire in Romantic Literature*. Durham, NC: Duke University Press.

——— (1985) *Dreadful Pleasures: An Anatomy of Modern Horror*. Oxford: Oxford University Press.

——— (1988) 'The Vampire Myth', in M. L. Carter (ed.) *Dracula: The Vampire and the Critics*. Ann Arbor: UMI Press, 109–16.

Tzevetan, T. (1990) *Genres in Discourse*, trans. C. Porter. Cambridge: Cambridge University Press.

Van Zoonen, L. (1994) *Feminist Media Studies*. London and New Delhi: Sage.

Varnado, S. L. (1987) *Haunted Presence: The Numinous in Gothic Fiction*. Tuscaloosa and London: University of Alabama Press.

Veeder, W. (1999) 'The nurture of the Gothic, or, how can a text be both popular and subversive?' in D. Punter and G. Byron (eds) *Spectral Readings: Towards a Gothic Geography*. London: Macmillan, 43–56.

Vermorel, F. and J. Vermorel (1985) *Starlust: The Secret Fantasies of Fans*. London: W. H. Allen.

——— (1989) *Fandemonium: The Book of Fan Cults and Dance Crazes*. London, New York and Sidney: Omnibus Press.

Viacom's Third Quarter Statement (2002) <viacom.com/pdf/grol93.pf>

Virey, J. J. (1819) 'Negre', *Dictionnaire des sciences medicales*, 35, 398–403, Paris.

Walkerdine, V. (1986) 'Video replay: families, films and fantasy', in V. Burgin, J. Donald and C. Kaplan (eds) *Formations of Fantasy*. London: Methuen.

Wallace, M. (1990) *Invisibility Blues*. London: Verso.

Waller, G. (1986) *The Living and the Undead: From Stoker's Dracula to Romero's Dawn of the Dead*. Urbana and Chicago, IL: University of Illinois Press.

Waller, G. (ed.) (1987) *American Horrors: Essays on the Modern American Horror Film*. Chicago, IL: University of Illinois Press.

Wasson, R. (1966) 'The Politics of *Dracula*', *English Literature in Transition*, 9, 1, 18–23.

Watson, P. (1997) 'There's No Accounting for Taste: Exploitation Cinema and the Limits of Film Theory', in D. Cartmell, I. Q. Hunter, H. Kaye and I. Whelehan (eds) *Trash Aesthetics: Popular Culture and its Audience*. London: Pluto Press, 66–83.

Weiss, A. (1992) *Vampires and Violets: Lesbians in the Cinema*. London: Jonathan Cape.

Weissman, J. (1988) 'Women and Vampires: *Dracula* as a Victorian Novel', in M. L. Carter (ed.) *Dracula: The Vampire and the Critics*. Ann Arbor: UMI Press, 69–78.

Wicke, J. (1992) 'Vampiric Typewriting: *Dracula* and its Media, *English Literary History*, 59, 476–93.

Wilcox, R. (1999) 'There will never be a "very special" Buffy: Buffy and the monsters of teen life', *Journal of Popular Film and Television Studies*, 27, 2, 16–23.

Wilcox, R. and D. Lavery (eds) (2002) *Fighting the Forces: What's at Stake in Buffy the Vampire Slayer*. Lanham, Boulder, New York, Oxford: Rowman and Littlefield.

Williams, A. (1994) 'The Fiction of Feminine Desires: not the mirror but the lamp', *Women's Writing*, 1, 2, 229–39.

Williams, L. (1984) 'When the Woman Looks', in M. A. Doane, P. Melencamp and L. Williams (eds) *Re-visions: Essays in Feminist Film Criticism*. Los Angeles: The American Film Institute Monograph Series, University Publications of America, 3–29.

Williamson, M. (2001) *Women and Vampire Fiction: Texts, Fandom and the Construction of Identity*, unpublished PhD thesis, Goldsmiths College, University of London.

Willis, P. (1980) 'Notes on Method', in S. Hall, A. Lowe and P. Willis (eds) *Culture, Media, Language*. London: Hutchinson, 64–79.

Wilson, E. (1985) *Adorned In Dreams*. London: Virago.

___ (2000) *Bohemians: The Glamorous Outcasts*. London: I. B. Tauris.

Wise, A. (1987) 'A framework for discussing ethical issues in feminist research: a review of the literature' in D. Farran, V. Griffiths, S. Scott and L. Stanley (eds) *Writing Feminist Biography: Using Life Histories, Studies in Sexual Politics*, 19, Sociology Department: University of Manchester.

Wisker, G. (2000) 'Love Bites: Contemporary Women's Vampire Fiction', in D. Punter (ed.) *A Companion to the Gothic*. Oxford: Blackwell, 167–79.

___ (2001) 'Vampires and School Girls: High School Jinks on the Hellmouth', *Slayage*, 2 <Slayage.tv/essays/slayage2/wisker.htm>

Wood, R. (1984) 'An Introduction to the American Horror Film', in B. K. Grant (ed.) *Planks of Reason: Essays on the Horror Film*. Metuchen: Scarecrow Press, 164–200.

___ (1986) *Hollywood Film from Vietnam to Reagan*. New York: Columbia University Press.

Wyman, M. (1998) 'Teen Kicks: *Buffy the Vampire Slayer*', *Xpose* Special, 5, 6–19.

Young, L. (1996) *Fear of the Dark: 'Race', Gender and Sexuality in the Cinema*. London: Routledge.

Zanger, J. (1997) 'Metaphor into Metonymy: The Vampire Next Door', in J. Gordon and V. Hollinger (eds) *Blood Read: The Vampire as Metaphor in Contemporary Culture*. Philadelphia: University of Pennsylvania Press, 17–26.

Zimmerman, J. (1984) 'Daughters of darkness: the lesbian on film', in B. K. Grant (ed.) *Planks of Reason: Essays on the Horror Film*. Metuchen: Scarecrow Press, 153–63.